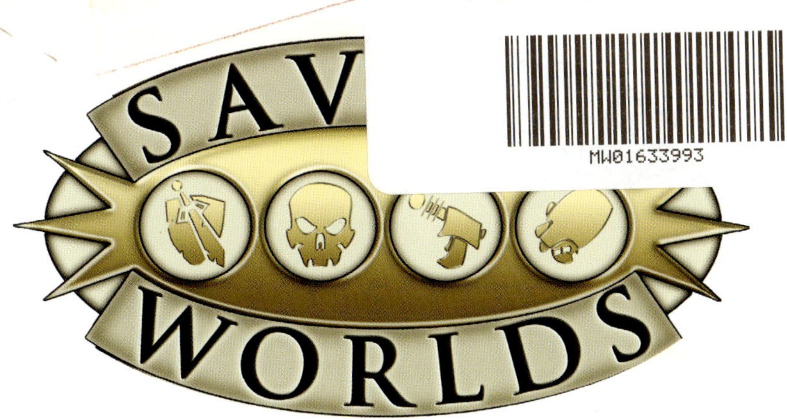

SAVAGE WORLDS

By Shane Lacy Hensley, with Clint & Jodi Black, Matthew Cutter, John Goff, Joel Kinstle, Piotr Koryś, Jordan Peacock, Teller, and Simon Lucas

Playtesting and Advice: "Evil" Mike McNeal, "Chaos" Steve Todd, Jay & Amy Kyle, Paul "Wiggy" Wade-Williams, Randy Mosiondz, Ed Wetterman, Preston DuBose, Cheyenne Wright, Sean Patrick Fannon, Sean Preston, Tappy, Bill, and Stu of The Happy Jacks RPG Podcast, Chris Fuchs, Bill Stilson, and Thomas Jakobsen

Cover and Graphics: Cheyenne Wright

Proofing: Matthew Cutter & Jodi Black

Interior Illustrations: Joewie Aderes, Chris Appel, Nate Bell, Leanne Buckley, Richard Clark, Storn Cook, Lecuona Esnaola, Bartłomiej Fedyczak, Gil Formosa, Carl Frank, Jesus Garcia, Andy Hopp, Emmo Huang, Jon Joseba, Tomek Jedruszek, Todd Lockwood, Chris Malidore, Carlos NCT, Magdalena Izabela Partyka, Jordan Peacock, Marta Poludnikiewicz, Daniel Rudnicki, Christophe Swal, Tomasz Tworek, and Cheyenne Wright

Special Thanks to Frank Uchmanowicz and Jim Searcy of Studio2, Dancin' Dirk Ringersma, and Ron and Veronica Blessing of Smiling Jack's Bar & Grill

To the pulp authors who inspire us—Burroughs, Howard, Lovecraft, and the rest. Your tales will forever echo in our own.

WWW.PEGINC.COM

Contents

Chapter Five: Powers 118

Chapter Six: Game Mastering 140

Chapter Seven: Bestiary 152

Sample Adventures 166

Collected Charts & Tables 184

Introduction: Savage Worlds

In barbaric worlds of fantasy and far-flung galaxies, great heroes battle for gold, glory, justice, or mere survival. Some wear mithril armor and wield massive swords glowing with magical energy. Others are commandos in the latest ballistic vests spraying lead from their submachine guns. Some aren't even human.

But they are all heroes, and their epic tales inspire those who read them. This game system attempts to simulate these incredible tales—at least in our imaginations—giving form, structure, and challenge to the heroes and the savage worlds they walk in with rules that are simple on the surface and comprehensive in their depth.

The game focuses on the action rather than statistics and bookkeeping, allowing the Game Master to concentrate on the player characters, their foes, and the fantastic settings they battle in.

For players, *Savage Worlds* has an extremely rich advancement system that lets you create everything from a swashbuckling rogue to a charismatic investigative reporter.

Some "generic" rules systems come up lacking in certain settings. *Savage Worlds* avoids this with Setting Rules (you'll find a list of common Setting Rules on page 108). These allow the Game Master to fundamentally alter the feel of the game without changing the basic mechanics. Players can explore haunted space hulks in power armor, battle dragons, or surf the matrix of a virtual computer world without having to learn all-new rules. But throw in something like Righteous Rage from Solomon Kane®—which makes a hero far more deadly in his most desperate moments—and the entire feel of the game changes in an instant.

What's New?

This deluxe version of the *Savage Worlds* rules system is the culmination of a decade's play with suggestions and comments gathered from our own campaigns and the thousands of adventures we've run at game stores and conventions across the globe. For those who have already played we think you'll find this the most complete and comprehensive edition of the rules we've ever published. We've compiled the best material from our setting books and added in web updates like gritty damage rules and interludes. Races and vehicles are back from the first edition, as well as the race creation rules from the Fantasy Companion and a consolidated list of all the best powers from our many expansions.

Veterans of our game will also find a number of Design Notes scattered throughout the book. These are insights into why a particular rule is written the way it is and the thinking that went into it.

For those who are new, we welcome you to the "Savages," and encourage you to join one of the most friendly, helpful, and enthusiastic communities in gaming on our forums and mailing lists.

And if you already own Savage Worlds and want a list of all the changes or additions we've made here **completely free,** just go to our website at www.peginc.com!

Now let your imagination wander to worlds of danger and adventure, where heroes are larger than life and monsters stalk the land. These are savage worlds—and those who survive them become legends...

Getting Started

You'll need a few other items besides this book to begin your journey:

Dice

Savage Worlds uses traditional gaming dice: 4-sided, 6-sided, 8-sided, 10-sided, 12-sided, and some settings use a 20-sided die as well. As a player, you'll also want a "Wild Die," a d6 of a different color which we'll explain in Chapter One. Dice are available from your favorite local gaming store, or online directly from Pinnacle.

We abbreviate the different dice as d4, d6, d8, d10, d12, and d20. If you see something like 2d6+1, that means to roll two six-sided dice, add the two together, then add 1 to the total.

Players need only one set of dice. The Game Master might want a couple of sets so she can roll attacks for several villains at once.

The Action Deck

Savage Worlds uses a standard deck of playing cards with the Jokers left in. Cards are used for initiative in combat and to help keep things moving fast and furious. You'll even find an official set of *Savage Worlds* cards where you found this book!

A Setting

Will you and your friends explore post-apocalyptic ruins? Lead a rugged warband in your favorite fantasy world? Take on the role of vampire lords? Or perhaps fight evil in the many theaters of *Weird Wars?*

Pick up the book for your favorite game setting at your local game store, or create your own. Official Savage Settings include new Edges and Hindrances, Setting Rules, spells, weapons, gear, monsters, and more! We talk more about some of our settings on pages 7 through 15.

The Adventure Deck

We also make an exciting Adventure Deck that adds an additional aspect of player control to the game. Your hero might find a new romance, make a lifelong enemy, or do additional damage in that critical fight. Look for it on our website or in better game and hobby stores.

Using Miniatures

The rules are written for the table-top because that requires exact measurements and precise rules. That's why all the weapon ranges and movement values are listed in inches (rather than yards or some other unit). Using miniatures and terrain or a battle-mat can really help your players understand the tactical situation and better interact with their environment, and we highly recommend this style of play for most games.

But miniatures certainly aren't required, and you'll find rules for "guesstimating" ranges, how many foes are caught in a blast radius, and other issues on page 73.

If you do decide to use miniatures, check the Pinnacle website for metal miniatures for our games as well as cardboard and cardstock variants.

Pinnacle has created many Savage Settings, from our award-winning Deadlands and its spin-offs Hell on Earth and Lost Colony to Rippers and Necessary Evil and Weird Wars. We've also licensed some of our favorite worlds, such as Frank Chadwick's Space 1889® and The Savage World of Solomon Kane®. A few of our settings, such as Andy Hopp's brilliant Low Life, are published by Pinnacle but owned by their creators.

You'll find a sneak peek at a few of these settings on the following pages.

Plot Point Campaigns

Like our rules system, our settings are designed to be easy for the Game Master to run. That's why many of our Savage Settings feature "Plot Point Campaigns," a backstory to the campaign world and a set of adventures that resolve the main plot. Interspersed between these Plot Points are Savage Tales—short adventures that can be run depending on where the party goes and what they do. Of course a Game Master can also insert his own adventures into the campaign, including those based around the player characters' backstories.

The idea is to communicate a big backstory—like the flooding of the world in 50 Fathoms—but still give Game Masters the freedom to construct and run their own stories in the foreground. In this game, the heroes are a crew of explorers, traders, or even pirates sailing about a drowning world. They can seek out whatever destiny they choose, but will become entangled in the fight against the Sea Hags—the creatures destroying Caribdus—as well.

Savage Tales

The adventures in our books are called "Savage Tales," short and direct adventure outlines the Game Master can run with only a few minutes of preparation. We do this by cutting to the most important details of an encounter.

Ideally, a Game Master can find out what his group is interested in doing that session, read no more than a page or so, and be ready to run the game. He can always put more into it if he wishes, but all the crucial ingredients for running a fun game are there in detail.

Savagery

If you decide you like Savage Worlds, you migh want to check out some of our settings and othe resources. Some basic information is found below and you can find more detail, free downloads, an support materials at our website: www.peginc.com.

Settings

From space opera to Western to Puritan adventures we make a lot of exciting settings. Our philosoph has always been to do things a little differently tha everyone else. Most of our worlds have a uniqu twist we think makes them special. For example Evernight begins in a typical fantasy world of elve and dwarves—but quickly changes as strange spike drop from the heavens and spill forth somethin terrible from beyond the stars.

Some of our largest game lines, such as Deadlands are open settings with multiple Plot Point Campaign presented separately. For example, The Floo revolves around fighting Reverend Ezekiah Grimm in what's left of California after the Great Quake—th Maze. Stone and a Hard Place is all about the game' deadliest gunslinger and killer of heroes: Stone Stand-alone adventures such as Coffin Rock, o add-ons like the Smith & Robards Catalog, featurin dozens of steampunk inventions, are also available

Companions

Our Companions focus on new Edges an Hindrances, powers, monsters, and Setting Rules fo particular genres such as Fantasy, Horror, Scienc Fiction, and more.

Adventures

Full-length adventures are available for most of ou settings, as well as unique tales set in worlds of thei own, such as Zombie Run, a survivor adventure se in America after a worldwide outbreak of undead.

Accessories

We've already mentioned our official Action Adventure Decks. We also manufacture custor Bennies for each of our lines—custom poker chip with images specific to the setting. Licensees als make plastic templates, dice, and other specialt items. Check our webstore at www.peginc.com fo the latest.

Forums

We're very proud of our forums, and think we hav the best community in all of gaming. If you have question, visit the forums and the other Savages, o our own writers, will happily answer it for you. You ca also find new world, campaign, or adventure ideas groups to play with, and Game Mastering advice, a from a friendly and welcoming community that love to game.

Space 1889: Red Sands

Mars needs heroes!

Frank Chadwick's classic *Space 1889*® gets savage in this intergalactic Plot Point Campaign!

While the Empires of Earth battle over Mars' red plains and crimson hills, a villain known as Kronos seizes the technology of a long-dead race to threaten to repel the "alien" invaders forever.

Deadlands: The Weird West

The year is 1876, but the history is not our own.
A vengeful shaman named Raven opened the doorway to Hell and released the manitous—demonic creatures that flooded the world with magic and monsters. Some heroes have learned to harness this arcane power to fight the growing evil. Others rely on their blazing six-guns or weird science.
And some are too tough to die and come back from the grave wrestling a manitou for incredible powers—and their very souls.

DEAD LANDS

Weird Wars: Weird War Two

In the violence and horror of war, dark things rise.
Monsters have always lurked in the shadows, feeding on the fear and terror of war. The occultists and scientists of the Third Reich have realized this, secretly researching forbidden lore, gathering ancient relics, and recruiting or creating inhuman monsters to subjugate the world.

Never before has such a conflict spread to so many corners of the globe or given rise to so many horrors. Time is running out. The Allies have gathered a secret organization of soldiers, sailors, and survivors to battle the monsters of the Third Reich and the creatures rising in the growing darkness.

WEIRD WARS

La G

The Savage World of Solomon Kane®

A landless man. A Wanderer. A Puritan.

He stalks the land, a wanderer of fate. He is Solomon Kane®, puritan, adventurer, hero. Kane punishes the wicked. Hundreds have fallen before his saber and pistols.

But rarely, Kane finds one who wants to atone—a tainted soul who realizes the evil he's done in his life. These hopeful few are tasked to wander the earth as Kane does, searching out the horrors of the world to battle and defeat them. Most will perish in this arduous quest. Others will find redemption. A few will become heroes.

All will walk the Path of Kane.

Rippers

Stalk the creatures of the night—or become one!

Rippers are a secret cabal of scholars, warriors, sages, and heroes who battle legendary horrors around the globe. But willpower, science, technology, and steel are not their only weapons. Abraham Van Helsing and "Dr. Jack" have shown the Rippers how to extract the essences or natural tools of the creatures they battle—and implant it in themselves.

Those who survive the process may become fearsome warriors, fighting with the claws of a werewolf or the teeth of a piranha-man. Others go mad from the procedure and become that which they once hunted.

And at least one has become the greatest traitor the Rippers have ever known…

Great heroes are more than a collection of statistics and numbers, but in a game system this is certainly where they begin. To make your hero, download a *Savage Worlds* character sheet from our website (www.peginc.com) or copy the one found at the back of this book and follow the steps below.

1. Race

Humans are the most common characters, but some settings may feature bizarre aliens, graceful elves, or other exotic races—some examples of which you'll find on page 20. You can choose to play any race available in your particular setting.

- Humans are the standard race in *Savage Worlds,* and start play with one free Edge (see Step 3).

2. Traits

Characters are defined by attributes and skills, collectively called "Traits," and both work in exactly the same way. Attributes and skills are ranked by die types, from a d4 to a d12, with d6 being the average for adult humans. Higher is better!

Attributes

Every character starts with a d4 in each attribute, and has 5 points with which to raise them. Raising a d4 to a d6, for example, costs 1 point. You're free to spend these points however you want with one exception: no attribute may be raised above a d12.

- **Agility** is your hero's nimbleness, quickness, and dexterity.
- **Smarts** is a measure of how well your character knows his world and culture, how well he thinks on his feet, and mental agility.
- **Spirit** reflects inner wisdom and willpower. Spirit is very important as it helps your character recover from being Shaken (see page 77).
- **Strength** is raw physical power and general fitness. Strength is also used to generate your warrior's damage in hand-to-hand combat.

- **Vigor** represents endurance, resistance to disease, poison, or toxins, and how much pain and physical damage a hero can shake off.

Skills

Skills are learned abilities such as Shooting, Fighting, scientific knowledge, professional aptitudes, and so on. These are very general descriptions which cover all related aspects. Shooting, for example, covers all types of guns, bows, rocket launchers, and other ranged weapons.

You have 15 skill points to distribute among your skills. Each die type costs 1 point (starting at d4) as long as the skill is equal to or less than the attribute it's linked to (listed beside the skill in parentheses). If you exceed the attribute, the cost becomes 2 points per die type.

As with attributes, no skill may be increased above d12.

Example: Fighting is linked to Agility. A character with a d8 Agility can buy Fighting for one point per die type to d8. Buying a d10 costs 2 points, and a d12 costs another 2 points.

Derived Statistics

Your character sheet contains a few other statistics you need to fill in, described below.

Charisma is a measure of your character's appearance, manner, and general likability. It's 0 unless you have Edges or Hindrances that modify it. Charisma is added to Persuasion and Streetwise rolls, and is used by the GM to figure out how nonplayer characters react to your hero.

Pace is how fast your character moves in a standard combat round. Humans walk 6" in a round and can move an additional 1d6" if they run. Write "6" on your character sheet beside the word Pace. This is 6" on the table-top—every inch there represents 2 yards in the "real world."

Parry is equal to 2 plus half your character's Fighting (2 if a character does not have Fighting), plus any bonuses for shields or certain weapons. This is the Target Number (TN) to hit your hero in hand-to-hand combat.

For stats such as d12+1, add half the fixed modifier, rounded down. For instance, a Fighting skill of d12+1 grants a Parry of 8 (2+half of d12), whereas a d12+2 gives a Parry of 9 (2+half of d12+2).

Toughness is your hero's damage threshold. Anything over this causes him to be rattled or worse. Toughness is 2 plus half your hero's Vigor, plus Armor (use the armor worn on his torso). Vigor over a d12 is calculated just like Parry.

3. Edges & Hindrances

Great heroes are far more than a collection of skills and attributes. It's their unique gifts, special powers, and tragic flaws that truly make them interesting characters.

Characters can take Edges by balancing them out with Hindrances. You'll find a complete list of Edges and Hindrances later in this chapter. Look for more in our Savage Settings.

You can take one Major Hindrance and two Minor Hindrances. A Major Hindrance is worth 2 points, and a Minor Hindrance is worth 1 point.

For 2 points you can:
- Raise an attribute one die type, or
- Choose an Edge

For 1 point you can:
- Gain another skill point, or
- Gain additional money equal to your starting funds (if you start with $500, you gain an additional $500)

4. Gear

Next you need to purchase equipment. Some settings may provide your hero with all the gear he needs. In others, you may be assigned a certain amount of money with which to purchase your starting gear. A list of some common gear and weapons can be found in Chapter Two.

Unless your setting book or GM says otherwise, the standard starting amount is $500.

5. Background Details

Finish your character by filling in any history or background you care to. Ask yourself why your hero is where she is and what her goals are. Or you can just start playing and fill in these details as they become important.

You might also want to talk to the other players. Maybe your characters know each other right from the start. Or you might collectively decide to optimize your group a bit and ensure you've got a good assortment of skills and abilities. If so, make sure you're playing what you want to play. There's no point in being the party's magical healer, for example, if that's not a role you're interested in.

Most of us tend to play a particular character type and stick with it regardless of genre or game system. There's certainly nothing wrong with that, and you should absolutely play what you enjoy most of the time.

It's also great to occasionally break out of your usual mold and try something different. Challenge yourself to play a different character type now and then. Maybe you always play big tough guys and like being the "brick" of the party. Next time your friend runs a swords & sorcery game, try being the mage. You may find you love being a spellcaster.

Game Masters are also encouraged to try new things now and then. Some of the most incredible sessions we've played in have featured very strange character types, such as kobold slaves, the elderly, and even intelligent animals. And nothing beats the bizarre and amazing world of Andy Hopp's Low Life.

We encourage you to try something new once in a while. You can always slip right back into that very comfortable and familiar role you already know you enjoy next time out.

Sometimes you may want to quickly create a character for a one-shot or convention adventure. For those occasions, an Archetype might be a good choice. Add a name, Hindrances, and gear, spend any remaining skill points, and you're ready to play!

The Archetypes below are all Novice humans with one free Edge.

Driver

Attributes: Agility d8, Smarts d6, Spirit d6, Strength d6, Vigor d6
Skills: Driving d8, Fighting d4, Notice d6, Shooting d6, +7 additional skill points
Charisma: –; **Pace:** 6; **Parry:** 4; **Toughness:** 5
Hindrances: One Major, two Minor
Edges: Ace, Quick

"Face"

Attributes: Agility d6, Smarts d6, Spirit d8, Strength d6, Vigor d6
Skills: Fighting d4, Intimidation d6, Notice d6, Persuasion d10, Shooting d4, Streetwise d6, Taunt d6
Charisma: +2; **Pace:** 6; **Parry:** 4; **Toughness:** 5
Hindrances: One Major, two Minor
Edges: Attractive, Strong Willed

Fighter, Fencer

Attributes: Agility d8, Smarts d6, Spirit d6, Strength d6, Vigor d6
Skills: Fighting d12, Notice d6, Stealth d6, Taunt d8
Charisma: –; **Pace:** 6; **Parry:** 8; **Toughness:** 5
Hindrances: One Major, two Minor
Edges: Florentine, Two Fisted

Fighter, Great Weapon

Attributes: Agility d6, Smarts d4, Spirit d6, Strength d10, Vigor d6
Skills: Fighting d10, Intimidation d6, Notice d6, +4 additional skill points
Charisma: –; **Pace:** 6; **Parry:** 7; **Toughness:** 6
Hindrances: One Major, two Minor
Edges: Brawny, Sweep

Investigator

Attributes: Agility d6, Smarts d8, Spirit d6, Strength d6, Vigor d6
Skills: Fighting d6, Investigation d8, Notice d8, Persuasion d6, Shooting d6, Streetwise d8
Charisma: –; **Pace:** 6; **Parry:** 5; **Toughness:** 5
Hindrances: One Major, two Minor
Edges: Connections, Investigator

Leader

Attributes: Agility d6, Smarts d6, Spirit d8, Strength d4, Vigor d6
Skills: Fighting d6, Intimidation d6, Knowledge (Battle) d6, Notice d6, Persuasion d6, Shooting d6, +3 additional skill points
Charisma: –; **Pace:** 6; **Parry:** 5; **Toughness:** 5
Hindrances: One Major, two Minor
Edges: Command, Natural Leader

Mage

Attributes: Agility d4, Smarts d10, Spirit d8, Strength d4, Vigor d4
Skills: Fighting d4, Investigation d6, Knowledge (Arcana) d6, Notice d6, Spellcasting d10, +4 additional skill points
Charisma: –; **Pace:** 6; **Parry:** 4; **Toughness:** 4
Hindrances: One Major, two Minor
Edges: Arcane Background (Magic), New Power, Power Points

Marksman

Attributes: Agility d10, Smarts d6, Spirit d6, Strength d6, Vigor d6
Skills: Fighting d6, Notice d6, Shooting d10, Taunt d6, +5 additional skill points
Charisma: –; **Pace:** 6; **Parry:** 5; **Toughness:** 5
Hindrances: One Major, two Minor
Edges: Alertness

Martial Artist

Attributes: Agility d8, Smarts d6, Spirit d6, Strength d8, Vigor d6
Skills: Fighting d10, Intimidation d6, Notice d6, +6 additional skill points
Charisma: –; **Pace:** 6; **Parry:** 7; **Toughness:** 5
Hindrances: One Major, two Minor
Edges: Martial Artist

Pilot

Attributes: Agility d8, Smarts d6, Spirit d6, Strength d6, Vigor d6
Skills: Fighting d4, Notice d8, Piloting d10, Repair d6, Shooting d6, +1 additional skill point
Charisma: –; **Pace:** 6; **Parry:** 4; **Toughness:** 5
Hindrances: One Major, two Minor
Edges: Ace, Alertness

Pirate

Attributes: Agility d8, Smarts d4, Spirit d6, Strength d6, Vigor d6
Skills: Boating d6, Fighting d8, Intimidation d6, Notice d6, Shooting d8, Taunt d6
Charisma: –; **Pace:** 6; **Parry:** 7; **Toughness:** 5
Hindrances: One Major, two Minor
Edges: Acrobat, Steady Hands

Pistoleer

Attributes: Agility d8, Smarts d6, Spirit d6, Strength d6, Vigor d6
Skills: Fighting d6, Notice d6, Shooting d10, Taunt d6, +4 additional skill points
Charisma: –; **Pace:** 6; **Parry:** 5; **Toughness:** 5
Hindrances: One Major, two Minor
Edges: Ambidextrous, Two-Fisted

Priest, Healer

Attributes: Agility d6, Smarts d6, Spirit d8, Strength d6, Vigor d6
Skills: Faith d8, Fighting d6, Healing d8, Notice d6, +4 additional skill points
Charisma: –; **Pace:** 6; **Parry:** 5; **Toughness:** 5
Hindrances: One Major, two Minor
Edges: Arcane Background (Miracles), Healer

Rogue

Attributes: Agility d8, Smarts d6, Spirit d6, Strength d6, Vigor d6
Skills: Climbing d6, Fighting d6, Lockpicking d6, Notice d6, Stealth d8, Streetwise d6, Taunt d6
Charisma: –; **Pace:** 6; **Parry:** 5; **Toughness:** 5
Hindrances: One Major, two Minor
Edges: Assassin, Thief

Scientist

Attributes: Agility d4, Smarts d10, Spirit d6, Strength d4, Vigor d6
Skills: Investigation d6, Knowledge (Science) d10, Knowledge (Other) d10, Notice d8, Repair d6
Charisma: –; **Pace:** 6; **Parry:** 2; **Toughness:** 5
Hindrances: One Major, two Minor
Edges: Jack-of-All-Trades, McGyver, Scholar

Scientist, Weird

Attributes: Agility d6, Smarts d8, Spirit d6, Strength d4, Vigor d6
Skills: Knowledge (Science) d8, Knowledge (Other) d6, Notice d6, Repair d8, Shooting d6, Weird Science d10
Charisma: –; **Pace:** 6; **Parry:** 2; **Toughness:** 5
Hindrances: One Major, two Minor
Edges: Arcane Background (Weird Science), Gadgeteer

Design Note - Archetypes

Making characters in Savage Worlds is easy, but it still takes a while for everyone to figure out what they want, make it, and look through the rulebook and the particular setting book to get it done.

These Archetypes let you jump right in with little effort. They're also a great tool to use with younger or more inexperienced roleplayers who may be more interested in hopping in and playing than making characters. Use the Archetypes as a base, then let the player fill in the more creative blanks—such as their hero's name, where he comes from, and what's special about him.

If you're the Game Master and you want to introduce new players to the game, use these to quickly fill out character sheets, then add some background and appropriate Hindrances to make them shine and you're all set.

Races

Not every hero is human. Below are sample races common to many science fiction and fantasy settings. Use them as they are or modify them to fit your particular world. Immediately after you'll also find guidelines on how to create your own races.

Android

Androids are sentient machines with a variety of appearances depending on the setting. Some appear almost human, some are purely mechanical. The android presented here is a basic version with normal human knowledge and emotions. Particular settings may alter, remove, or add other abilities based on their role and function in that world.

- **Asimov Circuits:** The android cannot harm, or by inaction bring harm to sentient beings. This gives him the Pacifist Hindrance (Major).
- **Construct:** Androids add +2 to recover from being Shaken, don't suffer wound modifiers, and are immune to poison and disease. Androids cannot heal naturally. To heal an android requires the Repair skill—which is used like the Healing skill only with no "Golden Hour."
- **Outsider:** Organic races often mistrust or misunderstand androids. They subtract 2 from their Charisma when dealing with races other than their own.
- **Programming:** Androids begin with a free d6 in one skill, representing their original programmed role.
- **Recharge:** During character creation, the player must determine the android's power source. If the android cannot access his power source at least once per day, he's automatically Fatigued each day until he's Incapacitated. The day after that, he goes "off-line" and must be revived with a Repair roll and a four-hour charge of energy. The power source replaces the need for food and water, unless they are the chosen power source.
- **Unnatural:** Arcane powers, both detrimental and beneficial, suffer a –2 penalty to affect androids. This has no effect on damaging powers, which affect them normally.

Atlantean

From the crushing depths come the mysterious folk known as Atlanteans. They are thick and sturdy beneath the waves but often vulnerable in the dry air or searing heat. Their civilization is advanced, and Atlantean science is a wonder to behold.

- **Advanced Civilization:** Atlanteans are generally more intelligent than the other races of their world. They start with a d6 in Smarts rather than a d4.
- **Aquatic:** Atlanteans live in and breathe water. They cannot drown in water, move at full Swimming skill, and get a free d6 Swimming.
- **Dehydration:** Atlanteans must immerse themselves in water one hour out of every 24 or become automatically Fatigued each day until they are Incapacitated. The day after that, they perish.
- **Tough:** The pressure of their deep homes make Atlanteans tougher than most. Increase Toughness by 1.

Avion

Avions are any basically human race with wings. They tend to be very slight of build owing to their hollow bones.

- **Flight:** Avions can fly at their basic Pace and even "run" while flying. It costs 2" of Pace to gain 1" of height.
- **Hollow-boned:** Avions have –1 Toughness.
- **Mostly Human:** Avions may choose one free Edge a character creation as long as they meet all requirements

Dwarves

Dwarves are short, stout, hardy people who come from massive caverns in the high mountains. They are a proud, warlike race, usually made so by frequent contact with savage races such as orcs and goblins.

Dwarves usually live upwards of 200 years. In most fantasy campaigns, they have ruddy skin and all human hair colors.

- **Low Light Vision:** Dwarven eyes are accustomed to the dark of the underearth. They ignore attack penalties for Dim and Dark lighting.
- **Slow:** Dwarves have a Pace of 5".
- **Tough:** Dwarves are stout and tough. They start with a d6 Vigor instead of a d4.

Elves

Elves are tall, thin souls with pointed ears and deep-set eyes of various colors. Whether they hail from the forests or hidden valleys, they are all born more graceful than humans, though somewhat slighter. Most elves live upwards of 300 years. They have fair skin and their hair includes all human colors, plus shades of silver and blue.

- **Agile:** Elves are graceful and agile. They start with a d6 in Agility instead of a d4.
- **All Thumbs:** Elves have an inbred dislike of mechanical objects, and thus have the All Thumbs Hindrance. They shun most mechanical items and designs.
- **Low Light Vision:** Elven eyes amplify light like a cat's, allowing them to see in the dark. Elves ignores attack penalties for Dim and Dark lighting.

Half-Elves

Half-elves are usually a solid mix of their two parents. They gain the elves' grace but none of their elegant frailty. Most half-elves are well-adjusted, but some are shunned by one side of the family or the other and grow resentful. Others may even be mistreated. Their lifespans are closer to their human parent than those of their elven kin. Most half-elves live only to about 100 years.

- **Heritage:** Some half-elves retain the grace of their elven parent. Others gain the adaptability of their human ancestry. A half-elf may either start with a free Edge of his choice (as a human), or a d6 in Agility instead of a d4.
- **Low Light Vision:** The character's eyes amplify light like a cat's, allowing him to see in the dark. He ignores attack penalties for Dim and Dark lighting.
- **Outsider:** Half-elves aren't true outsiders (as per the Hindrance of the same name), but neither are they ever quite comfortable around humans or elves as one of their own, so the effect is the same.

Half-Folk

Half-folk are small, nimble creatures with fuzzy brown or black hair. Though they are frail compared to most other races, their cheerful optimism (or wily cunning) gives them a "never say die" attitude that makes them more than a match for creatures twice their size.

Half-folk see no reason to invite trouble, and tend to live in their own little communities far off the beaten path.

- **Fortunate:** Half-folk draw one additional Benny per game session. This may be combined with the Luck and Great Luck Edges.
- **Short:** Half-folk average only about 4' tall. This gives them a Size of –1 and subtracts 1 from their Toughness.
- **Spirited:** Half-folk are generally optimistic beings. They start with a d6 Spirit instead of a d4.

Half-Orcs

Half-orcs are the offspring of either a human and an orc or an orc and another half-orc. Rarely is such a mating willingly accepted, so the character's "family tree" is likely more than a little troublesome to him or her.

Half-orcs are usually accepted by orcish communities, but are shunned by most other races, including humans, elves, and dwarves. Some half-orcs choose to join the "civilized" races, turning their backs on their barbaric roots, and are often looking to redeem themselves. Many are heroic souls trying to prove their worth.

Half-orcs have light-colored human skin with just a tinge of orcish coloration, with black hair and small eyes. Their features are harsh and angular, like that of orcs. Their natural life-span is the same as humans, though it is rare when one dies of old age.

- **Infravision:** Half-orcs can see in the infrared spectrum, halving attack penalties (round down) for bad lighting.
- **Outsider:** Half-orcs aren't trusted by most other civilized races, and so subtract 2 from their Charisma.
- **Strong:** Half-orcs have some of the strength of their ancestry. They start with a d6 Strength attribute instead of a d4.

Humans

Humans in most settings should get the usual benefit—one free Edge of their choice. This option reflects their versatility and adaptability compared to other races.

If you like more variety, you might also give humans abilities based on culture rather than race. For instance, a seafaring human culture may start with Boating and Swimming at d6. Cultural templates are designed just like making new races (see page 22).

Rakashans

Rakashans have the form of humans with the features of felines. They come in a wide variety: the bright colors of tigers, the speckled hides of leopards, and the exotic look of Siamese cats are all appropriate. They have sharp claws and teeth and a cruel nature when it comes to dealing with their prey.

Rakashans can be found in their own remote and exotic cities or as fringe elements of normal society. While they are too beautiful to be shunned, they are too foreign to be easily accepted.

- **Agile:** Rakashans have the feline grace of their ancestors. They start with a d6 Agility attribute instead of a d4.
- **Bloodthirsty:** Rakashans can be cruel to their foes, often toying with them for simple amusement. They rarely take prisoners and feel little compunction about punishing captured foes. This causes a –4 Charisma penalty among more "civilized" types.
- **Racial Enemy:** Rakashan society rose at the expense of another. Pick a common race in your setting. Members of each culture suffer a –4 Charisma when dealing with each other. Unless fettered by other authorities or common goals, individuals of the two races typically attack each other on sight.
- **Claws:** Rakashans have retractable claws that do Str+d6 damage and grant +2 to Climbing rolls on all but completely sheer surfaces.
- **Low Light Vision:** Rakashan eyes amplify light. They can see in the dark and ignore attack penalties for Dim and Dark lighting.

Saurians

Lizard men typically come from steaming jungles or deep deserts where they have unique civilizations unknown to other sentient races.

Few outsiders have penetrated their society, and persistent rumors that Saurian religion requires sentient sacrifices remain unconfirmed.

- **Outsider:** Most races distrust the unblinking saurians. Their habit of eating their meat still squirming is also less than appetizing. They suffer a –2 Charisma penalty.
- **Natural Weapons:** The tails, claws, and teeth of saurians allow them to tail slap, claw, or bite in combat for Str+d4 damage.
- **Saurian Senses:** Saurians' lizard tongues can "taste" the air, giving them +2 to Notice rolls. They are always considered active guards for Stealth checks.
- **Warm Natured:** Though not truly cold-blooded, saurians are not comfortable in cold environments. They suffer a –4 penalty to resist cold environmental effects.

Making Races

The following system allows you to make new races or cultural templates like those found on the previous pages. The Game Master can use this to create pre-built races for his world, or allow players to do so if the setting allows a great number of racial variations.

If you're the Game Master, decide on the maximum number of Racial Edge points allowed (usually between 2 and 4). This provides enough scope to make an interesting race or culture without unduly unbalancing the game.

Races and cultures begin with a free +2 Racial Ability. This is equivalent to a human's Free Edge. Additional positive abilities must be countered with an equal value of negative ones. A +2 ability, for example, may be countered by a single –2 ability or two –1 abilities.

Give each ability a suitable name. If you want your horse nomads to have Riding skill at d6, call it Born to the Saddle. It's all about creating a rich flavor rather than just giving long lists of abilities your players have to keep up with. Short and flavorful is far preferable to long and comprehensive.

If you want to include an ability we haven't listed here, simply assign it a value based on the examples here.

+3 Abilities
• Begin with a d8 in one attribute and may raise it to a d12+2 via normal advancement; the Expert and Master Edges may raise it to a d12+4
• Free Seasoned Edge (regardless of requirements—except those which require other Edges)
• Hardy (a second Shaken result in combat does not cause a Wound)

+2 Abilities
• +1 Parry
• +1 Size
• +1 Toughness
• +2 Armor (negated by AP weapons)
• +2 Charisma
• +4 bonus to resist all negative environmental effects (heat, cold, pressure, etc.)
• +10 Power Points for one specific Arcane Background (Magic or Miracles)
• Aquatic (cannot drown in water, moves at full Swimming skill, free d6 Swimming)
• Base Pace 10
• Construct (see page 152)
• Free Novice Edge (regardless of requirements—except for those that require other Edges)
• Multiple limbs (one extra non-movement action per limb, incurs no multi-action penalty, price is per additional limb)
• Poison (victims that suffer a Shaken result from your natural weapons must make a Vigor roll or be paralyzed for 2d6 rounds)
• Start with a d6 in one attribute
• The Flight ability (at base Pace; may "run"); see the monstrous ability on page 153

+1 Abilities
• +1 Reach
• +2 bonus to resist all negative environmental effects (heat, cold, pressure, etc.)
• +4 bonus to resist any single negative environmental effect (e.g., heat or cold)
• +5 Power Points for use with a specific Arcane Background (cannot be same AB as +2 Ability described above)
• Burrowing, Wall Walker, or similar
• Free d6 in a skill common to that race
• Immune to poison or disease
• Keen Sense (+2 to Notice when using one sense)
• Low light or infravision; see monstrous abilities on page 154
• Natural Weapons such as claws that cause Str+d6 damage
• Potent Poison (must have Poison, each level gives victims a –1 penalty to their Vigor roll)
• Semi-aquatic (gain Fatigue level every 15 minutes he holds his breath; on reaching Incapacitated, must make Vigor roll every minute or drown; Fatigue recovers one level per 15 minutes back in air)

–3 Abilities
• One attribute can never advance beyond a d6
• One attribute requires two points per step to raise during character generation and the character must dedicate two Advances to raising the attribute during game play

–2 Abilities
• –1 Parry
• –1 Toughness
• –4 penalty to resist all negative environmental effects (heat, cold, pressure, etc.)
• One attribute requires two points per step to raise during character generation
• Dehydration (the creature must immerse itself in water one hour out of every 24 or become automatically Fatigued each day until they are Incapacitated; the day after that, they perish)
• Major Hindrance (or equivalent effect)
• Pace 3 or less (d4 running die)

–1 Abilities
• –2 Charisma
• –4 penalty to resist any single negative environmental effect (e.g., heat or cold)
• Minor Hindrance (or equivalent effect)
• Pace 5
• Racial Enemy (–4 Charisma when dealing with one other race)

On the following pages are skills available in most Savage Settings. Normal use of a skill—guiding a boat in and out of a dock, repairing an engine with plenty of time and the proper tools, or riding a horse across a prairie—shouldn't require a skill roll. Only when a character is under pressure to perform a task quickly, or has a significant chance of failure and can't just keep trying until he's successful, should his player be asked to roll.

Familiarization

Skills are very broad for ease of play, but sometimes it's dramatically appropriate to emphasize when a character is out of his element.

When a hero finds himself using a skill in a dramatically different way than he's used to, he suffers a –2 penalty to his rolls. How long this lasts depends on the skill, but should typically be at least a few days of casual use, or a few hours of more intensive use.

What a character is familiar with should be based on his background and any character history the player has written up, with the Game Master having the final say.

If you want more in-depth rules, see the Skill Specialization Setting Rules on page 110.

Common Knowledge

Instead of asking characters to have dozens of background skills they rarely need in actual play, we use the concept of "Common Knowledge." Your hero knows the basic history of his land, common etiquette, how to get around geographically, how to operate common machinery or equipment native to his time period and location, and who the major players in his locality are. A Common Knowledge roll is made by rolling the adventurer's Smarts attribute.

If a character's background suggests he should know something about a subject and he must make a roll, add +2 if most in his area or profession would know the answer. If the subject is foreign to a character, subtract 2 or more from the roll. Everyone else breaks even and gets no modifier.

If it becomes important to know how well a character performs a common task, the GM can ask for whatever roll is appropriate. Knowing how to do a dance, for example, is a Common Knowledge roll. If it becomes important to see how well a character performs the dance, the GM might ask for an Agility roll (with no bonuses or penalties).

For example, an adventure might read: "Anyone who makes a Common Knowledge roll detects that this cavern was carved by civilized hands, not formed naturally." A dwarf knows more about stonework than an elf, so give the dwarf a +2 on the roll. A human has about average knowledge, so no bonus is granted. An elf who has spent most of his life in a forest won't know much about stonework, so the roll is at a –2 penalty.

Specific Knowledge

The Knowledge skill represents deeper specialization in a chosen subject. A dwarf with Knowledge (Stonework), for example, not only knows the dungeon was carved, but might just

know what race did it and the era in which it was first excavated. He might also be able to locate stress points that can cause a cave-in! Knowledge of a particular region is also handy. In a fantasy campaign, for example, locals might know the Dread Mountains are home to vicious harpies. A hero with Knowledge (Dread Mountains) might know a safe route or the specific peak the creatures' aerie is in.

Knowledge skills should be used for subjects that have a significant impact during the game. If the subject comes up very rarely, use Common Knowledge instead.

Skill List

Boating (Agility)

Characters with this skill can handle most any boat or ship common to their setting and character background. They generally know how to handle common tasks associated with their vessels as well (tying knots, rigging sails, etc.).

Climbing (Strength)

Characters may sometimes have to climb tall objects under duress, perhaps to scale a cliff to attack archers stationed above, or to evade a terrifying creature on the ground below!

No roll is usually needed to ascend ladders, ropes, or trees with lots of limbs unless the GM feels there's a good reason (being chased, wounded, etc.). In more stressful situations, a character makes a Climbing roll and checks the results below. Remember that these measurements are listed in table-top inches, with each inch representing two yards in the real world.

• **Fail:** The character makes no progress. If the Climbing roll is a total of 1 or less, he falls to the next level below—whatever that may be. See Falling damage on page 101. If the hero was secured by a rope or other restraint, he falls half the length of the restraint and suffers a Fatigue level instead.

• **Success:** The hero ascends a number of vertical inches on the table-top equal to half his Strength. A hero with a d6 Strength, for example, can climb 3" in a round if he makes his Climbing roll.

• **Raise:** As Success, above, but the character moves an additional 2".

Climbing Modifiers

Modifier	Situation
+2	Antique or medieval climbing equipment
+4	Modern climbing equipment
–2	Scarce or thin handholds
–2	Wet or slippery surface

► **Falling Damage:** See page 101.

► **Prepared Climbs:** Break lengthy ascents into three roughly even sections. Failing a Climbing roll after a break point typically means the hero falls that distance if free-climbing.

► **Ropes:** Those secured with a rope typically only suffer a level of Fatigue from Bumps and

Bruises (see page 99). Of course the Game Master might decide the rope has a chance of breaking under a sudden strain. This is rare in reality, but for dramatic effect, roll a d6. On a 1, the rope breaks and the character falls the entire length of the last section climbed.

Driving (Agility)

Driving allows your hero to control ground and hover vehicles common to his setting. Rules for handling vehicles on the table-top can be found on page 113. Driving is also frequently used with the Chase rules, described on page 94.

Fighting (Agility)

Fighting covers all hand-to-hand (melee) attacks, whether it's with fists, axes, laser swords, or martial arts. The TN to hit an opponent is his Parry (2 plus half his Fighting). See Chapter Three for the combat rules and numerous maneuvers your warrior might attempt.

Gambling (Smarts)

Gambling is useful from the saloons of the Old West to the barracks of most armies. Here's a quick way to simulate about a half-hour of gambling without having to roll for every single toss of the dice or hand of cards.

First have everyone agree on the stakes, such as $10, 10 gold coins, etc. Now have everyone in the game make a Gambling roll. The lowest total pays the highest total the difference times the stake. The next lowest pays the second highest the difference times the stake, and so on. If there's an odd man left in the middle, he breaks even.

Example: Kali rolls highest with a 10 and Yuri rolls lowest with a 4. The difference is 6, so Yuri pays Kali 6 x the stake of $10, or $60.

▶ **Cheating:** A character who cheats adds +2 to his roll. The GM may raise or lower this modifier depending on the particulars of the game or the method of cheating. If the player ever rolls a 1 on his skill die (regardless of his Wild Die), he's caught. The consequences of this depend on the setting, but are usually quite harsh.

Design Note - Guts

Where did the Guts skill go? We removed it. It's important to some settings (and you'll find it as a Setting Rule when it is), but rare in others. Where it's rare, however, even a mighty barbarian has to spend valuable skill points to prove his mettle with the Guts skill, and that really doesn't make much sense.

In the core rules and most settings (especially fantasy and sci-fi) characters now use Spirit to resist the effects of Fear. If a character in a previously published setting has Guts, ignore it. If you're using a published adventure that requires a Guts roll, use Spirit instead.

In a few settings (primarily horrific ones, like Deadlands), Guts is a Setting Rule that reflects the particular nature of the game world and remains intact.

Healing (Smarts)

Healing is the art of stopping wounds and treating existing injuries. In general, every success and raise on a Healing roll eliminates a wound. The healer must subtract not only his own wounds from the roll as usual, but those of his patient as well.

See the Healing rules on page 87 for specific information.

Intimidation (Spirit)

Intimidation is the art of frightening an opponent with sheer force of will, veiled or overt threats, or sometimes just really big guns. This is an opposed roll between the hero's Intimidation and his opponent's Spirit. See Tests of Will on page 86 for game effects.

Investigation (Smarts)

A character skilled in Investigation knows how to make good use of libraries, newspaper morgues, the internet, or other written sources of information. To get information from people rather than books and computers, use the Streetwise skill.

Knowledge (Smarts)

Knowledge is a catch-all skill that must have a focus of some sort, such as Knowledge (Occult) or Knowledge (Science). The player can choose the focus of his character's knowledge, which might reflect his background and education. The skill can be taken multiple times with different focuses to reflect different areas of expertise. An archaeologist, for example, should have Knowledge (History) and Knowledge (Archaeology).

General focuses such as Knowledge (Science) are acceptable, but the GM should give a bonus to a character who has a focus more relevant to a particular task, such as using Knowledge (Biology) to identify a plant or animal.

Some Common Knowledge focuses are: Area Knowledge, Battle (used in Mass Battles, see page 106), Computers, Electronics, History, Journalism, various languages, Law, Medicine (though actually caring for someone is the Healing skill), or Science.

▶ **Common Knowledge:** Characters don't need a Knowledge skill to know something about a particular field. Basic information should be covered by Common Knowledge (see page 26) assuming it makes sense within a character's background. A mercenary with a penchant for reading or a young history student, for example, doesn't necessarily need Knowledge (History). If tasked with a historical question, however, the two might roll normally while those without such a background roll at a penalty.

▶ **Languages:** Knowledge can also be used to reflect knowing a language other than one's own. The higher the level, the better the character can speak and mimic regional dialects, as shown below.

In settings where inhabitants typically speak many languages, see the Languages Setting Rule on page 109.

Knowledge (Language) Table

Skill	Ability
d4	The character can read, write, and speak common words and phrases
d6	The speaker can carry on a prolonged but occasionally halting conversation
d8	The character can speak fluently
d10	The hero can mimic other dialects within the language
d12	The speaker can masterfully recite important literary or oral works

Lockpicking (Agility)

Lockpicking is the ability to bypass mechanical and electronic locks. Lockpicking is also used to disarm the catches and triggers on traps, unless a more relevant skill seems appropriate for a particular trap.

Notice (Smarts)

Notice is a hero's general alertness and ability to search for items or clues. This covers hearing rolls, detecting ambushes, spotting hidden weapons and even scrutinizing other characters to see if they're lying, frightened, and so on. The more raises a character gets on a Notice roll, the more information the Game Master should reveal.

Persuasion (Spirit)

Persuasion is the ability to convince others to do what you want them to do.

Nonplayer characters start at one of five different attitudes: Hostile, Uncooperative, Neutral, Friendly, or Helpful. A successful Persuasion roll improves the Extra's attitude one step, or two with a raise. Failure, on the other hand, decreases the character's attitude by a step, or two if a 1 is rolled on the Persuasion die (regardless of the Wild Die). Most Extras won't change their reaction more than one or two levels during a single exchange, but that's entirely up to the Game Master and the situation.

▶ **Charisma:** Persuasion is always modified by a character's Charisma.

▶ **Player Characters:** Persuasion should never be used on other player characters. Their attitudes should be decided entirely by their players.

▶ **Reaction Table:** If the Game Master doesn't already have an initial attitude in mind for the Extra, he can roll on the chart below.

Reaction Table

2d6 Initial Reaction

2 Hostile: The target is openly hostile and does his best to stand in the hero's way. He won't help without an overwhelming reward or payment of some kind.

3-4 Uncooperative: The target isn't willing to help unless there's a significant advantage to himself.

5-9 Neutral: The target has no particular attitude and will help for little reward if the task at hand is very easy. If the task is difficult, he'll require substantial payment of some kind.

10-11 Friendly: The target will go out of his way for the hero. He'll likely do easy tasks for free (or very little), and is willing to do more dangerous tasks for fair pay or other favors.

12 Helpful: The target is anxious to help the hero, and will probably do so for little or no pay depending on the nature of the task.

Piloting (Agility)

Piloting allows a character to fly airplanes, helicopters, jet packs, and any other flying devices common to his setting and background.

Repair (Smarts)

Repair is the ability to fix gadgets, vehicles, weapons, and other machines. Characters suffer a −2 penalty to their rolls if they don't have access to basic tools. A raise on a Repair roll halves the time required by the specific task.

Riding (Agility)

Riding allows a hero to mount, control, and ride any beast common to his setting. Players should note that mounted characters use the lowest of their Fighting or Riding skills when fighting from horseback. Additional rules for fighting while mounted can be found on page 83.

Shooting (Agility)

Shooting covers all attempts to hit a target with a ranged weapon such as a bow, pistol, or rocket launcher. The basic Target Number to hit is 4 as usual, though there are a number of important modifiers such as range that frequently come into play. See Chapter Three for more details.

Stealth (Agility)

Stealth is the ability to both hide and move quietly, as well as palm objects and pick pockets. In many *Savage Worlds* games, knowing exactly when your hero has been spotted and when he hasn't can be critical.

For a character to sneak up on foes and infiltrate enemy lines, start by figuring out if the "guards" the heroes are sneaking up on are "active" or "inactive." *Inactive* guards aren't paying particularly close attention to their surroundings. The group need only score a standard success on their individual Stealth rolls to avoid being seen. Failing a Stealth roll in the presence of inactive guards makes them active.

Active guards make opposed Notice rolls against the sneaking characters' Stealth skills. Failing a roll against active guards means the character is spotted.

Apply the following modifiers to all Stealth rolls:

Stealth Modifiers

Situation	Modifier
Crawling	+2
Running	−2
Dim light	+1
Darkness	+2
Pitch darkness	+4
Light cover	+1
Medium cover	+2
Heavy cover	+4

▶ **The Last Step:** Sneaking to within 6" of a foe (usually to get close enough for a melee attack) requires an opposed Stealth roll versus the target's Notice, whether the guard is active or inactive.

▶ **Movement Rate:** Out of combat, each Stealth roll covers moving up to five times the character's Pace. In combat, the Stealth roll covers only a single round of movement.

▶ **Stealth for Groups:** Out of combat, make only one Stealth roll for each like group of characters (see Group Rolls on page 71). Use the lowest movement rate to determine how much ground is covered. The observers also make a group roll to Notice their foes. Once a combat breaks down into rounds, Stealth and Notice rolls are made on an individual basis.

Streetwise (Smarts)

Streetwise characters are able to gather information from the street, saloons, or other contacts through bribes, threats, or carousing. Finding written information in libraries and the like is covered by the Investigation skill. Streetwise is always modified by a character's Charisma modifier.

Survival (Smarts)

Survival allows a character to find food, water, or shelter in hostile environments. A character may only make one roll per day. A successful roll finds sustenance for one person, a raise on the roll finds food and water for five adults. Horses and other large beasts count as two adults. Children, camels or others with small appetites count as half. Those who benefit from the roll do not have to make Fatigue rolls for the day for food, water, or shelter.

Swimming (Agility)

Swimming determines if a character floats or sinks in water, as well as how fast he can move within it. A character's Pace is half his Swimming skill in inches per turn in normal water (round up). Choppy water counts as rough terrain and halves this rate. Characters may not "run" while swimming for extra movement.

▶ **Holding Your Breath:** Characters can hold their breath for a number of rounds equal to 2 plus their Vigor die, or half that if they weren't prepared for being submerged and didn't have time to get a good breath.

▶ **Drowning:** The rules for drowning are found on page 100.

Taunt (Smarts)

Taunt is a Test of Wills attack against a person's pride through ridicule, cruel jokes, or one-upmanship. This is an opposed roll against the target's Smarts. See Tests of Will on page 86 for the effects of a successful Taunt.

Throwing (Agility)

Throwing governs all sorts of thrown weapons, from hand grenades to knives, axes, and spears. Throwing works just like the Shooting skill, and uses all the same modifiers, including those for Range. The Rate of Fire of a thrown attack is 1 per hand, so a human character could throw two items at once (one with each hand), suffering the usual multi-action and off-hand penalties (see page 85).

Tracking (Smarts)

Tracking allows a character to follow the tracks of one or more individuals in any type of terrain. Each roll generally covers following the tracks for one mile, but the GM may adjust this dramatically for more specific or small scale searches.

Tracking Modifiers

Modifier	Situation
+2	Tracking more than 5 individuals
+4	Recent snow
+2	Mud
+1	Dusty area
−4	Raining
−2	Tracking in poor light
−2	Tracks are more than one day old
−2	Target attempted to hide tracks

Hindrances

Hindrances are character flaws and physical handicaps that occasionally make life a little tougher for your hero. Some Hindrances are more or less subjective (such as Overconfident). They're there to help you roleplay your character, and might even net you more Bennies since the Game Master awards them for properly playing your character.

A character may take one Major Hindrance and up to two Minor Hindrances. You're free to take more if you think they fit your character description, but you don't get additional points for them.

Design Note - Roleplaying Hindrances

Some Hindrances impose game penalties and some only really matter if the player roleplays them. That's intentional and not something you should worry about too much. The game is designed with the assumption that all heroes take their full complement of Hindrances and therefore have two additional attribute points, Edges, skills, or a combination thereof.

It's certainly true that a Hindrance like Big Mouth won't be worth much if the player doesn't occasionally roleplay it by blurting things out at inappropriate times. But the Game Master can pay a little attention here, too. For example, in a fantasy campaign, players don't roleplay every minute their characters are in a tavern. But it's easy to assume that while they're there—whether it was acted out or not—the Big Mouthed hero let spill their plans to raid the ancient tomb on the hill. Maybe the group will find another team of adventurers are there before them—or worse, waiting to see what they found when they come out.

Finally, Hindrances are more about helping a player figure out who his character is than inflicting a gameplay penalty on him. Being Loyal may never really be a problem—most characters are just naturally loyal to others in their party. But having it on the character sheet reminds the player that he's a "good guy," at least to his friends, and will help him indirectly roleplay his character and make decisions within that context he might have made differently if he was Mean instead.

All Thumbs (Minor)

Some people just aren't good with modern devices. Characters with this drawback suffer a −2 penalty to the Repair skill at all times. In addition, when a hero uses a mechanical or electronic device, a roll of 1 on his skill die (regardless of his Wild Die) means the device is broken. The damage usually requires a Repair roll at −2 and 1d6 hours to fix.

Anemic (Minor)

An anemic character is particularly susceptible to sickness, disease, environmental effects, and fatigue. He subtracts 2 from all Fatigue checks such as those made to resist poison and disease. (See page 99 for more information on Fatigue and the various hazards that lead to it.)

Arrogant (Major)

Your hero doesn't think he's the best—he knows he is. Whatever it is—swordsmanship, kung fu, running—few compare to his skills and he flaunts it every chance he gets.

Winning just isn't enough for your hero. He must completely dominate his opponent. Anytime there is even a shadow of a doubt as to who is better, he must humiliate his opponent and prove he can snatch victory any time he wishes. He is the kind of man who disarms an opponent in a duel just so he can pick the sword up and hand it back with a smirk.

Arrogant heroes always look for the "boss" in battle, attacking lesser minions only if they get in the way.

Bad Eyes (Minor or Major)

Your hero's eyes just aren't what they used to be. With glasses, there's no penalty and the Hindrance is only Minor. Should he lose his glasses (generally a 50% chance when he's wounded, or no chance with a "nerd-strap"), he suffers a −2 penalty to any Trait roll made to shoot or Notice something more than 5" (10 yards) distant.

In low-tech settings where the hero cannot wear glasses, Bad Eyes is a Major Hindrance. He must subtract 2 from Trait rolls made to attack or notice things 5" or more away.

Bad Luck (Major)

Your hero is a little less lucky than most. He gets one less Benny per game session than normal. A character cannot have both Bad Luck and the Luck Edge.

Big Mouth (Minor)

Loose lips sink ships, the saying goes. Your hero's mouth could drown an armada.

Your character can't keep a secret very well. He reveals plans and gives away things best kept among friends, usually at the worst possible times.

Blind (Major)

The individual is completely without sight. He suffers a –6 to all physical tasks that require vision (which is most everything) and –2 to most social tasks as he can't "read" those he's interacting with as well as others.

On the plus side, Blind characters gain their choice of a free Edge to compensate for this particularly difficult Hindrance.

Bloodthirsty (Major)

Your hero never takes prisoners unless under the direct supervision of a superior. This can cause major problems in a military campaign unless his superiors condone that sort of thing. Your killer suffers –4 to his Charisma, but only if his cruel habits are known.

Cautious (Minor)

Some folks gather too much intelligence. This character personifies over-cautiousness. He never makes rash decisions and likes to plot things out in detail long before any action is taken.

Clueless (Major)

Your hero isn't as aware of his world as most others. He suffers –2 to Common Knowledge rolls.

Code of Honor (Major)

Honor is very important to your character. He keeps his word, won't abuse or kill prisoners, and generally tries to operate within his world's particular notion of proper gentlemanly or ladylike behavior.

Curious (Major)

It killed the cat, and it might kill your hero as well. Curious characters are easily dragged into any adventure. They have to check out everything and always want to know what's behind a potential mystery.

Death Wish (Minor)

Having a death wish doesn't mean your adventurer is suicidal—but he does want to die *after* completing some important goal. Maybe he wants revenge for the murder of his family, or maybe he's dying from disease and wants to go out in a blaze of glory. He won't throw his life away for no reason, but when there's a chance to complete his goal, he'll do anything—and take any risk—to achieve it.

This Hindrance is usually Minor unless the goal is relatively easily fulfilled (very rare).

Delusional (Minor or Major)

Your hero believes something that is considered quite strange by everyone else. Minor Delusions are harmless or the character generally keeps it to himself (the government puts sedatives in soft drinks, dogs can talk, we're all just characters in some bizarre game, etc.).

With a Major Delusion, he expresses his view on the situation frequently and it can occasionally

lead to danger (the government is run by aliens, hospitals are deadly, I'm allergic to armor, zombies are my friends).

Doubting Thomas (Minor)

Some people don't believe in the supernatural until they're halfway down some creature's gullet. Doubting Thomases are skeptics who try their best to rationalize supernatural events. Even once a Doubting Thomas realizes the supernatural exists, he still tries to rationalize weird events, following red herrings or ignoring evidence.

Doubting Thomases suffer −2 to their Fear checks when confronted with undeniable supernatural horror.

Elderly (Major)

Your adventurer is getting on in years, but he's not quite ready for the nursing home. His Pace is reduced by 1, and his Strength and Vigor drop a die type to a minimum of d4, and cannot be raised thereafter.

On the plus side, the wisdom of his years grants the hero 5 extra skill points that may be used for any skills linked to Smarts.

Enemy (Minor or Major)

Someone out there hates the character and wants him dead. The value of the Hindrance depends on how powerful the enemy is and how often he might show up. A Minor Enemy might be a lone gunslinger out for vengeance. A Major Enemy might be a supernatural gunslinger who wants your hero dead.

If the enemy is one day defeated, the GM should gradually work in a replacement, or the hero may buy off the Hindrance by sacrificing an Advance.

Greedy (Minor or Major)

Your miserly hero measures his worth in treasure. If a Minor Hindrance, he argues bitterly over any loot acquired during play. If a Major Hindrance, he fights over anything he considers unfair, and may even kill for his "fair share."

Habit (Minor or Major)

Your warrior has an annoying and constant habit of some sort. Maybe she picks her nose, says "y'know" in every sentence, or chews gum like it's going out of style.

A Minor Habit irritates those around her but isn't dangerous. Your hero suffers a −1 Charisma.

A Major Habit is a physical or mental addiction of some sort that is debilitating or possibly even deadly. This includes drug use, chronic drinking, or perhaps even an addiction to virtual reality in a high-tech setting. A character who doesn't

get his fix must make a Fatigue check every 24 hours thereafter (see Fatigue on page 99). The first failed roll makes the character Fatigued, then Exhausted. The final result is a coma for hard drug use, or a bad case of the shakes for things like alcohol or VR. Medical care may ease the symptoms. Otherwise the victim must live with the penalties for 1d6 days. Afterward, the hero must buy off the Hindrance by sacrificing an opportunity to Advance or he eventually falls back into his dependency.

Hard of Hearing (Minor or Major)

Characters who have lost some or all of their hearing have this disadvantage. As a Minor Hindrance, it subtracts 2 from all Notice rolls made to hear, including awaking due to loud noises. A Major Hindrance means the character is deaf. She cannot hear and automatically fails all Notice rolls that depend on hearing.

Heroic (Major)

This noble soul never says no to a person in need. She doesn't have to be happy about it, but she always comes to the rescue of those she feels can't help themselves. She's the first one to run into a burning building, usually agrees to hunt monsters for little or no pay, and is generally a pushover for a sob story.

Illiterate (Minor)

Your hero cannot read. He can probably sign his name and knows what a STOP sign says, but can do little else. He also doesn't know much about math either. He can probably do 2+2=4, but multiplication and the like are beyond him.

Illiterates can't read or write in any language, by the way, no matter how many they actually speak.

Lame (Major)

A past wound has nearly crippled your hero. His basic Pace is reduced by 2 and he rolls only a d4 for running rolls. A character's Pace may never be reduced below 1.

Loyal (Minor)

Your character may not be a hero, but he'd give his life for his friends. This character can never leave a man behind if there's any chance at all he could help.

Mean (Minor)

This fellow is ill-tempered and disagreeable. No one really likes him, and he has trouble doing anything kind for anyone else. He must be paid for his troubles and doesn't even accept awards graciously. Your character suffers −2 to his Charisma.

Obese (Minor)

Particularly large people often have great difficulty in dangerous physical situations. Those who carry their weight well have the Brawny Edge. Those who don't handle it very well are Obese. A character cannot be both Brawny and Obese.

An Obese hero adds 1 to his Toughness, but his Pace is decreased by 1 and his running die is a d4. Obese characters may also have difficulty finding armor or clothing that fits, squeezing into tight spaces, or even riding in confined spaces such as coach airplane seats or compact cars.

One Arm (Major)

Whether by birth or battle, your hero has lost an arm. Fortunately, his other arm is (now) his "good" one. Tasks that require two hands, such as Climbing, suffer a –4 modifier.

One Eye (Major)

Your hero lost an eye for some unfortunate reason. If he doesn't wear a patch or buy a glass replacement (typically $500), he suffers –1 to his Charisma for the grotesque wound.

He suffers –2 to any Trait rolls that require depth perception, such as Shooting or Throwing, jumping a ravine or rooftop, and so on.

One Leg (Major)

With a prosthetic, One Leg acts exactly like the Lame Hindrance, reducing Pace by 2 and running rolls are now a d4. Without a prosthetic, the character's Pace is 2 and he can never run. He also suffers –2 to Traits that require mobility, such as Climbing and Fighting. A character with one leg also suffers a –2 penalty to his Swimming skill (and Pace).

Outsider (Minor)

In a society made up of only a few types of people, your hero isn't one of them. An Indian in a Western town, an alien in a sci-fi game of human marines, or a half-orc in a party of elves, dwarves, and humans are all examples of outsiders. Locals are likely to raise prices on the Outsider, ignore pleas for help, and generally treat him as if he's of a lower class than the rest of their society.

In addition to the roleplaying effects above, your hero's Charisma suffers a –2 modifier among all but his own people.

Overconfident (Major)

There's nothing out there your hero can't defeat. At least that's what he thinks. He believes he can do most anything and never wants to retreat from a challenge. He's not suicidal, but he certainly takes on more than common sense dictates.

Pacifist (Minor or Major)

Your hero absolutely despises violence. Minor pacifism means he only fights when given no other choice, and never allows the killing of prisoners or other defenseless victims.

Major Pacifists won't fight living characters under *any* circumstances. They may defend themselves, but won't do anything to permanently harm sentient, living creatures. Note that undeniably evil creatures, undead, demons, and the like are fair game. A Major Pacifist might also fight with nonlethal methods, such as with his fists. Such characters only do so when obviously threatened, however.

Phobia (Minor or Major)

Phobias are overwhelming and irrational fears that stay with a hero for the rest of his life. Whenever a character is in the presence of his phobia, he subtracts 2 from all his Trait tests as a Minor Hindrance, and 4 if the fear is a Major Phobia.

Phobias shouldn't be too obvious—everyone should be afraid of vampires, for example, so it's not a phobia—it's common sense. Instead, the phobia usually centers on some random element the mind focused on during whatever encounter caused such a fright. Remember, phobias are *irrational* fears.

Poverty (Minor)

It's said a fool and his money are soon parted. Your hero is that fool. He starts with half the usual money for your setting and just can't seem to hang onto funds acquired after play begins. In general, the player halves his total funds every game week.

Quirk (Minor)

Your hero has some minor foible that is usually humorous, but can occasionally cause him trouble. A swashbuckler may always try to first slash his initials on his foes before attacking, a dwarf may brag constantly about his culture, or a snobby debutante might not eat, drink, or socialize with the lower class.

Small (Major)

Your character is either very skinny, very short, or both relative to his particular race. Subtract 1 from his Toughness for his reduced stature.

Stubborn (Minor)

This stubborn individual always wants his way and never admits he's wrong. Even when it's painfully obvious he's made a mistake he tries to justify it with half-truths and rationalizations.

Ugly (Minor)

Unfortunately, this individual hit more than a few ugly sticks on his way down the tree of life. His Charisma is lowered by 2, and he is generally shunned by members of the opposite sex.

Vengeful (Minor or Major)

Your character always attempts to right a wrong he feels was done to him. If this is a Minor Hindrance, he usually seeks vengeance legally. The type and immediacy of his vengeance varies by character, of course. Some plot and scheme for months to extract what they see as justice. Others demand immediate results.

If this is a Major Hindrance, your character will kill to rectify his perceived injustice.

Vow (Minor or Major)

The character has a vow of some sort. Whether it's Major or Minor depends on the Vow itself. Some may have Vows to particular orders or causes, to the Hippocratic Oath, to rid the world of evil, and so on. The danger in fulfilling the Vow and how often it might occur determines the level of the Hindrance. Whatever the Vow, it's only a Hindrance if it actually comes into play from time to time and causes the character some discomfort.

Wanted (Minor or Major)

Your hero has committed some crime in his past and will be arrested if discovered by the authorities. This assumes the setting actually has laws and police officers to enforce them.

The level of the Hindrance depends on how serious the crime was. A hero with numerous unpaid parking tickets (in a game where he might have to drive occasionally) has a Minor Hindrance, as does someone wanted for more serious crimes away from the main campaign area. Being accused of murder is a Major Hindrance in almost any setting.

Yellow (Major)

Not everyone has ice water in his veins. Your hero is squeamish at the sight of blood and gore and terrified of coming to harm. He subtracts 2 from all of his fear-based Spirit checks.

Young (Major)

Children are sometimes forced to go on dangerous adventures through unfortunate circumstances. Think carefully before choosing this Hindrance, for your youngster starts at a significant disadvantage.

Young heroes are generally 8–12 years old (in human years—adjust this for races with different

aging paradigms). They have only 3 points to adjust their attributes and 10 skill points. On the plus side, youths like these have a fair amount of luck. They draw one extra Benny at the beginning of each game session in addition to any additional Bennies gained from such things as the Luck or Great Luck Edges.

If the character should live long enough to mature, the Hindrance doesn't have to be bought off, he's already paid the price for the Hindrance by starting at a disadvantage. He stops getting the extra Benny when he reaches 18 years of age however (or the age of adulthood in your particular setting).

Edges

Below is a list of Edges common to most settings. You'll find more Edges in official *Savage Worlds* setting books as well. The Edges are grouped by type to help during character creation. Unless an Edge specifically says otherwise, it may only be selected once.

► **Requirements:** Below each Edge are any skills and Rank required to take it. A Novice character can't buy a Legendary Edge, for instance. A character may always purchase an Edge of a Rank lower than his.

► **Improved Edges:** Some Edges have improved effects if you purchase additional "levels" in them, such as Attractive and Very Attractive, or Rich

and Filthy Rich. To buy an Improved Edge, you must have all previous versions of an Edge. You must choose Rich before buying Filthy Rich, for example.

Background Edges

These Edges are hereditary and background advantages or learned responses that develop in a character after prolonged training or exposure to certain events.

Players can choose these Edges after character creation but the Game Master might require a little more rationalization. An individual might choose the Attractive Edge, for example, by cleaning herself up, getting a makeover, and generally paying more attention to her looks. Characters might be able to gain the Arcane Background Edge as well, should they find a book of forbidden knowledge or train under another arcane type in their party.

Design Note - Background Edges

In previous versions of Savage Worlds, *Background Edges could only be taken at character creation without special permission by the Game Master. We've changed that rule and you may now take Background Edges as advances just like any other. If you care about the rationalization of such things, you may want to link them to an event in your game. If a player wants the Fast Healer Edge, for example, you might say (or the Game Master might require) that exposure to the party's magical healing, or a new emphasis on health and fitness, have given the hero this ability.*

Alertness

Requirements: Novice

Not much gets by your hero. He's very observant and perceptive, and adds +2 to his Notice rolls to hear, see, or otherwise sense the world around him.

Ambidextrous

Requirements: Novice, Agility d8+

Your hero is as deft with his left hand as he is with his right. Characters normally suffer a –2 penalty when performing physical tasks with the off-hand (characters are assumed to be right-handed). With this Edge, your warrior ignores the –2 penalty for using his off-hand (see page 85).

Arcane Background

Requirements: Novice, Special

This is the Edge your character must purchase to have any sort of magical, psionic, or other supernatural ability. See Chapter Five for a complete description of Arcane Backgrounds.

Arcane Resistance

Requirements: Novice, Spirit d8+

This individual is particularly resistant to magic (including psionics, weird science, etc.), whether by nature or by heritage. He acts as if he had 2 points of Armor when hit by damage-causing arcane powers, and adds +2 to his Trait rolls when resisting opposed powers. Even friendly arcane powers must subtract this modifier to affect the resistant hero.

Improved Arcane Resistance

Requirements: Novice, Arcane Resistance

As above but Armor and resistance are increased to 4.

Attractive

Requirements: Novice, Vigor d6+

It's no secret that beautiful people have an easier time getting their way in life. This Edge grants your beautiful or handsome character +2 to Charisma.

Very Attractive

Requirements: Novice, Attractive

Your hero is drop-dead gorgeous. His Charisma is increased to +4.

Berserk

Requirements: Novice

Immediately after suffering a wound (including a Shaken result from physical damage), your hero must make a Smarts roll or go Berserk.

While Berserk, his Parry is reduced by 2 but he adds +2 to all Fighting, Strength, melee damage rolls, and Toughness. The warrior ignores all wound modifiers while Berserk, but cannot use any skills, Edges, or maneuvers that require concentration, including Shooting and Taunt, but not Intimidation.

Berserkers attack with reckless abandon. Anytime his Fighting die is a 1 (regardless of his Wild Die), he hits a random adjacent target (not the original target). The attack may hit friend as well as foe. If there are no other adjacent targets, the blow simply misses.

The Berserker may end his rage by doing nothing (not even moving) for one full action and making a Smarts roll at –2.

Brave

Requirements: Novice, Spirit d6+

Those with this Edge have learned to master their fear. Or perhaps are so jaded or emotionally distant they've just lost their normal "fight or flight" responses. Either way, your hero adds +2 to Fear tests. If the character is in a setting that uses Guts as a Setting Rule, it adds to that as well.

Brawny

Requirements: Novice, Strength and Vigor d6+

Your bruiser is very large or perhaps just very fit. His bulk resists damage better than most and adds +1 to his Toughness. In addition, the character can carry more than most proportional to his Strength. He can carry 8 times his Strength in pounds without penalty instead of the usual 5 times his Strength.

Fast Healer

Requirements: Novice, Vigor d8+

Some individuals just seem to heal faster than others. Those with this blessing add +2 to Vigor rolls when checking for natural healing. See page 87 for complete rules on Healing.

Fleet-Footed

Requirements: Novice, Agility d6+

The hero's Pace is increased by +2 and he rolls a d10 instead of a d6 when running.

Linguist

Requirements: Novice, Smarts d6+

The character has an ear for languages and a rare talent for recognizing similarities between them. A character with this Edge starts with a number of languages equal to his Smarts die, and can make a Smarts roll at –2 to make herself understood in any language or dialect she has heard spoken for at least a week.

Luck

Requirements: Novice

The adventurer seems to be blessed by fate, karma, the gods, or whatever external forces he believes in (or believe in him!)

He draws one extra Benny at the beginning of each game session, allowing him to succeed at important tasks more often than most, and survive incredible dangers.

Great Luck

Requirements: Novice, Luck

The player draws two extra Bennies instead of one at the start of each session.

Noble

Requirements: Novice

Those born of noble blood have many perks in life, but often have just as many responsibilities. Nobles have high status in their societies, are entitled to special treatment from their foes, gain +2 Charisma, and also have the Rich Edge. This gives the hero several Edges for the price of one, but the responsibilities more than offset the additional perks. Nobles often have troops under their control, as well as land, a family home, and other assets. All of this must be determined by the GM, and balanced by the grave responsibilities the character faces.

As an example, a character in a fantasy campaign might have a company of swordsmen, a small keep, and even a magical sword he inherited from his father. But he also has an entire region to manage, criminals to judge, justice to mete out, and a jealous neighbor who covets his lands and constantly plots against him at court.

Quick

Requirements: Novice, Agility d8+

Quick characters have lightning-fast reflexes and a cool head. Whenever you are dealt a 5 or lower in combat, you may discard and draw again until you get a card higher than 5.

Characters with both the Level Headed and Quick Edges draw their additional card and take the best as usual. If that card is a Five or less, the Quick Edge may be used to draw a replacement until it's Six or higher.

Rich

Requirements: Novice

Whether the individual was born with a silver spoon in his mouth or earned it through hard work, he's got more money than most. Rich heroes start with three times the normal starting funds for the setting. If a regular income is appropriate for this setting, the hero receives the modern day equivalent of a $150,000 annual salary.

Filthy Rich

Requirements: Novice, Rich or Noble

This character is very wealthy. He has five times the starting funds for the setting and, if appropriate, a yearly income of around $500,000.

Wealthier characters should have a very complete background as well. This needs to be worked out with the GM, and comes with many more assets as well as onerous responsibilities.

Combat Edges

These Edges are designed to help your hero dish out terrible damage—or survive it—in the bloody battles of *Savage Worlds*.

Block

Requirements: Seasoned, Fighting d8+

Warriors who engage in frequent hand-to-hand combat are far more skilled in personal defense than most others. They've learned not only how to attack, but how to block their opponent's blows as well. A fighter with this Edge adds +1 to his Parry.

Improved Block

Requirements: Veteran, Block

As above, but the hero adds +2 to his Parry.

Brawler

Requirements: Novice, Str d8+

Frequent fights with his bare hands have given this thug a powerful punch. When he hits a foe with a successful bare-handed Fighting roll, he adds +2 to his damage.

Bruiser

Requirements: Seasoned, Brawler

When the bruiser gets a raise on his bare-handed Fighting attack, he rolls a d8 instead of a d6.

Combat Reflexes

Requirements: Seasoned

Your adventurer recovers quickly from shock and trauma. He adds +2 to his Spirit roll when attempting to recover from being Shaken.

Counterattack

Requirements: Seasoned, Fighting d8+

Fighters with this Edge know how to respond instantly to an enemy's mistakes. Once per round (if not Shaken), the character receives one free Fighting attack against one adjacent foe who failed a Fighting attack against him. This attack is made at –2, and the Counterattack must be a normal attack (no Disarm, Wild Attack, or other maneuvers), and may not be combined with Frenzy or Sweep. It may be used with the Defend maneuver, but not Full Defense.

Improved Counterattack

Requirements: Veteran, Counterattack

As above but the character may ignore the –2 penalty.

Dodge

Requirements: Seasoned, Agility d8+

Some crafty types know how to get out of harm's way. This Edge allows them to use cover, movement, and concealment to make them harder to hit. Unless they are the victim of a surprise attack and taken completely unaware, attackers must subtract 1 from their ranged attack rolls when targeting them (even in close combat).

Characters who attempt to evade area effect attacks may add +1 to their Agility roll as well (when allowed).

Improved Dodge

Requirements: Veteran, Dodge

As above but attackers subtract 2 from their attack rolls, and the character adds +2 to evade area effect weapons when allowed.

Elan

Requirements: Novice, Spirit d8+

When this spirited hero puts his heart into something it tends to pay off in big ways. When you spend a Benny on a Trait roll (including Soak rolls), add +2 to the final total.

Extraction

Requirements: Novice, Agility d8+

When a character normally withdraws from a melee, his attacker gets a free attack before he does so—a very dangerous proposition for most. Your hero is adept at retreating from an engagement.

Make an Agility roll. If successful, one opponent doesn't get a free attack anytime you disengage (see page 87).

Improved Extraction

Requirements: Novice, Extraction

As above but if you succeed with a raise all opponents currently in melee with the character lose their free attack as your warrior withdraws.

First Strike

Requirements: Novice, Agility d8+

Once per turn the hero (if not Shaken) gets a free Fighting attack against a single foe who moves adjacent to him. This automatically interrupts the opponent's action and does not cost the hero his action if he is on Hold or has not yet acted this round.

Improved First Strike

Requirements: Heroic, First Strike

As above but the hero may make one free attack against each and every foe who moves adjacent to him.

Florentine

Requirements: Novice, Agility d8+, Fighting d8+

A character trained to fight "Florentine" is a master at wielding two weapons at once. He adds +1 to his Fighting rolls versus an opponent with a single weapon and no shield. In addition, opponents subtract 1 from any "gang up" bonuses they would normally get against the fighter as his two flashing blades parry their blows.

Frenzy

Requirements: Seasoned, Fighting d10+

Frenzied fighters make fast and furious melee attacks, sacrificing finesse for raw speed. This allows them to make an extra Fighting attack per round at a –2 penalty to all Fighting rolls. This attack must be taken at the same time as another Fighting attack though it may target any two foes adjacent to the hero (Wild Cards roll two Fighting dice and one Wild Die). The –2 penalty is subtracted from all attacks.

A character armed with two weapons still only makes one extra attack.

Improved Frenzy

Requirements: Veteran, Frenzy

As above but the character may ignore the –2 Frenzy penalty.

Giant Killer

Requirements: Veteran

The bigger they are, the harder they are to kill. At least for most. But your hero knows how to find the weak points in massive creatures.

Your hero does +1d6 damage when attacking creatures three sizes or more larger than himself. An ogre (Size +3) with this ability, for example, gains the bonus only against creatures of Size +6 or greater. A human Giant Killer (Size 0), can claim the bonus against the ogre, however.

Hard to Kill

Requirements: Wild Card, Novice, Spirit d8+

This adventurer has more lives than a truckload of cats. When forced to make Vigor rolls due to Incapacitation, he may ignore his wound modifiers. This only applies to Vigor rolls called for to resist Incapacitation or death (see page 77). He still suffers from wound modifiers for other Trait rolls normally.

Harder to Kill

Requirements: Veteran, Hard to Kill

Your hero is tougher to kill than Rasputin. If he is ever "killed," roll a die. On an odd result, he's dead as usual. On an even roll, he's Incapacitated but somehow escapes death. He may be captured, stripped of all his belongings, or mistakenly left for dead, but he somehow survives.

Improvisational Fighter

Requirements: Seasoned, Smarts d6+

Heroes often find themselves fighting with pieces of equipment or furnishings not designed for combat. A character with this Edge has a knack for using such improvised weapons, and does not suffer the usual −1 penalty to attack and Parry when wielding them. See page 83 for details.

Killer Instinct

Requirements: Heroic

This hero hates losing. If he ties on an opposed roll of any sort, he wins. In addition, if his skill die on an opposed skill roll is a 1, he can reroll it (but must keep the second result, even if it's another 1).

Level Headed

Requirements: Seasoned, Smarts d8+

Fighters who can keep their cool when everyone else is running for cover are deadly customers in combat.

A hero with this Edge draws an additional Action Card in combat and acts on the best of the draw.

Improved Level Headed

Requirements: Seasoned, Level Headed

As above but the hero draws 3 cards.

Marksman

Requirements: Seasoned

The hero excels at taking controlled, measured shots. If he does not move in a turn, he may fire as if he took the Aim maneuver. Marksman may never be used with a Rate of Fire greater than 1.

Marksman works with both Shooting and Throwing.

Martial Artist

Requirements: Novice, Fighting d6+

This character is highly trained in hand-to-hand fighting. He is never considered unarmed in combat and so is never subject to the Unarmed Defender rule (page 87). With a successful unarmed attack, he adds +d4 to his Strength roll (as if he were using a small weapon).

Improved Martial Artist

Requirements: Veteran, Martial Artist, Fighting d10+

The character now adds +d6 to his bare-handed damage.

Nerves of Steel

Requirements: Wild Card, Novice, Vigor d8+

Your hero has learned to fight on through the most intense pain. He may ignore 1 point of wound penalties.

Improved Nerves of Steel

Requirements: Novice, Nerves of Steel

The hero ignores 2 points of wound penalties.

No Mercy

Requirements: Seasoned

The character may spend a Benny to reroll any one damage roll, including those made for area effect attacks.

Quick Draw

Requirements: Novice, Agility d8+

This Edge allows a hero to draw a weapon as a free action (and thus ignore the usual −2 multi-action penalty if he chooses to fire as well). If the character must make an Agility roll to draw a weapon (see page 74), he adds +2 to the roll.

Rock and Roll!

Requirements: Seasoned, Shooting d8+

Some veteran shooters learn to compensate for the recoil of fully automatic weapons. If a character with this Edge does not move, he may ignore the recoil penalty for firing a weapon on full automatic.

Steady Hands

Requirements: Novice, Agility d8+

Your hero ignores the "unstable platform" penalty for firing from the backs of animals or while riding in moving vehicles. In addition, when performing actions while Running (see page 74), his penalty is −1 instead of −2.

Sweep

Requirements: Novice, Strength d8+, Fighting d8+

Sweep allows a character to make a single Fighting attack and apply it against all currently adjacent targets at a −2 penalty (friends and foes alike—be careful). Resolve each damage roll separately. The attack is applied immediately when rolled and only affects targets adjacent at that time.

A character may not use Sweep in the same round she uses Frenzy, nor may she Sweep more than once per round, or with a second weapon held in another hand. In effect, the hero may only perform Sweep once per action unless she somehow gets two entire actions (perhaps under the effects of a spell or power, for example).

Improved Sweep

Requirements: Veteran, Sweep

As above but the hero may ignore the –2 penalty.

Trademark Weapon

Requirements: Novice, Fighting or Shooting of d10+

The hero knows one unique weapon (*Excalibur, Old Betsy, Sting*) like the back of his hand. When using that weapon, he adds +1 to his Fighting, Shooting, or Throwing rolls. A hero can take this Edge multiple times, applying it to a different weapon each time. If a Trademark Weapon is lost, the hero can replace it, but the benefit of the Edge doesn't kick in for two game weeks.

Improved Trademark Weapon

Requirements: Veteran, Trademark Weapon

As above but the bonus when using the weapon increases to +2.

Two-Fisted

Requirements: Novice, Agility d8+

A Two-Fisted hero isn't ambidextrous—he's simply learned to fight with two weapons (or both fists) at once. When attacking with a weapon in each hand, he rolls each attack separately but ignores the multi-action penalty (see page 75).

Leadership Edges

Leadership Edges grant bonuses to subordinates, making them more effective, reliable, or durable. These Edges apply only to a number of subordinates within 5" (the "command radius"), and are not cumulative with the same Edge from other leaders. Subordinates may benefit from different Leadership Edges by the same or different leaders.

Command

Requirements: Novice, Smarts d6+

Command is the ability to give clear instructions to surrounding allies and enforce your hero's will upon them. This makes your character's compatriots more willing to fight on despite their wounds, and so adds +1 to their Spirit rolls to recover from being Shaken.

Command Presence

Requirements: Novice, Command

A booming voice, effective commands, natural charisma, or simple training results in a much more effective combat element. At the center of that element is the officer in command. A hero with this Edge has a "command radius" of 10" instead of the usual 5".

Fervor

Requirements: Veteran, Command, Spirit d8+

A simple phrase uttered by a great leader can sometimes have momentous results. A leader with this ability can inspire his men to bloody fervor by yelling a motto, slogan, or other inspirational words. Those in the command radius add +1 to their Fighting damage rolls.

Hold the Line!

Requirements: Seasoned, Command, Smarts d8+

This Edge strengthens the will of the men under the hero's command. The troops add +1 to their Toughness.

Inspire

Requirements: Seasoned, Command

Leaders with exceptional reputations and experience in battle inspire the soldiers around them. They add +2 to Spirit rolls when recovering from being Shaken (this includes the original +1 bonus for the Command Edge).

Leader of Men

Requirements: Veteran, Command

Command comes easy to this commander. Those under his command work like a well-oiled machine when he's in charge.

Allies under the leader's command roll a d10 as the Wild Die instead of a d6 when making group rolls.

Natural Leader

Requirements: Novice, Command, Spirit d8+

This Edge signifies a special link between a leader and his men. With it, he may share his Bennies with any troops under his command.

Tactician

Requirements: Seasoned, Command, Wild Card, Smarts d8+, Knowledge (Battle) d6+

The leader has a natural grasp of small unit tactics and can frequently take advantage of a rapidly changing situation.

At the beginning of a fight and before any Action Cards are dealt, the hero makes a Knowledge (Battle) roll. For each success and raise he receives one Action Card. These are kept separate from his regular Action Cards and are not placed back into the deck until used or the combat ends (including Jokers!). At the start of any round, the hero may give one or more of these extra cards to his allies, whether Extras or Wild Cards, who then use it as their Action Card for the round in place of the one dealt them. This allows Extras to operate independently of Wild Card characters for one round if they receive their own card.

Only one character per encounter may use this Edge.

Power Edges

Power Edges are for those with Arcane Backgrounds. See Chapter Five for more information on each type of Arcane Background, how to use them, and the powers available.

New Power

Requirements: Novice, Arcane Background

An arcane character may learn a new power by choosing this Edge (which may be taken multiple times). He may choose from any powers normally available to his particular Arcane Background.

Power Points

Requirements: Novice, Arcane Background

Wizards, weird scientists, and other arcane types always want more power. This Edge grants them an additional 5 Power Points.

Power Points may be selected more than once, but only once per Rank.

Rapid Recharge

Requirements: Seasoned, Spirit d6+, Arcane Background

This Edge allows an arcane character to regain 1 Power Point every 30 minutes.

Improved Rapid Recharge

Requirements: Veteran, Rapid Recharge

The character regains 1 Power Point every 15 minutes.

Soul Drain

Rank: Seasoned, Arcane Background (any but Weird Science), Knowledge (Arcana) d10+

Spellcasters, mentalists, and other arcane types in dire need of Power Points may use this Edge to drain energy from their own souls. To use this dangerous ability, the arcane character first decides how many Power Points he wants to draw from himself. Then he makes a Spirit roll minus the number of points he's trying to drain. (This is a free action.) On a Spirit total of 1 or less, the character suffers a wound and falls unconscious for 1d6 hours. On a failure, the character suffers a wound. On a success or better, the character gets the points he needed and may attempt to cast a spell with them immediately (they may not be saved).

Professional Edges

Professional Edges are very special abilities that reflect many years of practicing a particular trade. In some cases they may also represent special blessings from higher powers as well.

These Edges help you create a character who is far more competent in his chosen field than most others. If you want to make a very effective Mad Scientist, for example, you could combine the Arcane Background (Weird Science) with the Gadgeteer and Mr. Fix It Edges.

Professional Edges represent many years of training so their Requirements are quite high. Players may purchase Professional Edges after character creation, but should usually lead up to it story-wise by practicing the affected trade during down-time or in between adventures. The time spent acquiring one of these abilities is subjective and up to the Game Master, but makes the game much more believable if a little narrative time is spent training.

▶ **Stacking:** Bonuses to the same Trait from different Professional Edges do not stack. If you make a hero with both the Woodsman and the Thief Edges, for example, he gains +2 to his Stealth skill, not +4.

Ace

Requirements: Novice, Agility d8+

Aces are special pilots and drivers who feel more comfortable behind the wheel, throttle, or flight stick than on their own two feet.

Aces add +2 to Boating, Driving, and Piloting rolls. In addition, they may also spend Bennies to make Soak rolls for any vehicle or vessel they control. This is a Boating, Driving, or Piloting roll at −2 (cancelling their usual +2). Each success and raise negates a wound and any critical hit that would have resulted from it.

Acrobat

Requirements: Novice, Agility d8+, Strength d6+

Those who have formal training in the acrobatic arts or are naturally agile may take this Edge. It adds +2 to all Agility rolls made to perform acrobatic maneuvers (including Trick maneuvers), and also adds +1 to a character's Parry as long as he has no encumbrance penalty.

Adept

Requirements: Novice, Arcane Background (Miracles), Martial Artist, Faith d8+, Fighting d8+

Adepts are holy warriors who have trained themselves to be living weapons. Some do so to be ultimate warriors; others do it in the service of a cause or deity.

As a free action, an adept can spend 1 Power Point to gain AP 2 with all of his unarmed attacks until his next action.

In addition, upon taking this Edge and at each new Rank, they may choose to change the trappings of one of the following powers to work only on themselves but be activated as a free action: *boost/lower trait, deflection, healing, smite,* or *speed*. The Adept must have the power to begin with, and this does not allow him to activate more than one power in a round.

Assassin

Requirements: Novice, Agility d8+, Climbing d6+, Fighting d6+, Stealth d8+

Assassins are trained killers who know how to kill with deadly precision—if they can properly approach their prey. Assassins add +2 to any damage roll where they strike a foe unawares (even with ranged attacks).

Champion

Requirements: Novice, Arcane Background (Miracles), Spirit d8+, Strength d6+, Vigor d8+, Faith d6+, Fighting d8+

Champions are holy (or unholy) men and women chosen to fight for a particular deity or religion. Most are pious souls ready and willing to lay down their lives for a greater cause, but some may have been born into the role and follow their path with some reluctance.

Champions fight the forces of darkness (or good). They add +2 damage when attacking supernaturally evil (or good) creatures, and have +2 Toughness when suffering damage from supernaturally evil (or good) sources, including arcane powers and the weapons, claws, teeth, etc., of such creatures.

Gadgeteer

Requirements: Novice, Arcane Background (Weird Science), Smarts d8+, Repair d8+, Weird Science d8+, at least two other scientific Knowledge skills at d6+

These mechanical gurus are so technically savvy they can quickly build a machine to handle nearly any situation.

Once per game session, a gadgeteer can create a "jury-rigged" device from spare parts. The device functions just like any other Weird Science device, and uses any power available to Weird Scientists in that setting (though this is still subject to Rank restrictions). It has half the inventor's Power Points, and once these are used up, the gadget burns out and does not recharge. The inventor must have access to some parts and a reasonable amount of time (GM's call, but at least 1d20 minutes) to create the gizmo.

Holy/Unholy Warrior

Requirements: Novice, Arcane Background (Miracles), Spirit d8+, Faith d6+

Acolytes, clerics, paladins, holy slayers, and other avatars of the gods are frequently tasked with battling the forces of evil in the mortal world. This Edge gives them a slight advantage against such foes.

As an action, a priest or other holy person may call upon his chosen deity to repulse supernaturally evil creatures, such as the undead, demons, and the like. It also works on evil characters with the Arcane Background (Miracles) Edge.

Repulsing evil costs 1 Power Point and has a range of the character's Spirit. Targeted creatures within that range must make a Spirit roll. Failure means the creature is Shaken; a 1 means it is destroyed. Wild Cards suffer an automatic Wound instead.

A character may also be an Unholy Warrior working for the forces of evil. In this case, he repulses good creatures, such as angels, paladins, or good characters with Arcane Background (Miracles).

Investigator

Requirements: Novice, Smarts d8+, Investigation d8+, Streetwise d8+

Investigators have spent a great deal of time researching ancient legends, working the streets, or deducing devilish mysteries. Some of these heroes are actual Private Investigators for hire while others may be sleuthing mages in a fantasy world or perhaps inquisitive college professors stumbling upon Things Man Was Not Meant to Know in the dark of night. Investigators add +2 to Investigation and Streetwise rolls, as well as Notice rolls made to search through evidence.

Jack-of-All-Trades

Requirements: Novice, Smarts d10+

Through advanced schooling, book-learning, computer-enhanced skill programs, or just amazing intuitive perception, your hero has a talent for picking up skills on the fly. There is little he can't figure out given a little time and a dash of luck.

Any time he makes an unskilled roll for a Smarts-based skill, he may do so at d4 instead of the usual d4–2.

McGyver

Requirements: Novice, Smarts d6+, Repair d6+, Notice d8+

This character can improvise something when the need for a tool arises. He suffers no negative penalties on Trait rolls for lack of equipment in most situations.

In addition, given a few simple tools, props, or devices, he can generally rig devices to help escape from death-traps, weapons to match some bizarre need, or otherwise create something that's needed when such a thing isn't actually present. The extent of this is completely up to the Game Master, but creativity should be rewarded, particularly in dire situations where few other answers are possible.

Mentalist

Requirements: Novice, Arcane Background (Psionics), Smarts d8+, Psionics d6+

Mentalists are masters of mind control and psionics. Some are pulp heroes, others are trained in secret government academies to root out traitors. Their frequent toying with human minds gives them a +2 on any opposed Psionics roll, whether they are using their powers against a foe or are trying to defend against a rival Mentalist.

Mr. Fix It

Requirements: Novice, Arcane Background (Weird Science), Smarts d10+, Repair d8+, Weird Science d8+, at least two other scientific Knowledge skills at d6+

The inventor adds +2 to Repair rolls. With a raise, he halves the time normally required to fix something. This means that if a particular Repair job already states that a raise repairs it in half the time, a Mr. Fix It could finish the job in one-quarter the time with a raise.

Scholar

Requirements: Novice, d8+ in affected skill

Learned professors, devoted students, and amateur enthusiasts spend months of their lives studying particular subjects. They become experts in these fields, and rarely fail to answer questions in their particular area of expertise.

Pick any two Knowledge skills the Scholar has a d8 or better in. Add +2 to your total whenever these skills are used. Those who study military history have a natural edge when commanding troops in Mass Battles (see page 106)—a +2 to a Knowledge (Battle) roll can mean the difference between a rousing victory and a crushing defeat.

Thief

Requirements: Novice, Agility d8+, Climbing d6+, Lockpicking d6+, Stealth d8+

Thieves specialize in deceit, treachery, and acrobatics. They can be invaluable where traps must be detected, walls must be climbed, and locks must be picked.

Thieves add +2 to Climbing, Lockpick, Stealth, as well as Notice or Repair rolls that relate to traps and similar devices. The bonus to Stealth does not apply when the character is in a wilderness environment—only in urban areas.

Wizard

Requirements: Novice, Arcane Background (Magic), Smarts d8+, Knowledge (Arcana) d8+, Spellcasting d6+

Wizards range from young apprentices to frighteningly powerful supreme sorcerers. They are often physically weak, however, and rarely have the divine powers or healing abilities of priestly spellcasters. What they lack in spiritual favor, however, they more than make up for in utility and eldritch might.

Wizards tend to learn their craft in formalized institutions or under the tutelage of experienced masters. Each raise a Wizard gets on his Spellcasting roll reduces the cost of the spell by 1 Power Point. The Wizard must have the points available to cast the spell in the first place before rolling.

Woodsman

Requirements: Novice, Spirit d6+, Survival d8+, Tracking d8+

Woodsmen are rangers, scouts, and hunters who are more at home in the wilderness than in urban areas. They are skilled trackers and scouts, and know how to live off the land for months at a time. Woodsmen gain +2 to Tracking, Survival, and Stealth rolls made in the wilderness (not towns, ruins, or underground).

Social Edges

Getting people to do what you want is a critical skill in most any setting. These Edges help your hero do just that.

Charismatic

Requirements: Novice, Spirit d8+

Your hero has learned how to work with others, even those who might be somewhat opposed to him or his efforts. This adds +2 to his Charisma.

Common Bond

Requirements: Wild Card, Novice, Spirit d8+

This Edge signifies a special link between close companions—such as a typical party. It doesn't matter whether or not the characters get along perfectly or not, they've just formed a close and common bond during their epic adventures.

A character with this Edge may freely give his Bennies to any other Wild Card he can communicate with. This represents the character giving his verbal or spiritual support to the ally. The player should say what his character is doing to give the support. The gesture could be as complex as a rousing speech, or as simple as a knowing nod.

Connections

Requirements: Novice

Whether it's to the Feds, the cops, the Mob, or some big corporation, your heroine knows someone on the inside—someone who is willing to lend her a hand on occasion (usually once per game session).

This Edge may be taken more than once, but each time must be applied to a different organization. The GM should also ensure the organization is limited to a single, unique organization. A hero may, for instance, have Connections (US Army), but he shouldn't have a blanket Connections (Military).

To use a character's Connections requires that she first get in touch with one of her contacts. This requires a Streetwise roll. Failure means the particular contact wasn't available, their cell phone wasn't on, or they were otherwise tied up.

Once in contact, the hero must make a Persuasion roll. The GM should feel free to modify both the Persuasion roll and any results based on the circumstances.

A failure indicates the heroine's contacts just couldn't come through this time, or perhaps just weren't persuaded that their help was really necessary.

On a success, the contact might share information, but won't do anything too risky to help. On a raise, the contact is willing to leak sensitive information, but stops short of outright betrayal.

Two or more raises means the heroine has pushed the right buttons and can count on serious help. The Connection will risk serious consequences for the heroine, and if she needs financial assistance, may provide more than he's comfortable with. If the heroine asks for muscle, the contact delivers either one expert (a safe-cracker, wheel-man, security expert, etc.) or five average fighter-types for the contact's particular organization (a mob boss sends five thugs, the Army sends five infantrymen, etc.).

Strong Willed

Requirements: Novice, Intimidation d6+, Taunt d6+

Characters with strong willpower use their voice, steely stares, or quick wits to unnerve their opponents. Strong Willed adds +2 to a character's Intimidation and Taunt rolls, as well as his Spirit and Smarts rolls when resisting Test of Wills attacks.

Weird Edges

Weird Edges are slightly supernatural and only appropriate in games with those elements.

Beast Bond

Requirements: Novice

Some individuals can exert incredible will over their animal companions. These characters may spend their own Bennies for any animals under their control, including mounts, pet dogs, familiars, and so on.

Beast Master

Requirements: Novice, Spirit d8+

Animals like your hero, and won't attack him unless he attacks them first or they are enraged for some reason. His "animal magnetism" is so great he's attracted a loyal animal of some sort as well. This is typically a dog, wolf, or raptor, though the GM may allow other companions if it fits the setting.

The beast is an Extra (not a Wild Card). If it should be killed, the hero finds a replacement in 2d6 days.

Danger Sense

Requirements: Novice

Your hero can sense when something bad is about to happen. Anytime he's about to be the victim of a surprise attack, ambush, or other nasty surprise, he gets a Notice roll at −2 just before the attack or event occurs. If successful, the character knows something is about to happen and may take appropriate action against it. This means the hero is on Hold for the first round of a combat. Should the hero fail his roll, he still follows the normal Surprise rules, if applicable (see page 73).

Healer

Requirements: Novice, Spirit d8+

A hero with this Edge adds +2 to all Healing rolls (including natural healing rolls for his own wounds), whether natural or magical in nature. Up to five companions traveling with a Healer add the bonus to their natural healing rolls as well.

Liquid Courage

Requirements: Novice, Vigor d8+

Your hero processes alcohol far differently than most. The round after consuming a stiff drink (at least 8 ounces of hard liquor or equivalent), the character's Vigor increases by one die type (increasing Toughness as well). The hard drinker can also ignore one level of wound modifiers (which stacks with other abilities that do the same).

The effect lasts for one hour after it begins. If the drunkard seeks inebriation he suffers −2 to Smarts and Agility-based rolls for as long as he continues to drink and the next 1d6 hours thereafter.

Scavenger

Requirements: Novice, Luck

Once per session the hero may "suddenly remember" that he has a much-needed piece of equipment on his person. The item must be capable of being stored in the hero's pocket or bag (assuming he has one), and the Game Master has the final word on what can be found.

Wild Card Edges

The following Edges work only when the character is dealt a Joker during combat. The Edge's effects are in addition to the usual effects of being dealt a Joker.

Dead Shot

Requirements: Wild Card, Seasoned, Shooting/Throwing d10+

The character doubles his total damage when making a successful Shooting or Throwing attack this round.

Mighty Blow

Requirements: Wild Card, Seasoned, Fighting d10+

The character doubles his total damage when making a successful Fighting attack this round.

Power Surge

Requirements: Wild Card, Seasoned, arcane skill d10+

This Edge is for those characters with Arcane Backgrounds. When dealt a Joker, the character recovers 2d6 Power Points. He may not exceed his usual limit.

Legendary Edges

Most Legendary Edges are very specific to their campaign world—such as gaining a stronghold or divine favor—but a few fit most anywhere, as shown below.

Followers

Requirements: Wild Card, Legendary

Heroes often acquire dedicated warbands, "merry men," or others who voluntarily follow the hero on his adventures.

Each time this Edge is chosen, five followers join the hero's band. Casualties are not automatically replaced, so a hero may need to choose this Edge again on occasion to replenish his losses. The followers must have some way to eat and earn income, and generally want a piece of whatever loot, treasure, or other rewards the hero acquires. Otherwise, they are completely dedicated to their idol and risk their lives for him under any normal conditions. They won't knowingly throw their lives away except under very special circumstances.

The GM determines the followers' statistics, but in general, use the Soldier statistics presented on page 93. Followers generally come with only basic equipment depending on their particular setting (warriors in fantasy come with at least leather armor and short swords, for example). The hero must purchase any additional equipment for his Followers himself.

Martial Arts Master

Requirements: Legendary, Improved Martial Artist, Fighting d12+

The warrior is deadly with his hands. He adds +2 to his bare-handed damage every time he takes this Edge, up to a maximum of five times for a total damage bonus of +10.

Professional

Requirements: Legendary, d12 in affected Trait

The character is an expert at a particular skill or attribute (his choice). That Trait becomes d12+1. This Edge may be selected more than once, but it may never be applied to the same skill or attribute twice.

Expert

Requirements: Legendary, Professional in affected Trait

As above, but the Trait increases to d12+2.

Master

Requirements: Wild Card, Legendary, Expert in affected Trait

The character's Wild Die increases to a d10 when rolling a particular Trait of his choice. This Edge may be chosen multiple times, though it only affects a particular Trait once.

Sidekick

Requirements: Wild Card, Legendary

A character who triumphs over evil time and time again becomes an inspiration to others. Eventually, one of these young crusaders may attempt to join the hero in his epic quests.

The hero gains a Novice Rank sidekick. The sidekick is a Wild Card, gains experience as usual, and has abilities that complement or mimic his hero's.

The player character should control his sidekick just like any other ally. Of course, the sidekick may occasionally cause trouble (by getting captured, running into danger when he's not supposed to, etc.). The player should be prepared for his "Edge" to occasionally become a "Hindrance."

If the sidekick dies, he isn't replaced unless the hero chooses this Edge again.

Tough as Nails

Requirements: Legendary

Your hero is a grizzled veteran. Increase his Toughness by +1.

Improved Tough as Nails

Requirements: Legendary, Tough as Nails

Increase your hero's Toughness by another +1.

Weapon Master

Requirements: Legendary, Fighting d12

Increase your hero's Parry by +1.

Master of Arms

Requirements: Legendary, Weapon Master

Increase your hero's Parry by another +1.

Advancement

At the end of each game session (usually 4-6 hours of gaming), the GM awards 1 to 3 Experience Points to everyone in the group, based on these guidelines.

Experience Awards

Award	Situation
1	The group accomplished little or had a very short session.
2	The group had more successes than failures.
3	The group succeeded greatly, and their adventure had a significant impact on the overall story.

Ranks

As a character gains more Experience Points, he goes up in "Rank." This is a rough measure of how powerful the hero is. As characters progress in experience, new Ranks allow access to more powerful Edges.

Rank Table

Experience Points	Rank
0-19	Novice
20-39	Seasoned
40-59	Veteran
60-79	Heroic
80+	Legendary

Every 5 points accumulated grants a hero an Advance. An Advance lets a character do one of the following:

- Gain a new Edge.
- Increase a skill that is equal to or greater than its linked attribute by one die type.
- Increase two skills that are lower than their linked attributes by one die type each.
- Buy a new skill at d4.
- Increase one attribute by a die type.*

You may only choose this option once per Rank. No Trait may be raised above a d12 (but see the Professional and Expert Legendary Edges). Legendary characters may raise an attribute every other Advance.

Starting With Experienced Characters

If the GM lets you make a character who has already earned some experience, simply make a character as usual and then grant her that many Advances. A Veteran character, for example, has 40 Experience Points, so you would make a normal character and grant her eight Advances.

Additional goods, equipment, or other assets must be determined by the Game Master and the particular setting. As a quick rule of thumb, a character's starting funds double with each Rank after Novice.

▶ **Replacement Characters:** When a character dies, his new hero begins play with one less Advance than his last.

Legendary Characters

Legendary characters are major forces in their worlds, and often have political power and influence as well as a host of Edges to defeat those who oppose them.

Once a hero reaches Legendary status, the rules for Advances change a bit. The character now Advances every time he accumulates 10 Experience Points instead of 5, but a world of new Edges opens up to him as well. "Legendary Edges" allow heroes to accumulate followers, build castles, start massive corporations, and otherwise become major players in their campaign world.

Legendary characters may also choose to improve an attribute every other Advance. A few Legendary Edges are included in this book. Many more are quite specific to their particular campaign worlds, and so are covered in other Savage Settings.

Character Creation Summary

1) Race
• Choose any race available in your setting.

2) Traits
• Your hero starts with a d4 in each attribute, and has 5 points with which to raise them. Raising an attribute a die type costs 1 point.

• You have 15 points for skills. Each die type in a skill costs 1 point up to the linked attribute. Going over the linked attribute costs 2 points per level.

• Charisma is equal to the total bonuses or penalties given by Edges and Hindrances.

• Pace is 6".

• Parry is equal to 2 plus half Fighting.

• Toughness is equal to 2 plus half Vigor. Go ahead and add the bonus granted by the armor worn on your torso to this value as well for speed's sake, but remember it may not count if attacks target other parts of the body.

3) Edges & Hindrances
• You gain additional points for taking up to one Major Hindrance (2 points) and two Minor Hindrances (1 point each).

For 2 points you can:
• Gain another attribute point, or
• Choose an Edge

For 1 point you can:
• Gain another skill point, or
• Increase starting funds by 100%

4) Gear
• Start with $500 unless your setting book says otherwise.

5) Background Details
• Fill in any other background details you care to add.

Skills

Skill	Attribute
Boating	Agility
Climbing	Strength
Driving	Agility
Fighting	Agility
Gambling	Smarts
Healing	Smarts
Intimidation	Spirit
Investigation	Smarts
Knowledge	Smarts
Lockpicking	Agility
Notice	Smarts
Persuasion	Spirit
Piloting	Agility
Repair	Smarts
Riding	Agility
Shooting	Agility
Stealth	Agility
Streetwise	Smarts
Survival	Smarts
Swimming	Agility
Taunt	Smarts
Throwing	Agility
Tracking	Smarts

Hindrance	Type	Effects
All Thumbs	Minor	–2 Repair; Roll of 1 causes malfunction
Anemic	Minor	–2 to Fatigue tests
Arrogant	Major	Must humiliate opponent, challenge the 'leader'
Bad Eyes	Minor/Major	–2 to attack or notice something more than 5" distant
Bad Luck	Major	One less Benny per session
Big Mouth	Minor	Unable to keep a secret, blabs at the worst time
Blind	Major	–6 to all actions that rely on vision; –2 on social rolls, gain additional Edge
Bloodthirsty	Major	Never takes prisoners
Cautious	Minor	Character is overly careful
Clueless	Major	–2 to most Common Knowledge rolls
Code of Honor	Major	Character keeps his word and acts like a gentleman
Curious	Major	Character wants to know about everything
Death Wish	Minor	Hero wants to die after completing some task
Delusional	Minor/Major	Character suffers from grave delusions
Doubting Thomas	Minor	Character doesn't believe in the supernatural
Elderly	Major	Pace –1, –1 to Strength and Vigor die types; +5 skill points for any skill linked to Smarts
Enemy	Minor/Major	Character has a recurring nemesis of some sort
Greedy	Minor/Major	Character is obsessed with wealth
Habit	Minor/Major	Charisma –1; Fatigue rolls when deprived of Major Habits
Hard of Hearing	Minor/Major	–2 to Notice sounds; automatic failure if completely deaf
Heroic	Major	Character always helps those in need
Illiterate	Minor	Hero is unable to read or write
Lame	Major	–2 Pace and running die is a d4
Loyal	Minor	The hero tries to never betray or disappoint his friends
Mean	Minor	–2 to his Charisma for ill-temper and surliness
Obese	Minor	+1 Toughness, –1 Pace, d4 running die
One Arm	Major	–4 to tasks requiring two arms
One Eye	Major	–1 Charisma, –2 to rolls requiring depth perception
One Leg	Major	Pace –2, d4 running die, –2 to rolls requiring mobility, –2 to Swimming skill
Outsider	Minor	–2 Charisma, treated badly by those of dominant society
Overconfident	Major	The hero believes he can do anything
Pacifist	Minor/Major	Character fights only in self-defense as a Minor Hindrance; won't harm living creatures as Major Hindrance
Phobia	Minor/Major	–2 or –4 to Trait tests when near the phobia
Poverty	Minor	Half starting funds, inability to hang onto future income
Quirk	Minor	Character has some minor but persistent foible
Small	Major	–1 Toughness
Stubborn	Minor	Hero always wants his way
Ugly	Minor	–2 Charisma due to appearance
Vengeful	Minor/Major	Character holds a grudge; will kill as a Major Hindrance
Vow	Minor/Major	A pledge to a group, deity, or religion
Wanted	Minor/Major	The character is a criminal of some sort
Yellow	Major	The character is cowardly and suffers –2 to Fear checks
Young	Major	3 points for Attributes, 10 skill points, +1 Benny per session

Edges Summary

Edge	Requirements	Effects
Ace	N, A d8	+2 to Boating, Driving, Piloting; may make Soak rolls for vehicle at −2
Acrobat	N, A d8, St d6	+2 to nimbleness-based Agility rolls; +1 Parry if unencumbered
Adept	N, AB (Miracles), Faith d8+, Fighting d8+	Str+d4 unarmed attacks; always considered armed; may choose certain powers to active as a free action (see text)
Alertness	N	+2 Notice
Ambidextrous	N, A d8	Ignore −2 penalty for using off-hand
Arcane Background	N, Special	Allows access to supernatural powers
Arcane Resistance	N, Sp d8	Armor 2 vs. magic, +2 to resist powers
Imp. Arcane Res	N, Arcane Res.	Armor 4 vs. magic, +4 to resist magic effects
Assassin	N, A d8+, Climbing d6+, Fighting d6+, Stealth d8+	+2 to damage when striking a foe unawares
Attractive	N, V d6	Charisma +2
Very Attractive	N, Attractive	Charisma +4
Beast Bond	N	Character may spend Bennies for his animals
Beast Master	N, Sp d8	The hero gains an animal companion
Berserk	N	See text
Block	S, Fighting d8	Parry +1
Improved Block	V, Block	Parry +2
Brave	N, Sp d6	+2 to Fear tests
Brawler	N, St d8	+2 to unarmed damage rolls
Bruiser	S, Brawler	Bonus die to unarmed damage is d8 instead of d6
Brawny	N, St d6, V d6	Toughness +1; load limit is 8 x Str
Champion	N, See text	+2 damage / Toughness vs. supernatural evil
Charismatic	N, Sp d8	Charisma +2
Combat Reflexes	S	+2 to recover from being Shaken
Command	N, Sm d6	+1 to troops recovering from being Shaken
Command Presence	N, Command	Increase command radius to 10"
Common Bond	WC, N, Sp d8	May give Bennies to companions
Connections	N	Call upon powerful friends
Counterattack	S, Fighting d8	Receive free Fighting attack at −2 once per round when a foe fails a Fighting attack
Improved Counterattack	V, Counterattack	As above but ignore the −2 penalty
Danger Sense	N	Notice at −2 to detect surprise attacks/danger
Dead Shot	WC, S, Shooting / Throwing d10	Double ranged damage when dealt Joker
Dodge	S, A d8	−1 to be hit with ranged attacks
Improved Dodge	V, Dodge	−2 to be hit with ranged attacks
Elan	N, Sp d8	+2 when spending a Benny on a Trait roll (including Soak rolls)
Extraction	N, A d8	Ignore one foe's free attack when withdrawing from melee with an Agility roll
Improved Extraction	N, Extraction	As above. With a raise, no foes get their free melee attack.
Fast Healer	N, V d8	+2 to natural healing rolls
Fervor	V, Sp d8, Command	+1 melee damage to troops in command
First Strike	N, A d8	May attack one foe who moves adjacent
Imp. First Strike	H, First Strike	May attack every foe who moves adjacent
Fleet-Footed	N, A d6	+2 Pace, d10 running die instead of d6

Edge	Requirements	Effect
Florentine	N, A d8, Fighting d8	+1 vs. foes with single weapon and no shield; ignore 1 point of gang up bonus
Followers	L, WC	Attract 5 henchmen
Frenzy	S, Fighting d10	1 extra Fighting attack at –2
Imp. Frenzy	V, Frenzy	As above but no penalty
Gadgeteer	N, See text	May "jury-rig" a device once per game session
Giant Killer	V	+1d6 damage when attacking large creatures
Hard to Kill	N, WC, Sp d8	Ignore wound penalties for Vigor rolls made on the Injury Table
Harder to Kill	V, Hard to Kill	50% chance of surviving "death"
Healer	N, Sp d8	+2 Healing
Hold the Line!	S, Sm d8, Command	Troops have +1 Toughness
Holy/Unholy Warrior	N, See text	See text
Improvisational Fighter	S, Sm d6+	Ignores the usual –1 penalty to attack and Parry for improvised weapons
Inspire	S, Command	+1 to Spirit rolls of all troops in command
Investigator	N, Sm d8, Inv. d8, Streetwise d8	+2 Investigation and Streetwise
Jack-of-All-Trades	N, Sm d10	No –2 for unskilled Smarts-based tests
Killer Instinct	H	Wins tied opposed rolls, may reroll opposed skill die if it comes up a "1"
Leader of Men	V, Command	Roll a d10 as the Wild Die for subordinates' group rolls
Level Headed	S, Sm d8	Act on best of two cards in combat
Imp. Level Headed	S, Level Headed	Act on best of three cards in combat
Linguist	N, Sm d6	Begin play with a number of languages equal to Smarts; Smarts –2 to be understood in any language heard for a week
Liquid Courage	N, V d8	Gain Vigor die type after imbibing at least 8 oz of alcohol
Luck	N	+1 Benny per session
Great Luck	N, Luck	+2 Bennies per session
Marksman	S	Aim maneuver (+2 Shooting) if hero does not move
Martial Artist	N, Fighting d6	Never considered unarmed, +d4 to unarmed damage rolls
Improved Martial Artist	V, Martial Artist, Fighting d10	+d6 to unarmed damage rolls
Martial Arts Master	L, Imp. Martial Artist, Fighting d12	+2 to unarmed damage rolls; may take this Edge up to five times
McGyver	N, Sm d6, Repair d6, Notice d8	May improvise temporary gadgets
Mentalist	N, AB (Psionics), Sm d8, Psionics d6	+2 to any opposed Psionics roll
Mighty Blow	WC, S, Fighting d10	Double melee damage when dealt Joker
Mr. Fix It	N, See text	+2 to Repair rolls, 1/2 Repair time with raise
Natural Leader	N, Sp d8, Command	Leader may give Bennies to troops in command
Nerves of Steel	N, WC, V d8	Ignore 1 point of wound penalties
Imp. Nerves of Steel	N, Nerves of Steel	Ignore 2 points of wound penalties
New Power	N, AB	Character gains one new power
Noble	N	Rich; +2 Charisma; Status and wealth
No Mercy	S	May spend Bennies on damage rolls
Power Points	N, AB	+5 Power Points, once per rank only
Power Surge	WC, S, arcane skill d10	+2d6 Power Points when dealt a Joker

Edge	Requirements	Effect
Professional	L, d12 in Trait	Trait becomes d12+1
Expert	L, Prof. in Trait	Trait becomes d12+2
Master	L, WC, Expert in Trait	Wild Die is d10 for one Trait
Quick	N, A d8	Discard draw of 5 or less for new card
Quick Draw	N, A d8	May draw weapon as a free action
Rapid Recharge	S, Sp d6, AB	Regain 1 Power Point every 30 minutes
Imp. Rapid Recharge	V, Rapid Recharge	Regain 1 Power Point every 15 minutes
Rich	N	3x starting funds, $150K annual salary
Filthy Rich	N, Noble Birth or Rich	5x starting funds, $500K annual salary
Rock and Roll!	S, Shooting d8	Ignore full-auto penalty if shooter doesn't move
Scavenger	N, Luck	Find an essential piece of equipment once per session
Scholar	N, d8 in affected skills	+2 to two different Knowledge skills
Sidekick	L, WC	Character gains a Novice WC sidekick
Soul Drain	S, See Text	Special
Steady Hands	N, A d8	Ignore unstable platform penalty; Running penalty reduced to −1
Sweep	N, St d8, Fighting d8	Attack all adjacent foes at −2
Imp. Sweep	V, Sweep	As above but with no penalty
Strong Willed	N, Intimidation d6, Taunt d6	+2 Intimidation and Taunt, +2 to resist Tests of Will
Tactician	S, See text	Make a Knowledge (Battle) roll at the beginning of a fight to get an Action Card per success and raise; these may be given to any allies throughout the course of the battle
Thief	N, A d8, Climbing d6, Lockpicking d6, Stealth d8	+2 Climb, Lockpick, Stealth, or to disarm traps
Tough as Nails	L	Toughness +1
Imp. Tough as Nails	L, Tough as Nails	Toughness +2
Trademark Weapon	N, Fighting or Shooting d10	+1 Fighting or Shooting with particular weapon
Imp. Tr. Weapon	V, Trademark Weapon	+2 Fighting or Shooting with particular weapon
Two-Fisted	N, A d8	May attack with a weapon in each hand without multi-action penalty
Weapon Master	L, Fighting d12	Parry +1
Master of Arms	L, Weapon Master	Parry +2
Wizard	N, See text	Each raise reduces cost of spell by 1 point
Woodsman	N, Sp d6, Survival d8, Tracking d8	+2 Tracking Survival, and Stealth

In the following section is a sampling of gear from the ancient era to the near future. Below are some notes you'll need to understand the equipment lists.

3RB: The weapon has a three-round burst selector (see page 81).

AP (Armor Piercing): The weapon or round ignores this many points of Armor. A weapon with an AP value of 4, for instance, ignores 4 points of Armor. Excess AP is simply lost.

Auto: This full-auto weapon may fire in automatic (single shot) mode.

Armor: This is the amount of Armor provided by the equipment, which is added to the wearer's Toughness when the covered location is hit in combat. A character who wears multiple layers of armor only gains the highest bonus—they do not stack. Note that unless an attacker states otherwise, hits are always directed at the victim's torso.

Caliber: The number listed in parentheses after firearms is the caliber of bullet it fires. Use this when figuring ammunition costs or trying to figure out if the ammo from one weapon fits in another.

Cost: Equipment prices are relative both to the starting funds of $500 *and* to their tech level, so a Springfield musket doesn't really cost $250 in 1862. That's just the "worth" of the weapon relative to the tech level and the typical setting it's intended for. Remember that when comparing the $150 musket to the $150 AK47—the weapons are both "standard" for the typical environment they're found in, even though the AK is vastly superior to the musket. Characters in military campaigns shouldn't buy equipment at all—they're simply assigned their gear. Some items simply list "Military" as their cost, meaning they are typically bought by large national militaries and then supplied to the troops under their command. Such weapons are not normally available on the open market.

Economies are critical to balancing game worlds, so the Game Master is encouraged to re-price goods for his particular campaign.

Damage: Damage is listed in terms of dice. Projectile weapons have fixed damage (such as 2d6). Melee weapons have damage based on the wielder's Strength die plus another die, as listed under individual weapon entries. A dagger, for instance, inflicts Str+1d4 damage.

Double Tap: The weapon can rapidly fire two rounds. Rather than rolling twice, add +1 to the Shooting and damage rolls.

HW (Heavy Weapon): The weapon can affect vehicles or other devices with Heavy Armor.

HE (High Explosive): High explosive rounds use a burst template, the size of which is noted in the weapon or ammunition's notes. See the rules for Area of Effect attacks in Chapter Three.

Minimum Strength: A character whose Strength is lower than the weapon die can use the weapon, but there are penalties. First, the weapon die can't be higher than his Strength die. So if a scrawny kid (d4 Str) picks up a long sword (d8), he rolls 2d4 damage, not d4+d8. A brawny hero with Str d10 rolls d10+d8 when using the same long sword.

Second, if the Strength die isn't at least equal to the weapon die, the attacker doesn't get any of the weapon's inherent bonuses, such as +1 Parry or Reach. He still retains any penalties, however (like –1 Parry).

If a weapon has a damage listed as Str+d8+2, for instance, then the minimum Strength the wielder must have is a d8.

Some ranged weapons list a minimum Strength to use as well. A character with a lower Strength can use the weapon, but suffers a –1 penalty to his attack roll for every step of difference between his Strength and the minimum Strength required. The penalty is ignored if the weapon can be braced on a bipod or other support.

Parry +X: The weapon adds the bonus to the character's Parry score when used.

Range: This lists the weapon's Short, Medium, and Long range. Ranges are listed in inches so that you can use a ruler to move, shoot, and fight on the table-top with miniatures. Each inch is equal to 2 yards in the real world, so that 5" is really 10 yards, or 30 feet.

Weapon ranges are "effective" ranges for the table-top. If you need to know the real world range of a weapon (for battles that don't take place on the table-top, for instance), multiply each range bracket by 2.5. A tank round with a Long range of 300, for example, has a "real world" Long range of 750", or 1500 yards.

Rate of Fire: This is the maximum number of shots that may be taken by this weapon per action. Unless a weapon says otherwise, the user can fire up to the weapon's Rate of Fire (rather than its full Rate of Fire). If a single shot is taken, it uses a single round of ammunition and does not incur any recoil penalties. Two or more shots with such weapons always incurs the –2 autofire penalty.

Reach: Weapons with "reach" allow their user to make Fighting attacks at the listed range. A reach of 1", for example, allows a character to strike a target 1" distant. Weapons without a reach value can only strike targets at arm's length (adjacent).

Reach can be very important when fighting from horseback and *against* mounted foes (see page 83).

Reloading: Antique weapons, such as muskets and crossbows, are very slow to reload. Each weapon tells you how many actions it requires to reload, such as 1/3, which means the weapon can fire every third round if the firer does nothing but load every action. Characters can load and walk at no penalty. If the character tries to run and load, he must make an Agility roll (at the usual –2 penalty for running). Failure simply means no progress toward reloading was made that action.

Semi-Auto: The weapon fires on semi-auto and can take advantage of the double-tap rules (page 81).

Snapfire Penalty: Certain weapons, such as sniper rifles, are very inaccurate if fired "from the hip" rather than using their excellent sights or scopes. If the character moves in the action he fires, he suffers a –2 penalty.

Three Round Burst: The weapon can fire 3 rounds with one pull of the trigger. This adds +2 to the Shooting and damage rolls at the cost of the extra ammunition.

Encumbrance

In general, you shouldn't worry about Encumbrance. Characters will usually carry no more than their characters think they actually need. But occasionally it may become dramatically important—such as during a chase or when attempting to lug a heavy treasure away from a roaring dragon! When that occurs, use the guidelines below.

A character can carry five times his Strength die type in pounds without incurring any penalties. This is called his "Load Limit." A character with a Strength of d8, for example, can comfortably carry 40 pounds. (Ignore normal clothes when figuring weight.)

Carrying too much weight inflicts a –1 penalty for every additional multiple of your Load Limit. The penalty applies to all Agility and Strength totals, as well as skills linked to either of those two attributes.

A hero with a d8 Strength, for example, has a Load Limit of 40 pounds. He can carry 41-80 pounds at a –1 penalty to his Strength, Agility, and related skill rolls. He could also carry 81-120 pounds at –2, or 121-160 pounds at –3.

Characters cannot regularly carry weight that inflicts a penalty of more than –3. They may be able to lift greater weights (up to a –4 penalty) for a few short steps at the discretion of the GM, however.

Below are notes for some of the weapons, armor, and other devices you'll find on the Equipment Lists.

Armor

Note that the weights listed for most large suits of armor such as hauberks, plate, and power armor, are figured for their "distributed" weight. This assumes the armor is properly fitted, which takes a Knowledge (Armorsmithing) roll, some basic tools, and 1d6 hours. If armor is not properly fitted (such as when wearing armor taken from a foe), the weight is typically doubled.

Kevlar

Kevlar offers 2 points of protection against most attacks. Kevlar weave "binds" spinning bullets and so negates up to 4 points of AP from bullets, and provides +4 protection from them as well.

Power Armor

Power armor suits carry much of their own mass, hence the low weight values. Scout suits weigh 100 pounds when powered down, Battle suits weigh 150, and Heavy Suits weigh 220 pounds. All power armor contains comm-units with a 5-mile range. Powered armor typically lasts for one week without recharge. It requires a special recharging facility and 10 hours to return to full power. The GM may decide suits lose power faster under excessive use.

- **Scout Suit:** These suits are made for reconnaissance. In addition to the standard comm-unit, they are coated in stealth paint that adds +4 to Stealth rolls vs. radar and other automated detection systems (but not people).
- **Battle Suit:** This is the standard power armor worn by most heavy troopers in futuristic settings. It increases Strength by one die type, adds +2 to Pace, and allows users to jump 2d6" horizontally or 1d6" vertically. A Heads Up Display provides targeting information for linked weapons, adding +1 to the wearer's Shooting rolls.
- **Heavy Suit:** Heavy suits (or assault suits) are designed for hard fighting under the most intense combat conditions. They subtract 2 from Pace and boost Strength by two

die types. They mount at least one heavy weapon of some sort such as a flamethrower or a minigun, and feature enhanced targeting computers that add +2 to the character's Shooting rolls.

Shields

If a character with a shield is hit by a ranged attack from the protected side, roll damage normally, but add the Armor bonus of the shield to the character's Toughness (it acts as an obstacle).

Ranged Weapons & Accessories

Bipods

Most full machine guns are also equipped with either an integral or detachable bipod. Once deployed, these provide a more stable shooting position and help control recoil. It takes one action to deploy a bipod and set the weapon up. Once in position the autofire penalty is reduced to –1. If the hero moves, this benefit is negated and he will have to spend another action to redeploy the bipod.

Scopes

Optical scopes can be attached to all manner of firearms from rifles to hand guns, and magnify targets to make distance shooting easier. A scope provides a +2 Shooting bonus to shots at Medium Range or higher as long as the firer does not move this round.

Shotguns

Shotguns fire a spread of metal balls (also called "shot"), and so do more damage at close range where the spread is less and more of the shot hits the target. Farther away, the shot spreads more and causes less damage. Because of the increased chance of hitting someone due to the spread, shotguns add +2 to their user's Shooting rolls. They cause 1d6 damage at Long range, 2d6 at Medium, and 3d6 at Short range.

▶ **Double Barrels:** Shotguns with two attached barrels are called "double barrels." If the attacker wants to fire both barrels at once, he rolls an additional Shooting die just like when firing Full Auto (plus Wild Die), including recoil (which cancels out the usual

+2 for shotguns). Roll damage for each successful shot separately.

► **Slugs:** Shotguns can also fire slugs. The attacker doesn't get the +2 shotgun bonus to his Shooting roll, but the damage is 2d10 regardless of the range increment.

Special Weapons

Bouncing Betties

These deadly mines are designed to pop up into the air and rain shrapnel down from about head-height. Only full overhead cover offers an Armor bonus against such devices. Simply being prone offers no protection from these deadly explosives.

Cannons

Cannons can fire three different types of shells: solid shot, shrapnel, and canister. The crew can pick the type of ammunition to be loaded each time it reloads.

Solid Shot is just that—big round balls made to batter walls or plow through packed ranks of troops. To fire, the leader of the crew makes a Shooting roll as usual. A target directly behind and adjacent to the first is also hit on a d6 roll of 1-3, and takes full damage. This continues until there are no more adjacent foes.

Shrapnel is an explosive shell filled with metal balls, nails, and other scraps. The debris is hurled outward when the shell explodes, shredding lightly armored targets in a shower of steel. Shrapnel is an area effect attack, and uses the Medium Burst Template.

Canister is a shell made to detonate inside the barrel of the cannon. The jagged metal inside the "canister" then sprays out of the cannon to shred anything within its deadly cone like a giant shotgun. To determine the effects of canister, place a ruler in front of the cannon in the direction you want it to fire and make a Shooting roll with no range modifiers. If the shot is missed, move the far end of the ruler 1" left or right (roll randomly).

Now place a Medium Burst Template at the near end of the ruler and move it directly forward along that path for 24". Every target under the template is hit for 2d6 damage. Cover acts as Armor just as with any area effect weapon, meaning prone characters add +2 to their Toughness.

► **Reloading:** Cannons require one action to reload with a crew of four, or two actions with less crewmen.

► **Line of Sight:** Cannon crews must be able to see their targets to hit them. Howitzers, mortars, and bombards may fire at targets they cannot see (assuming they know roughly where the target is) at a —4 penalty, and double deviation (see **Combat**).

Flamethrowers

Flamethrowers include any device that squirts an incendiary liquid or even pure flame. To use it, the attacker places the small end of the Cone Template at the tip of his character's weapon, and the large end on as many targets as he's able. The attacker then makes a Shooting roll at +2. Defenders who make an Agility roll equal to or greater than the attacker's Shooting total move out of the way and are unaffected. The rest suffer the weapon's damage (typically 2d10) and roll to see if they catch fire (see **Fire**).

Like other area effect weapons, flamethrowers typically bypass most body armor (see **Area Effect Attacks**).

► **Vehicular Flamethrowers:** Military organizations often have flamethrowers with much longer ranges. The flame fired from a British Crocodile, for example, has a range of about 70 yards (35"). The flame must be arced to reach these distances however, so a character may choose to use a Medium Burst Template instead of the Cone Template when using such weapons. The center of the template may be placed up to the maximum range of the particular flamethrower, as listed in its notes. This is treated just like any other area effect attack, though targets still get a chance to dodge out of the cone as detailed above.

Grenades

A character within the burst radius has two additional options. To pick up and throw the grenade before it goes off, he must make an Agility roll at —4 (or —2 if he was on Hold). Failure means it goes off and he takes an additional die of damage.

► **Covering Grenades:** A character may also throw himself on a grenade. He takes double the normal dice of damage for his heroic act, but his total Toughness is subtracted from the damage inflicted on other characters in the blast radius. Allies won't normally perform such a suicidal act, though the GM might rule otherwise in specific situations, such as when an ally has a "loyal" personality.

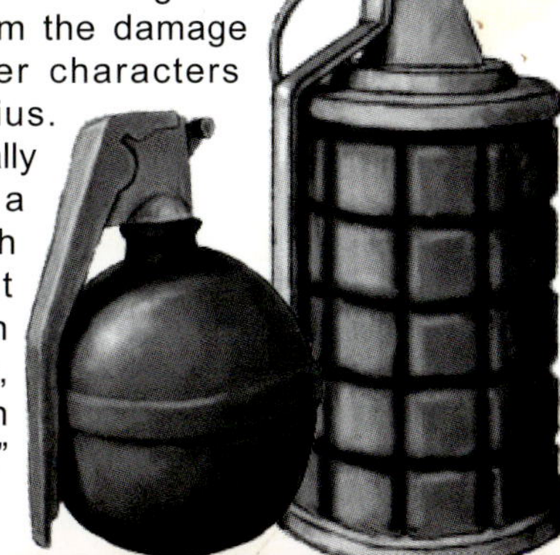

Missiles

Air-to-air (or space-to-space) weapons are designed to destroy enemy fighters and other small targets with a focused warhead. To activate, the pilot must first "capture" the target's signature on his own control panel. This is accomplished by various means including heat-signature, radar, emissions, or even profile, depending on tech level.

To get a lock, the pilot picks his target and must then succeed at an opposed Piloting roll. The attacker must subtract range modifiers from the Piloting roll just as if he were Shooting.

Once locked, the pilot decides how many missiles to release (usually up to his full payload depending on his craft). At Short Range, the target has one round to evade. He has two rounds (and chances) at Medium Range, and three at Long Range.

Evading a missile requires a Piloting roll at –4. Note that many craft contain additional evasion systems, such as chaff or flares, that add +4 to this roll if they're of the right type (flares for heat-seeking missiles and chaff for radar-guided missiles).

▶ **Air to Ground Targets:** Use the same procedure as above but the target makes a Driving or Boating roll against the attacker's Piloting skill.

▶ **Surface to Air Missiles:** As above, but the attacker makes a Shooting roll and the defender makes a Piloting roll.

▶ **Anti-Missile Systems:** Larger ships often have anti-missile systems designed to shoot down missiles with targeted lasers, walls of matter, or hails of lead. All systems require a modicum of skill and a lot of luck. First the crewman in charge of the particular AMS battery makes a Shooting roll minus the range. (Don't subtract for the size or speed of the missile—the AMS already accounts for that.) Each successful hit has a 1 in 6 chance of shooting down the torpedo. A Phalanx system with a RoF of 5, for example, rolls 5 dice, and each die that comes up a "1" shoots a missile down.

▶ **Obstacles:** Evading prey can add +2 to the Piloting roll with substantial cover—such as asteroids, canyon walls, or the hull of a capital ship.

Item Weight	Cost*	
Adventuring Gear		
Backpack	50	2
Bedroll (sleeping bag; winterized)	25	4
Blanket	10	4
Camera (disposable)	10	1
Camera (regular)	75	2
Camera (digital)	300	1
Candle (provides light in 2" radius)	1	1
Canteen (waterskin)	5	1
Cellular Phone	100	–
Crowbar	10	2
Flashlight (10" beam)	20	3
Flask (ceramic)	5	1
Flint and Steel	3	1
Grappling Hook	100	2
Hammer	10	1
Lantern (provides light in 4" radius)	25	3
Lighter	2	–
Lockpicks	200	1
Handcuffs (manacles)	15	2
Oil (for lantern; 1 pint)	2	1
Quiver (holds 20 arrows/bolts)	25	2
Rope (10")	10	15
Shovel	5	5
Soap	1	1/5
Tool Kit	200	5
Torch (1 hour, 4" radius)	5	1
Umbrella	5	2
Whistle	2	–
Whetstone	5	1
Clothing		
Camouflage Fatigues	-20	–
Hiking Boots	100	–
Normal Clothing	20	–
Formal Clothing	200	–
Winter Gear (cloak/parka)	200	3
Winter Boots	100	1

Item	Cost*	
Food		
Fast Food Meal (cheap meal)	5	1
Good Meal (restaurant)	15+	–
MRE (Meal Ready to Eat)	10	1
Trail Rations (5 meals; keeps 1 week)	10	5
Animals & Tack		
Horse	300	–
War Horse	750	–
Saddle	10	10
Elaborate Saddle	50	10
War Horse Barding (+3)	1250	30
Computers		
Desktop	800	20
Laptop	1200	5
Handheld	250	1
GPS	250	1
Surveillance		
Cellular Interceptor	650	5
Lineman's Telephone	150	2
(Repair roll to tap into a phone line)		
Night Vision Goggles		
Passive	1000	3
(no penalties for Dim or Dark)		
Active	2500	4
(no penalties for any level of darkness)		
Parabolic Microphone	750	4
(good to 200 yards)		
Telephone Tap (Bug)	250	–
Transmitter Detector	525	1

Costs for mundane items depend entirely on the setting and the tech level available. A horse in most fantasy campaigns, for instance, is fairly common and costs about $300. In the modern world, horses cost thousands of dollars.

Medieval

Blades

Type	Damage	Weight	Cost	Notes
Dagger	Str+d4	1	25	
Great Sword	Str+d10	12	400	Parry −1, 2 hands
Flail	Str+d6	8	200	Ignores Shield Parry and Cover bonus
Katana	Str+d6+2	6	1000	AP 2
Long Sword	Str+d8	8	300	Includes scimitars
Rapier	Str+d4	3	150	Parry +1
Short Sword	Str+d6	4	200	Includes cavalry sabers

Axes and Mauls

Type	Damage	Weight	Cost	Notes
Axe	Str+d6	2	200	
Battle Axe	Str+d8	10	300	
Great Axe	Str+d10	15	500	AP 1, Parry −1, 2 hands
Maul	Str+d8	20	400	AP 2 vs. rigid armor, Parry −1, 2 hands
Warhammer	Str+d6	8	250	AP 1 vs. rigid armor (plate mail)

Pole Arms

Type	Damage	Weight	Cost	Notes
Halberd	Str+d8	15	250	Reach 1, 2 hands
Lance	Str+d8	10	300	AP 2 when charging, Reach 2, only usable in mounted combat
Pike	Str+d8	25	400	Reach 2, requires 2 hands
Staff	Str+d4	8	10	Parry +1, Reach 1, 2 hands
Spear	Str+d6	5	100	Parry +1, Reach 1, 2 hands

Modern

Type	Damage	Weight	Cost	Notes
Bangstick	3d6	2	5	Basically a shotgun shell on a stick used in melee; must be reloaded with a fresh shell (1 action)
Bayonet	Str+d4	1	25	A bayonet affixed to a rifle increases the damage to Str+d6, Parry +1, Reach 1, 2 hands
Billy Club/Baton	Str+d4	1	10	Carried by most law-enforcement officials
Brass Knuckles	Str+d4	1	20	A hero wearing brass knuckles is considered to be an Unarmed Attacker
Chainsaw	2d6+4	20	200	A natural 1 on the Fighting die (regardless of the Wild Die) hits the user instead
Switchblade	Str+d4	1	10	−2 to be Noticed if hidden
Survival knife	Str+d4	3	50	Contains supplies that add +1 to Survival rolls

Futuristic

Type	Damage	Weight	Cost	Notes
Molecular Knife	Str+d4+2	1	250	AP 2, Cannot be thrown
Molecular Sword	Str+d8+2	8	500	AP 4
Laser Sword	Str+d6+8	5	1000	AP 12, Laser swords aren't terribly realistic, but are staples in many space-opera campaigns

Medieval Armor

Type	Armor	Weight*	Cost	Notes
Personal				
Leather	+1	15	50	Covers torso, arms, legs
Chain Hauberk (long coat)	+2	25	300	Covers torso, arms, legs
Plate Corselet	+3	25	400	Covers torso
Plate Arms (vambrace)	+3	10	200	Covers arms
Plate Leggings (greaves)	+3	15	300	Covers legs
Pot Helm	+3	4	75	50% vs. head shot
Steel Helmet (enclosed)	+3	8	150	Covers head
Barding				
Plate Barding	+3	30	1250	For horses
Shields**				
Small Shield (buckler)	—	8	25	+1 Parry
Medium Shield	—	12	50	+1 Parry, +2 Armor to ranged shots that hit
Large Shield (kite, pavise)	—	20	200	+2 Parry, +2 Armor to ranged shots that hit

***Shields protect only against attacks from the front and left (assuming a right-handed character).*

Modern Armor

Type	Armor	Weight*	Cost	Notes
Flak Jacket	+2/+4	12	80	Covers torso
Kevlar Vest	+2/+4	8	250	Covers torso only, negates 4 AP, see notes
Kevlar Vest w/inserts	+4/+8	12	2500	As Kevlar, but ceramic inserts are +8 vs. bullets
Motorcycle Helmet	+3	5	75	50% chance vs. head shot
Steel Pot (helmet)	+4	5	80	50% chance vs. head shot

Futuristic Armor

Type	Armor	Weight*	Cost	Notes
Infantry Battle Suit	+6	20	Mil	Covers entire body, near-future military, bomb suit
Hard Armor	+8	30	Mil	Covers entire body, future military
Powered Armor (scout suit)	+10	0	Mil	Covers entire body, far future military
Powered Armor (battle suit)	+12	0	Mil	Covers entire body, far future military
Powered Armor (heavy suit)	+14	0	Mil	Covers entire body, far future military
Reflective Vest	+10	5	200	Covers torso, far future, works against lasers only

**Effective weight when worn. Most armor weighs quite a bit more when carried rather than worn.*

Medieval

Type	Range	Damage	RoF	Cost	Weight	Shots	Min Str.
Axe, Throwing	3/6/12	Str+d6	1	75	2	—	—
Bow	12/24/48	2d6	1	250	3	—	d6
Crossbow	15/30/60	2d6	1	500	10	—	d6
AP 2, 1 action to reload							
English Long Bow	15/30/60	2d6	1	200	5	—	d8
Knife/Dagger	3/6/12	Str+d4	1	25	1	—	—
Sling	4/8/16	Str+d4	1	10	1	—	—
Spear	3/6/12	Str+d6	1	100	5	—	d6

Black Powder

Type	Range	Damage	RoF	Cost	Weight	Shots	Min Str
Brown Bess (.75)	10/20/40	2d8	1	300	15	—	d6
Notes: 2 actions to reload							
Blunderbuss (8G)*	10/20/40	1-3d6*	1	300	12	—	d6
Notes: 2 actions to reload							
Flintlock Pistol (.60)	5/10/20	2d6+1	1	150	3	—	—
Notes: 2 actions to reload							
Kentucky Rifle (.45)	15/30/60	2d8	1	300	8	—	d6
Notes: AP 2, 3 actions to reload							
Springfield (.52)	15/30/60	2d8	1	250	11	—	d6
Notes: 2 actions to reload							

*A blunderbuss does 1d6 at Long range, 2d6 at Medium range, and 3d6 at Close range.

Modern

Type	Range	Damage	RoF	Cost	Weight	Shots	Min Str
Pistols							
Derringer (.44)	5/10/20	2d6+1	1	150	2	2	—
Notes: AP 1							
Colt Dragoon (.44)	12/24/48	2d6+1	1	200	4	6	—
Notes: Revolver							
Colt 1911 (.45)	12/24/48	2d6+1	1	200	4	7	—
Notes: AP 1, Semi-Auto							
S&W (.44)	12/24/48	2d6+1	1	250	5	6	—
Notes: AP 1, Revolver							
Desert Eagle (.50)	15/30/60	2d8	1	300	8	7	—
Notes: AP 2, Semi-Auto							
Glock (9mm)	12/24/48	2d6	1	200	3	17	—
Notes: AP 1, Semi-Auto							
Peacemaker (.45)	12/24/48	2d6+1	1	200	3	6	—
Notes: AP 1, Revolver							
Ruger (.22)	10/20/40	2d6-1	1	100	2	9	—
Notes: Semi-Auto							
S&W (.357)	12/24/48	2d6+1	1	250	4	6	—
Notes: AP 1, Revolver							
Submachine Guns							
H&K MP5 (9mm)	12/24/48	2d6	3	300	10	30	—
Notes: AP 1, Auto							
MP40 (9mm)	12/24/48	2d6	3	300	11	32	—
Notes: AP 1, Auto							
Tommy Gun (.45)	12/24/48	2d6+1	3	350	13	50	—
Notes: AP 1, Auto							
Uzi (9mm)	12/24/48	2d6	3	300	9	32	—
Notes: AP 1, Auto							

Shotguns

Type	Range	Damage	RoF	Cost	Weight	Shots	Min Str
Double-Barrel (12g)	12/24/48	1-3d6	1-2	150	11	2	—
Notes: See text							
Pump Action (12g)	12/24/48	1-3d6	1	150	8	6	—
Notes: See text							
Sawed-Off DB (12g)	5/10/20	1-3d6	1-2	150	6	2	—
Notes: See text							
Streetsweeper (12g)	12/24/48	1-3d6	1	450	10	12	—
Notes: See text							

Rifles

Type	Range	Damage	RoF	Cost	Weight	Shots	Min Str
Barrett (.50)	50/100/200	2d10	1	750	35	11	d8
Notes: AP 4, Snapfire, HW							
M1 (.30)	24/48/96	2d8	1	300	10	8	d6
Notes: AP 2, Semi-Auto							
Kar98 (7.92)	24/48/96	2d8	1	300	9	5	d6
Notes: AP 2							
Sharps Big 50 (.50)	30/60/120	2d10	1	400	11	1	d8
Notes: AP 2, Snapfire Penalty							
Spencer Carbine (.52)	20/40/80	2d8	1	250	8	7	—
Notes: AP 2							
Winchester '76 (.45-.47)	24/48/96	2d8	1	300	10	15	d6
Notes: AP 2							

Assault Rifles

Type	Range	Damage	RoF	Cost	Weight	Shots	Min Str
AK47 (7.62)	24/48/96	2d8+1	3	450	10	30	d6
Notes: AP 2, Auto							
H&K G3 (.308)	24/48/96	2d8	3	400	10	20	d6
Notes: AP 2, Auto							
M-16 (5.56)	24/48/96	2d8	3	400	8	20 or 30	—
Notes: AP 2, Auto, 3RB							
Steyr AUG (5.56)	24/48/96	2d8	3	400	8	30	—
Notes: AP 2, Auto, 3RB							

Machine Guns

Type	Range	Damage	RoF	Cost	Weight	Shots	Min Str
Gatling (.45)	24/48/96	2d8	3	500	40	100	—
Notes: AP 2, May not move							
M2 Browning (.50 Cal)	50/100/200	2d10	3	1000	84	200	—
Notes: AP 4, Auto, May not move, HW							
M1919 (.30)	24/48/96	2d8	3	750	32	250	—
Notes: AP 2, May not move							
M60 (7.62)	30/60/120	2d8+1	3	1000	33	250	d8
Notes: AP 2, Snapfire							
7.7 MG (Japanese)	30/60/120	2d8	3	1000	30	250	—
Notes: AP 2, Auto, Snapfire							
MG34 (7.92)	30/60/120	2d8+1	3	500	26	200	d8
Notes: AP 2, Snapfire							
MG42 (7.92)	30/60/120	2d8+1	4	500	26	200	d8
Notes: AP 2, Snapfire							
SAW (5.56)	30/60/120	2d8	4	750	20	200	d8
Notes: AP 2, Snapfire							
Besa MG (7.92)	40/80/160	2d8	3	1000	54	50	—
Notes: AP 2, Auto, May not move							
DTMG (7.62)	30/60/120	2d8+1	3	1000	26	60	—
Notes: AP 2, Auto, May not move							
14.5mm MG	50/100/200	3d6	3	5000	30	100	—
Notes: AP 2, Auto, May not move							

Futuristic

Type	Range	Damage*	RoF	Cost	Weight	Shots	Min Str
Laser Pistol	15/30/60	1-3d6	1	200	4	24	—
Notes: Semi-Auto							
Laser Rifle	30/60/120	1-3d6	3	300	8	48	d6
Notes: Auto, 3RB							
Laser MG	50/100/200	1-3d6	5	500	15	200	d8
Notes: Auto							

Increasing the damage per attack uses a like number of shots. A 3d6 attack, for instance, uses up 3 shots.

Vehicle Mounted & AT Guns

Note that most tank guns can fire Armor Piercing (AP) or High Explosive (HE) shells. A 37mm tank gun, for example, can fire an Armor Piercing round at 4d8 damage with an AP value of 3, or a High Explosive shell that causes 4d6 damage, has an AP of 3, and impacts with a Medium Burst Template.

AT and Tank Guns

Type	Range	AP Rounds	HE Rounds	RoF
20mm Cannon	50/100/200	2d12, AP 4	—	4
25mm Cannon	50/100/200	3d8, AP 4	—	3
30mm Cannon	50/100/200	3d8, AP 6	—	3
37mm AT Gun	50/100/200	4d8, AP 3	4d6, AP 3, MBT	3
40mm Cannon	75/150/300	4d8, AP 5	3d8, AP 2, MBT	4
2pdr Tank Gun	75/150/300	4d8, AP 5	3d6, AP 2, MBT	1
57mm AT Gun	75/150/300	4d8, AP 4	3d8, AP 2, MBT	1
75mm Tank Gun	75/150/300	4d10, AP 6	3d8, AP 4, MBT	1
75mm (German)	75/150/300	4d10, AP 13	3d8, AP 5, MBT	1
76mm Tank Gun (US)	75/150/300	4d10, AP 12	3d8, AP 5, MBT	1
88mm (German)	100/200/400	4d10+1, AP 24	4d8, AP 8, MBT	1
120mm Tank Gun	100/200/400	5d10, AP 68	4d8, AP 30, MBT	1
76mm AT Gun (USSR)	75/150/300	4d10, AP 11	3d8, AP 4, MBT	1
125mm Tank Gun	100/200/400	5d10, AP 64	4d8, AP 45, MBT	1
100MGW Laser	150/300/600	5d10, AP 100	—	1
20MGW Pulse Laser	75/150/300	—	3d6+2, AP 10, LBT	3

**All are Heavy Weapons*

Ammunition

Ammo	Weight	Cost	Notes
Arrow*	1/5	1/2	—
Man-Killer Arrow	1/5	1	+1 damage, usually found only in Oriental settings
Teflon Arrow	1/5	5	AP 2, modern eras only
Bullets, Small	3/50	10/50	Includes .22 to .32 caliber weapons
Bullets, Medium	5/50	25/50	Includes 9mm to .45
Bullets, Large	8/50	50/50	Includes .50 and most rifle rounds
Quarrel*	1/5	2	AP 2 (standard crossbow bolt)
Laser Battery	1	25	Provides one full magazine for the laser pistol, rifle, or MG
Shot (w/powder)	1/10	3	For black powder weapons
Sling Stone	1/10	1/20	Stones can also be found for free with a Notice roll and 1d10 minutes searching, depending on terrain

If it's important arrows and quarrels can be recovered on a d6 roll of 4-6.

Type	Range	Damage	RoF	AP	Min Str	Burst	Weight
Cannon (shot)	50/100/200	3d6+1	1	4	—	None	—
Notes: Heavy Weapon							
Shrapnel	50/100/200	3d6	1	—	—	MBT	—
Canister	24" path	2d6	1	—	—	MBT	—
Catapult	24/48/96	3d6	1/3	4	—	MBT	—
Notes: Heavy Weapon							
Rocket Launchers							
Bazooka	24/48/96	4d8	1	9	—	MBT	12
Notes: Heavy Weapon, Snapfire, 3lbs / additional round							
Panzershrek	15/30/60	4d8	1	17	d6	MBT	20
Notes: Heavy Weapon, Snapfire, 7lbs / additional round							
Panzerfaust	12/24/48	4d8	1	20	d4	MBT	10
Notes: Heavy Weapon, Snapfire							
M203 40MM	24/48/96	4d8	1	—	d4	MBT	3
Notes: Heavy Weapon, Snapfire							
M72 Law	24/48/96	4d8+2	1	30	d4	MBT	5
Notes: Heavy Weapon, Snapfire							
AT-4	24/48/96	4d8+2	1	40	d4	MBT	15
Notes: Heavy Weapon, Snapfire							
Missiles							
TOW Missile	100/200/400	4d6	1	140	—	MBT	—
Notes: Heavy Weapon, Snapfire							
Hellfire Missile	75/150/300	5d8	4	150	—	MBT	—
Notes: Heavy Weapon							
Sidewinder	100/200/400	4d8	2	6	—	MBT	—
Notes: Heavy Weapon							
Sparrow	150/300/600	5d8	2	6	—	MBT	—
Notes: Heavy Weapon							
Mines							
Anti-Personnel Mine	—	2d6+2	—	—	—	SBT	10
Anti-Tank Mine	—	4d6	—	—	—	MBT	20
Notes: Heavy Weapon, AP 5 vs. ½ lowest Armor (round up)							
Bouncing Betty	—	3d6	—	—	—	SBT	9
Notes: See text							
Claymore Mine	—	3d6	—	—	—	MBT	4
Notes: Treat as canister							
Flamethrowers							
Flamethrower	Cone Template	2d10	1	—	d8	Cone	70
Notes: Ignores Armor							
Grenade							
Mk67 Pineaple (US)	5/10/20	3d6	—	—	—	MBT	2
Potato Masher (Ger)	5/10/20	3d6–2	—	—	—	MBT	2

Cost is dependent on the setting, but the weapons above are usually provided by military or government forces

Vehicles

On the following pages are a number of sample vehicles for land, air, and water, including some military vehicles such as tanks and armored personnel carriers.

Acc/Top Speed is the vehicle's Acceleration and Top Speed in inches per round. The Top Speed of vehicles is set for battlefields (not the open highway, where they can usually double their speed). They're adapted to work on the table-top, which means they're not entirely realistic but work well for the game. Top Speed is typically half the vehicle's operational speed for military vehicles, or one-quarter speed for civilian cars. Acceleration varies far more widely—use the examples from the Vehicle Table as a guide.

Climb is a relative value used to determine if an aircraft has a better ability to gain altitude than another, as you'll see in the Chase Rules on page 82. If converting vehicles of your own, use the following guidelines:

Climb	Example Aircraft
−2	Balloons, steampunk helicopters
−1	Craft which ascend relatively slowly, such as civilian helicopters
0	WWII bombers, "heavy" aircraft, modern helicopters
1	Light civilian aircraft, medium fighters
2	Early light fighters
3	Jets, very agile fighters, aircraft which ascend very quickly

Previous editions of *Savage Worlds* used Climb as an actual measurement of inches an aircraft could ascend in a round. In setting books where Climb uses the previous Climb values, simply estimate based on the table above.

Toughness is the vehicle's base durability including Armor (in parentheses); vehicles with three numbers listed have different values for Front/Sides/Rear. Figuring Toughness for vehicles is very difficult due to different types of materials or armor, weak points vs. strong points, and so on, but in general you can use this chart to set the base Toughness:

Weight in Tons	Base Toughness
<1	6–8
2–4	9–11
5–25	11–12
26–60	13–14
61–100	15–18
100–200	19–22
Every 100 tons thereafter	+3–5 Toughness

For Armor, figure the average thickness in inches of any metal on the vehicle and multiply by 2.5. This is a good baseline and will need more tinkering if it's really important based on the type of metal, how much of the vehicle it covers, and so on.

Passengers lists the number of crew plus any additional passengers it can transport. A notation of "2+8," for example, means it has a crew of 2 and can carry 8 additional passengers.

Cost is the average price of the vehicle. If the cost is "Military," the cost is beyond the means of most characters and is typically purchased only by state militaries.

Special Notes

Air Bags: Passengers with air bags roll half the normal damage dice in a collision (round down), minus one.

Amphibious: The vehicle can enter water without flooding or capsizing. See the individual descriptions for their movement rates while in water.

AMCM (Anti-Missile Counter Measures): Some jets or spacecraft are equipped with anti-missile counter measures, such as chaff, flares, or decoy pods. The number of AMCM is a reflection of "bursts," not actual flares or decoys. When used, an AMCM adds +2 to the user's Piloting roll *that round only* for purposes of evading missiles.

Fixed Gun: The vehicle's weapon cannot rotate.

Four Wheel Drive (4WD): These vehicles treat each inch of difficult terrain as 1.5 (instead of 2).

Heavy Armor: Only weapons marked as Heavy Weapons can hurt this vehicle, regardless of the damage roll. This keeps a really lucky pistol shot from destroying a tank. Vehicles with Heavy Armor halve damage they take from colliding with other obstacles (including vehicles) that don't have Heavy Armor.

Heavy Weapon: This weapon can harm vehicles equipped with Heavy Armor.

Hover: The vehicle is a hovercraft and can ignore most low terrain obstacles and water.

Infrared Night Vision: Thermal imaging devices halve darkness penalties (round down) for heat-producing targets.

Night Vision: "Starlight" and other night vision equipment eliminate Dim and Dark lighting penalties.

Sloped Armor: In the best armored vehicles, armor is sloped so as to increase the chance that a hit will be deflected off the tank's armor. Ballistic attacks against this target suffer a –2 penalty.

Spacecraft: The vehicle is designed for use in outer space. Those followed with /Atmospheric can enter and exit planetary orbits as well.

Stabilizer: A stabilizer reduces the Unstable Platform penalty for whatever weapon it's attached to (usually its main gun unless stated otherwise) to –1 (rather than the usual –2). An Improved Stabilizer negates the penalty entirely.

Stealth Paint: This is black paint that imposes a –4 to rolls made to spot the vehicle with sensors.

Tracked: Unless otherwise noted, the vehicle is assumed to have wheels. Tracked vehicles can climb over most low obstacles such as logs, and treat each inch of difficult terrain as 1.5 (instead of 2).

Weapons: Weapons are statted in the vehicle's text. Note that the Rate of Fire for missiles and rockets indicates how many may be fired in one action.

Vehicles

Civilian Vehicles

Vehicle	Acc/TS	Toughness	Crew	Cost	Examples
Horse & Carriage	Animal's Pace	10 (2)	1+3	$1-3K	See horse, p. 160
Early Car	5/16	8 (2)	1+3	$1000	Model Ts and the like
Motorcycle	20/36	8 (2)	1+1	$3000	Street bike
Dirt Bike	15/32	8 (2)	1	$2000	

Notes: +4 Toughness vs. jumps; Off Road (4WD)

Vehicle	Acc/TS	Toughness	Crew	Cost	Examples
Compact Car	10/36	10 (3)	1+3	$5-14K	Neons, Chevettes
Mid-Sized Car	20/40	11 (3)	1+4	$20-60K	

Notes: Air bags, luxury features

Vehicle	Acc/TS	Toughness	Crew	Cost	Examples
SUV	20/40	14 (3)	1+7	$20-60K	

Notes: Luxury features; 4WD

Vehicle	Acc/TS	Toughness	Crew	Cost	Examples
Sports Car	30/56	10 (3)	1+3	$15-$300K	Mustang to Lamborghini
Semi	5/30	16 (4)	1+1	$150-300K	

Notes: Trailer is Toughness 14 (2)

World War II Fighting Vehicles

Vehicle	Acc/TS	Toughness	Crew	Cost
Jeep	10/40	7 (1)	2+3	Military

Notes: Four Wheel Drive
Weapons: M2 .50 cal on center pintle mount

Vehicle	Acc/TS	Toughness	Crew	Cost
M4 Sherman	5/12	21/16//16 (9/4/4)	5	Military

Notes: Heavy Armor, Stabilizer, Tracked
Weapons: US 75mm tank gun, M1919 coax, M1919 hull, M2 .50 cal on commander's hatch

Vehicle	Acc/TS	Toughness	Crew	Cost
M5A1 Stuart	5/14	15/13/13 (5/3/3)	4	Military

Notes: Heavy Armor, Stabilizer, Tracked
Weapons: US 37mm tank gun, M1919 bow, M2 .50 cal on commander's hatch

Vehicle	Acc/TS	Toughness	Crew	Cost
Churchill VII	5/5	23/22/21 (9/8/7)	5	Military

Notes: Heavy Armor, Tracked
Weapons: UK 40mm tank gun, Besa MG bow, Besa MG coax

Vehicle	Acc/TS	Toughness	Crew	Cost
Daimler	10/18	11/11/11 (1/1/1)	2+3	Military

Notes: Heavy Armor, All Wheel Drive
Weapons: UK 2pdr cannon, Besa MG coax

Vehicle	Acc/TS	Toughness	Crew	Cost
T-34/76	5/14	19/17/18 (7/5/6)	4	Military

Notes: Heavy Armor, Tracked
Weapons: USSR 76mm tank gun, DTMG 7.62 coax, DTMG 7.62 bow

Vehicle	Acc/TS	Toughness	Crew	Cost
BA-64B	5/20	12/11/11 (2/1/1)	2	Military

Notes: Heavy Armor, Sloped Armor, Tracked
Weapons: DT 7.62 turret

SDKfz 234/2 (Puma)	5/20	15/12/12 (4/1/1)	4	Military

Notes: Heavy Armor, Four Wheel Drive
Weapons: 50mm cannon, MG34 coax

PzIVJ   5/10   20/15/14 (8/3/2)   5   Military
Notes: Heavy Armor, Tracked
Weapons: German 75mm gun, MG34 bow, MG34 coax

PzVI Tiger   4/9   25/23/23 (10/8/8)   5   Military
Notes: Heavy Armor, Tracked
Weapons: German 88mm gun, MG34 bow, MG34 coax

Modern Fighting Vehicles

Vehicle	Acc/TS	Toughness	Crew	Cost
M1A1 Abrams	5/24	77/58/29 (60/41/12)	4	Military

Notes: Heavy Armor, Stabilizer, Tracked
Weapons: 120mm Gun, M60MG coax, M60MG hull, .50 cal MG on commander's hatch

M2 Bradley   5/14   16/15/14 (4/3/2)   3+7   Military
Notes: Heavy Armor, Stabilizer, Tracked
Weapons: 25mm Autocannon, TOW Launcher

T-72 MBT   5/20   61/31/26 (45/15/10)   3   Military
Notes: Heavy Armor, Stabilizer, Tracked
Weapons: 125mm Gun, DTMG coax, DTMG on commander's hatch

T-80 MBT   5/22   66/35/26 (50/19/10)   3   Military
Notes: Heavy Armor, Stabilizer, Tracked
Weapons: 125mm Gun, DTMG coax, DTMG on commander's hatch

BTR 70 APC   7/20   15/14/14 (3/2/2)   2+8   Military
Notes: Amphibious, Four Wheel Drive
Weapons: 14.5mm MG and 7.62mm MG in turret

Futuristic Military Vehicles

Vehicle	Acc/TS	Toughness	Crew	Cost
Hover Tank	8/32	116/96/76 (100/80/60)	3	Military

Notes: Heavy Armor, Hover, Night Vision, Improved Stabilizer
Weapons: 100MGW Laser in turret, 20MGW Pulse Laser in hull

Hover APC   10/30   75/60/60 (60/50/50)   2+12   Military
Notes: Heavy Armor, Hover, Improved Stabilizer
Weapons: 20MGW Pulse Laser in hull

Watercraft

Vehicle	Acc/TS	Toughness	Crew	Cost
Rowboat	1/2	8 (2)	1+3	$500
Cigarette Boat	20/40	10 (2)	1+3	$60K+
Small Yacht	2/10	13 (2)	1+9	$500K+
Hydrofoil	4/13	15 (3)	1+9	$400K+

Notes: Various armament

PT Boat   3/10   13 (2)   10   Military
Notes: Heavy Armor
Weapons: 50 cal MG (forward), .50 cal MG (stern), 4 torpedo tubes (forward)

Patrol Boat, River   3/12   15 (4)   4   Military
Notes: Heavy Armor
Weapons: 2 x .50 cal MG (forward), 2 x M60 MG (port and starboard), .50 cal MG (stern)

Galleon   2/6   20 (4)   20+80 $300K+
Notes: Heavy Armor
Weapons: 46 x Cannon

Galley   2/8   19 (4)   20+100 $150K
Notes: Heavy Armor, Acc/TS is 1/3 under sail, most are equipped with catapults

Civilian

Vehicle	Acc/TS	Toughness	Crew	Cost	Climb
Helicopter	20/50	11 (2)	1+3	$500K+	−1
Cessna Skyhawk	20/48	12 (2)	1+3	$150K+	1
Biplane	10/30	11 (1)	1	$150K+	0
Learjet	25/200	14 (2)	2+10	$20M+	3
Space Shuttle	70/800	16 (4)	1+40	$250M+	3

World War II Era Aircraft

Vehicle	Acc/TS	Toughness	Crew	Cost	Climb
P-47 Thunderbolt	20/172	14 (2)	1	Military	1

Weapons: 8 x .50 cal MG

Vehicle	Acc/TS	Toughness	Crew	Cost	Climb
P-51 Mustang	20/175	13 (2)	1	Military	2

Weapons: B 6 x .50 cal MG

Vehicle	Acc/TS	Toughness	Crew	Cost	Climb
B-17 Flying Fortress	10/126	17 (2)	10	Military	−1

Weapons: B 2 x .50 cal MG nose, 2 x .50 cal MG top turret, 2 x .50 cal MG ball turret, 1 x .50 cal MG left and right waist slot, Bombs

Vehicle	Acc/TS	Toughness	Crew	Cost	Climb
Spitfire Mk IIA	15/145	10 (1)	1	Military	1

Weapons: 8 x 3.03 MG

Vehicle	Acc/TS	Toughness	Crew	Cost	Climb
Japanese Zero	20/140	12 (2)	1	Military	1

Weapons: 2 x 7.7 MGs, 2 x 20mm Cannons

Vehicle	Acc/TS	Toughness	Crew	Cost	Climb
BF-109	20/140	11 (2)	1	Military	1

Weapons: 20mm Cannon, 2 x 13mm MG

Modern Military Aircraft

Vehicle	Acc/TS	Toughness	Crew	Cost	Climb
UH-1 (Huey)	15/48	14 (2)	4+12	Military	0

Weapons: 2 x M60 MG

Vehicle	Acc/TS	Toughness	Crew	Cost	Climb
AH-64 Apache	20/60	16 (4)	2	Military	0

Notes: Night Vision

Weapons: 30mm Cannon, 16 x Hellfire Missiles

Vehicle	Acc/TS	Toughness	Crew	Cost	Climb
AV-8B Harrier	20/180	15 (3)	1	Military	Special

Notes: −1 Climb in VTOL mode, +2 Climb as jet

Weapons: 25mm Cannon, 2 x Sidewinder Missiles, Bombs

Vehicle	Acc/TS	Toughness	Crew	Cost	Climb
F-15 Eagle	50/700	16 (4)	1	Military	4

Notes: Night Vision

Weapons: 20mm Cannon, 4 x Sidewinder Missiles, 4 x Sparrow Missiles, Bombs

Vehicle	Acc/TS	Toughness	Crew	Cost	Climb
SU-27	40/625	16 (4)	1	Military	4

Notes: Night Vision

Weapons: 30mm Cannon, 4 x Sidewinder Missiles (Soviet equivalent)

The *Savage Worlds* rules provide a simple framework for your tales of adventure and glory. In this chapter we'll show you how to make basic skill and attribute checks and make your combats Fast, Furious, and Fun!

Wild Cards & Extras

Your hero (a player character), and unique allies, villains, and monsters are collectively called "Wild Cards." These beings have a little better chance at doing things, are a little tougher to put down, and are generally more detailed than common guards, minions, or lackeys—collectively called "Extras."

Wild Cards are noted with a design of some sort before their name, like this:

✠ Serious Chapel

The actual Wild Card symbol varies and is usually themed for the particular setting, such as a skull-and-crossbones for a pirate game like *50 Fathoms,* or the visage of the puritan himself in *Solomon Kane®,* but a symbol in front of the name always means the character is a Wild Card.

Besides your own characters, it's up to the Game Master to decide which characters are Wild Cards. The sergeant of the City Watch probably isn't a Wild Card, but Sergeant Grimlock of the City Watch, a veteran of many wars and an important character in your campaign, certainly is. Skytch the Dragon is also a Wild Card, though his three young wyrms aren't. You'll see the difference between Wild Cards and Extras as you continue to read, but for later reference, the differences are:

- Wild Cards can suffer multiple wounds.
- Wild Cards always roll a Wild Die along with their Trait die when making tests and take the better of the two.

Trait Tests

To use an attribute or skill, simply roll the die assigned to it. If the result is a 4 or better (the "Target Number" or TN), the action is successful. For example, if a character's Strength is a d6, he rolls a six-sided die. On a 4 or better, he's successful.

▶ **Modifiers:** Circumstances modify the die roll, such as shooting at something at long range or finding a well-hidden clue. Some things, such as ranged attacks, have standard modifiers. It's up to the GM to determine any modifiers for more subjective tasks, such as spotting an ambush or eavesdropping on a conversation through a door.

In general, an easy task, such as finding tracks in the mud, is made at +2. A difficult task, such as finding tracks by torchlight, is made at –2. A very difficult task, such as finding tracks in a rainstorm, is made at –4.

Aces

All Trait tests and damage rolls in *Savage Worlds* are open-ended. That means that when you roll the highest number possible on a die (a 6 on a d6, an 8 on a d8, and so on), you get to roll that die again and add it to the total. This is called an "Ace." Any modifiers to the die roll should be tacked on after adding up an Aced roll.

Raises

Sometimes it's important to know just how successful a Trait test was. Every 4 points over what you need for success is called a "raise." If your hero needs a 4 to Shoot an opponent and rolls an 11, he hits with one raise (and would have two raises with a roll of 12). Figure raises after adjusting for any modifiers.

Unskilled Attempts

If a character doesn't have a skill for an action he's attempting, he rolls a d4 and subtracts 2 from the total. Wild Card characters still get their Wild Die for these rolls (which are also subject to the –2 penalty). The GM may decide that a character has no chance at a particular skill if he has no training in it—such as performing surgery or flying a plane.

Opposed Rolls

Sometimes rolls are "opposed" by an opponent. If two characters are wrestling for control of an ancient artifact, for example, they both make Strength rolls and compare results.

When this happens, the acting character gets his Trait total first. If he wants to spend Bennies (see the next section), he does so now. When he's satisfied with his total, his opponent gets to roll. The highest total wins. In a tie, the two foes continue to struggle with no clear victor.

The winner of an opposed roll considers his opponent's total as his TN for purposes of determining any raises.

Cooperative Rolls

Sometimes characters may want to cooperate and help a friend complete some kind of urgent task. If two or more characters want to perform a task together (and the GM decides it's possible for them to do so), the lead character makes his roll and adds +1 for every success and raise his companions achieved on their own rolls. This has a normal maximum of +4 for all tasks except those of Strength, which have no maximum.

Characters may *not* make cooperative rolls if they don't actually have the skill in question. (You can't make default rolls to aid with Boating, for example, if your character doesn't actually have the Boating skill.)

Group Rolls

When you want to make a noncombat Trait roll for a group of Extras, roll one Trait die as usual along with a Wild Die. Take the better of the two as always and treat this as the group's total. This way you get a nice average without having to make individual Fear rolls for every Extra who sees a dragon, or watch one clumsy soldier ruin a stealthy approach for his 49 companions.

The Wild Die

Extras roll a single die as described above. But Wild Cards roll an extra d6 and take the highest of their normal die or the "Wild Die" when making skill or attribute rolls. Wild Dice are rolled just like the Trait die, and can Ace as well (see above).

▶ **Critical Failure:** The downside is that snake-eyes (double 1s) on one of these rolls is a critical failure. The GM gets to make up something rotten to happen to your character. That's the price Fate charges for making someone a hero.

> *Example: Buck Savage, international adventurer, faces wild-eyed cultists. He has a d10 Shooting and rolls his d6 Wild Die. The Wild Die comes up 4, but he Aces (a 10) on the d10. He sets the Wild Die aside and rolls the d10 again. He gets another 10, then rolls again and gets a 3. His total is (10+10+3=) 23!*

Bennies

Every now and then the dice may not work for you. That's why *Savage Worlds* gives you, the player, a little control over your hero's fate.

Every player starts each game session with three "Bennies" (American slang for "benefits"), represented by gaming stones or other tokens that signify a little bit of good luck or fate. The Game Master may also give you more Bennies for great roleplaying, overcoming major obstacles, or even entertaining everyone with an outlandish action, side-splitting comment, or other memorable act. (Tips for awarding Bennies can be found in the Game Master's section on page 145.)

You can use Bennies to reroll any Trait test. Make the entire roll from scratch. If you're firing three shots on full-auto and don't like the results, pick up all three dice and your Wild Die and roll again. You can keep spending Bennies and rerolling as long as you like, and take the best of your attempts. If you roll a 5, for example, and a Benny gets you a 4, keep the original 5 instead.

Bennies cannot be spent on tables, damage rolls (unless a character has the No Mercy Edge), or any other roll that isn't a Trait roll.

▶ **Soak Rolls:** Bennies can also be used to save your bacon from deadly attacks. Choose carefully where you spend them! See **Damage** for complete information on how to make Soak rolls.

Game Master Bennies

Game Masters get Bennies too. At the start of each session, the GM gets one Benny for each player character. He may use these for any of his villains throughout the course of the game.

Each of the GM's Wild Cards also gets two Bennies per game session. They can use these or any of the Bennies in the common pool to save their evil skins, but they can't share their own Bennies with other nonplayer characters.

As with heroes, Bennies are not saved between sessions.

Whether they are the blood-soaked plains of Mars or the corpse-strewn battlefields of the far future—these are *Savage Worlds* and there will be violence. We recommend using miniatures or markers of some sort so that players understand their surroundings and can use the terrain to their advantage. If miniatures aren't your thing, see the sidebar on page 73.

► **Distance:** Because the game assumes you are using terrain or a battle-mat and standard 28mm miniatures, movement and weapon ranges are listed in inches. If you need to translate that to regular distance, each inch is equal to 2 yards.

If the GM needs a different scale to accommodate a larger battle, such as a long-range firefight between tank platoons, simply divide weapon and movement ranges as needed.

► **Time:** When a fight breaks out, game time breaks down into rounds of six seconds each. Ten rounds, then, is one minute.

Using Allies

Allied Extras are divided up among all the players to control. This is a very important part of *Savage Worlds* because our settings often feature allied bands of skilled hirelings, fellow grunts, or loyal retainers, and the game is designed to handle them quickly and easily. It's also designed for the *players* to control them—not the Game Master.

It doesn't matter whether or not the *characters* control the allies, only that the *players* do. This keeps everyone involved in the action even if his hero is out of the fight, and makes running large combats much easier and fun for everyone. Of course the GM can always take charge of Extras when the need arises, but with good roleplayers, this should rarely be necessary. Some tips for the Game Master on using Allies can be found on page 146.

Initiative

The action in *Savage Worlds* is fast and furious. To help the Game Master keep track of who goes in what order and add a little randomness to the game, we use a single deck of playing cards with both Jokers left in to determine everyone's initiative.

Deal in characters as follows:

- Every Wild Card is dealt a single card. Any allies under that player's control act on his initiative card as well.
- Each group of Game Master characters, such as all zombies, all wolves, and so on, share a card.

Exactly which nonplayer character groups get their own cards is up to the GM. If he wants to break his 30 zombies into 5 groups of 6, that's fine. Your goal is to do whatever makes running the battle as quick and easy as possible. Generally, Wild Cards and other unique characters get their own card.

► **Shuffle:** Shuffle the deck after any round in which a Joker was dealt.

► **Large Groups:** In very large groups, or time-sensitive games, the Game Master might want to try dealing a single card per side (heroes and villains). On the heroes' turn, simply start at one end of the group and work quickly around. This will speed things up dramatically if that's more important than varying initiative order. If one or more characters have Level Headed or Quick, let that apply to the draw (but only once).

The Countdown

Once the cards are dealt, the Game Master starts the round by counting down from the Ace to the Deuce, with each group resolving its actions when its card comes up.

► **Ties:** Ties are resolved by suit order: Spades are first, then Hearts, Diamonds, and Clubs (reverse alphabetical order).

Jokers

When a player draws a Joker, his character can go whenever he wants in the round, even interrupting another character's action if he wants. In addition, add +2 to all Trait tests this round, and +2 to damage totals as well!

Hold

A hero may choose to wait and see what happens by taking a Hold action. He may then go later in the round if he chooses. A Held action lasts until it's used. If a character has a Held card when a new round starts, he's not dealt in.

If a character is Shaken while on Hold, he immediately loses his "Hold" status and any remaining actions for the round. If the victim soaks the attack and avoids the Shaken result, he remains on Hold.

► **Interrupting Actions:** If a character on Hold wants to interrupt an action (including a rival who was also on Hold), he and the opponent make opposed Agility rolls. Whoever rolls highest goes first. In the rare case of a tie, the actions are simultaneous.

Surprise

Combat often starts before everyone involved is prepared. An ambush, a sudden double-cross, or a trap might all give one side in a fight an edge over the other.

When this happens, the side that started the fight is not dealt cards but begins the fight on Hold. Victims of the surprise attack must make Notice rolls. Those who make it are dealt in as usual. Those who fail get no card in the first round of combat.

Design Note - Action Cards

Some new players have been hesitant to use cards for initiative. We've presented optional die-rolling systems in previous editions, but the truth is, the card-based initiative system works and is a lot of fun. If you're new to it, try it.

We've found the excitement of drawing a Joker—or getting a Queen when the monster that's about to kill your hero is on a Jack—is a major part of the game and those who give it a chance quickly realize how well it works for Savage Worlds—particularly when it comes to keeping track of large groups of heroes and villains.

Games Without Miniatures

Weapon ranges, character and vehicle movement rates, and even the templates are all based on using figures on a table-top. That's why they're measured in inches rather than yards, miles-per-hour, and so on.

But many times you won't want to use miniatures. Here are some quick and dirty ways to handle those situations that are usually dependent on table-top measurements.

► **Range:** The GM should simply decide how far away targets are. Mentally, it's much easier for most people to think in yards. Remember that every two yards is one inch on the table-top, so if a target is about 20 yards away, it's 10" away.

► **Templates:** Without exact placement of miniatures it's tricky to know how many foes might be caught by an area-effect attack (like a grenade). For these occasions, figure a Small Burst Template affects 1d3 foes, a Medium Burst or Cone Template affects 2d4 foes, and a Large Burst Template catches 2d6 opponents.

Allies adjacent or in combat with these foes suffer damage as well unless the attack hits with a raise.

Movement

Characters may move their full Pace (usually 6" for humans) in a round. This is considered a free action and doesn't inflict a penalty to any other actions, such as firing a weapon or taunting a foe.

▶ **Crawling:** A character may crawl 2" per turn. This counts as being prone when being fired upon.

▶ **Crouching:** A character may move while crouching at half Pace. He may run while crouched (halve his total Pace after rolling for running). Ranged attacks against him suffer a –1 penalty.

▶ **Going Prone:** A character may fall prone at any time during his action. Getting up costs 2" of movement. See Prone on page 85 for the benefits of being prone.

▶ **Difficult Ground:** Difficult ground such as mud, steep hills, or snow, slows characters down. Count each inch of difficult ground as two inches for purposes of movement.

▶ **Jumping:** A character can jump 1" horizontally from a dead stop, or up to 2" with a "run and go." A successful Strength roll grants one extra inch of distance.

Running

A character may run an additional 1d6" during his turn if he wishes. Characters suffer a –2 penalty (the standard multi-action penalty) to all other actions made while running.

▶ **Group Running Rolls:** When rolling for a group of nonplayer characters, villains, or monsters, the GM or controlling player makes a single running roll. The whole group doesn't actually *have to* run—it's just a convenient way to save a little time in the heat of battle.

Actions

Characters perform "actions" when their card comes up each round. A character can move (see Movement) and perform one regular action—attacking, running, casting a spell, and so on—without penalty.

Characters can perform a multitude of actions when their card comes up in combat. The most common actions are making Tests of Will, using a power, or attacking with the Fighting or Shooting skill. These are all covered on the following pages.

Simpler actions such as readying an item, drawing a sword, or other quick tasks usually take one action. More complex actions, such as lighting a torch, digging through a backpack to find a small item, and so on, might require a random amount of time (such as 1d6 rounds). The Game Master has the final say.

▶ **Readying Weapons:** Drawing a weapon usually takes an entire round, but a character can do it faster if she wants. This is an action, however, and so inflicts the standard multi-action penalty of –2 to the character's attack roll.

Drawing two weapons at once, drawing a weapon from a difficult location (such as an ankle holster or inside a coat), or drawing a large or unwieldy weapon (a rifle, a shotgun, etc.), still inflicts a single –2 penalty, but requires an Agility roll. If the roll is failed, the weapons are drawn but the character may not attack that round.

Multiple Actions

Characters may perform multiple actions such as Intimidating someone while blasting away with a shotgun, running and Fighting, attacking with a weapon in each hand, and so on. Two important rules apply:

- A character can't fire more than his weapon's Rate of Fire in one round
- A character may not make more than one Fighting attack with the same weapon in one round

In essence, a hero may not perform the same action twice in a round—he can't make two simultaneous Intimidation rolls or cast two different spells. He could make a Fighting and a Shooting attack if he had a gun in one hand and a knife in the other, however, and could even issue a Taunt at the same time. He could only make two Fighting attacks if he had a knife in each hand, however (or had the Frenzy Edge).

Each additional action attempted in a round subtracts 2 from all the hero's rolls. If an adventurer wants to fire a gun with one hand and slice at an adjacent foe with a sword in the other, for instance, he subtracts 2 from both rolls. If he also wanted to make a Test of Wills against someone at the same time, he subtracts 4 from all his rolls.

Wild Cards get their Wild Die on each action as usual.

A moving character may perform these actions at different points in his movement, but still suffers the multi-action penalty. This might seem a little odd in practice—a character might shoot a pistol, move a few inches, then issue a Taunt—suffering a –2 penalty to both even though the Taunt roll has yet to be resolved—so make sure the player is committed to both actions before resolving either.

▶ **Free Actions:** Some minor actions are "free" and don't inflict multi-action penalties. Speaking a short sentence or two, moving up to the character's Pace, falling prone, resisting opposed rolls, or dropping an item are all examples of free actions.

▶ **One Wild Die Per Action:** When Wild Cards roll multiple dice for a single action, such as when firing a machine gun, they roll only one Wild Die. A warrior with the Frenzy Edge, for example, rolls

two Fighting dice and one Wild Die. He can use the Wild Die's total to replace either of his Fighting dice if he chooses. The Wild Die must either replace one of the regular dice or be ignored—it never adds another action or attack to the roll.

Attacks

The heart of *Savage Worlds* is its fast, furious combat. Here's everything you need to know to decimate your foes and keep your hero alive.

Melee Attacks

The Target Number to hit an opponent is equal to the opponent's Parry score (2 plus half his Fighting ability; that's a 2 if he has no Fighting skill).

▶ **Bonus Damage:** If your attack hits with a raise, add +1d6 to your damage total as well! The d6 may Ace just like any other damage roll.

Ranged Attacks

The Shooting skill covers everything from pistols to rocket launchers. The base TN to hit something at Short range is 4 as usual. Shots at Medium range subtract 2 from the Shooting roll, and shots at Long range subtract 4 from the roll.

▶ **Bonus Damage:** If you hit your target with a raise, add +1d6 to the damage total. This roll may Ace just like any other damage roll.

Range Modifiers

Range	Modifier
Short	—
Medium	–2
Long	–4

▶ **Rate of Fire:** The Rate of Fire is how many Shooting dice the character rolls when firing the weapon. These additional shots must be taken at the same time, and each point of RoF grants the hero another Shooting die. A pistol with a RoF of 2, for example, gives a character two Shooting dice, which may be aimed at two different targets.

A submachine gun with a RoF of 3, for example, allows the player to roll up to three Shooting dice at once at up to three different targets. These shots can be split among all possible targets as the player desires, but must all be taken at the same time. A shooter with an Uzi can't fire one shot, then move and fire two more, for instance.

Wild Cards roll one Wild Die with the Shooting roll, and can use it in place of one of the Shooting dice if they choose.

Example: A special agent fires a submachine gun (RoF 3) at two terrorists. The agent is a Wild Card with a Shooting of d8, so he rolls 3d8 plus a Wild Die (d6). The player decides to put two shots into the closest terrorist and one at the further target. He rolls the two at the closest terrorist first, then rolls a third d8 for the second. He also rolls his Wild Die.

He scores a hit on each with his Shooting dice and misses with the third, but his Wild Die hit so he replaces one of the failed Shooting dice with it and gets his maximum three hits (since that was his RoF).

▶ **Firing Blind:** Sometimes a character may want to fire at targets they have no fix on whatsoever. In these cases, allow the attacker to make a Shooting roll at –4 as above. Should he hit, the target may make a simple Stealth roll to ignore the attack (it misses). The Stealth roll is made at –2 if the attack was made with a RoF of 3 or more.

Attack Modifiers

▶ **Cover:** Attackers suffer a penalty when attempting to hit a target behind cover:

- **Light Cover:** Characters subtract 1 from their attack rolls if half or less of their target is obscured.
- **Medium Cover:** The penalty is increased to –2 if more than half of the target is hidden from view. This is the usual penalty for attacking a prone character (see **Prone**).
- **Heavy Cover:** The penalty is –4 if only a small part of the target is visible (prone beside a tree, behind a high wall, peeking around the corner of a building, etc.).
- **Near Total Cover:** Attacking through a very tight opening that provides near total cover, such as an arrow slit, subtracts 6 from enemy attack rolls.

▶ **Illumination:** Attacking a poorly-illuminated target is more difficult than a similar attack with good lighting, and incurs the following penalties:

- **Dim:** Twilight, light fog, night with a full moon, and so on subtract 1 from combatants' attack rolls.
- **Dark:** Normal darkness with some ambient light (starlight, partial moon) inflicts a –2 penalty, and targets aren't visible outside of 10".
- **Pitch Darkness:** Targets aren't visible at all in pitch blackness, but if a character knows roughly where a victim is (he can hear him, target is in a confined space, a glint of light shines off his blade, etc.), he may be attacked at –4.

Damage

After a successful close combat or ranged hit, the attacker rolls damage. Ranged weapons do fixed damage as listed in the Gear section. Most pistols, for example, cause 2d6 damage.

Hand weapons cause damage equal to the attacker's Strength die plus a second die, which depends on the weapon. A barbarian with a d12 Strength and a long sword (d8 damage) rolls d12+d8 damage. Even though Strength is used to determine melee damage, this isn't a Trait roll. Wild Cards don't add a Wild Die to the roll and they can't spend Bennies if they're unhappy with the results.

All damage rolls can Ace.

▶ **Unarmed Combat Damage:** An unarmed combatant rolls only his Strength die.

▶ **Bonus Damage:** Well-placed attacks are more likely to hit vital areas, and so do more damage. If your hero gets a raise on his attack roll (regardless of how *many* raises), he adds +1d6 to the final total. This roll may also Ace!

Applying Damage

The damage of an attack is compared to the victim's Toughness just like a Trait roll (though it isn't one so you can't spend a Benny on it). With a success, the victim is Shaken. For each raise over his Toughness he suffers a wound as well, as shown below:

- **Success:** The character is Shaken. If he was already Shaken, he suffers a wound and remains Shaken. To cause a wound, the latter Shaken result must come from a physical attack of some kind—not a Test of Wills or other maneuver.
- **Raise:** The character suffers a wound for every raise on the damage roll, and is Shaken. (When wounds are caused, it doesn't matter if the victim was already Shaken beforehand.)

Example: A barbarian hits an ogre with a Toughness of 11. The barbarian's friend, a rogue, has already taunted the beast (a Test of Wills, see page 86) and Shaken it.

If the barbarian's damage is 11-14, that's a success and would normally Shake the ogre. Since it's already Shaken, he suffers a wound and remains Shaken.

If the barbarian's damage is 15+—a raise or more—he'd simply cause wounds. The ogre is already Shaken, and since a wound was caused, there's no further effect.

One of the core principles of Savage Worlds is that figures are up, down, or off the table. This assumes you're using figures, but the concept applies even if you're not. Up, down, or off the table means the Game Master can have dozens of actors (allies, enemies, etc.) and easily keep track of them all because those that are up are fine and operating normally, those that are down are Shaken, and those who are Incapacitated are removed. Understanding that may help you better understand why the Shaken rules work the way they do.

Of course the Game Master shouldn't fill the table with miniatures simply because he can. Instead, the ability to handle such large fights is a tool to let the player characters adopt different strategies than they would in most games where this just isn't practical. Want to recruit a warband to help you take down that orc horde? No problem! Want to add several platoons of tanks to help storm that enemy trench? Can do! One of our most infamous convention scenarios is a dozen tanks and 50 soldiers per side supporting a raid by the player characters—all handled in about two hours with roleplaying, puzzle-solving, and a massive combat. The power and flexibility to do that, while still maintaining a high level of character customization and detail, is one of the features we think makes Savage Worlds so special.

Damage Effects

Damage can result in three effects: Shaken, wounds, and Incapacitation.

Shaken

If the damage of an attack is a simple success (0-3 points over Toughness), the target is Shaken. Shaken characters are rattled, distracted, or momentarily shocked. They aren't stunned but are temporarily suppressed enough that they must make a Spirit roll to be effective.

On their action, a Shaken character must attempt to recover from being Shaken by making a Spirit roll:

- **Failure:** The character remains Shaken. He can only perform free actions (see page 75).
- **Success:** The character is no longer Shaken, but can still only perform free actions.
- **Raise:** The character is no longer Shaken and may act normally.

▶ **Spending Bennies:** A player may spend a Benny at any time to remove his Shaken status. If it's currently his action, he may act as if he gained a raise on the Spirit roll.

Wounds

Every raise on the damage roll inflicts a wound.

Wounded Extras are removed from play. They're dead, injured, or otherwise out of the fight.

Wild Cards can take three wounds and still function. If another wound would be caused after that, they're Incapacitated (see below). Wild Cards never have more than three wounds—anything beyond that is just considered three wounds and Incapacitated (see below).

▶ **Wound Penalties:** Each wound a Wild Card suffers causes a –1 cumulative penalty to his Pace (minimum of 1) and to all further Trait tests—up to the maximum of a hero's 3 wounds. A hero with 2 wounds, for example, suffers a –2 penalty to his Pace and any Trait tests.

▶ **Timing:** Characters sometimes take multiple hits on the same Action Card. Resolve each damage roll separately and completely before moving on to the next (including any Soak rolls).

Incapacitation

Incapacitated characters aren't necessarily dead, but are generally too beaten, battered, or bruised to do anything useful. They may not perform actions and are not dealt Action Cards in combat. Incapacitated Extras are removed from play.

Wild Cards are Incapacitated if they suffer more than three wounds (cumulatively or all at once). When a Wild Card becomes Incapacitated, make an immediate Vigor roll:

- **Total of 1 or Less:** The character dies.
- **Failure:** Roll on the Injury Table. The Injury is permanent and the victim is Bleeding Out (see below).
- **Success:** Roll on the Injury Table. The Injury goes away when all wounds are healed.
- **Raise:** Roll on the Injury Table. The Injury goes away in 24 hours, or when all wounds are healed.

Injury Table

2d6 Wound

2 Unmentionables: If the injury is permanent, reproduction is out of the question without miracle surgery or magic. There is no other effect from this result.

3-4 Arm: Roll left or right arm randomly; it's unusable like the One Arm Hindrance (though if the primary arm is affected, off-hand penalties still apply to the other).

5-9 Guts: Your hero catches one somewhere between the crotch and the chin. Roll 1d6:

1-2 Broken: Agility reduced a die type (minimum d4).

3-4 Battered: Vigor reduced a die type (minimum d4).

5-6 Busted: Strength reduced a die type (minimum d4).

10 Leg: Gain the Lame Hindrance (or the One Leg Hindrance if already Lame).

11-12 Head: A grievous injury to the head. Roll 1d6:

1-2 Hideous Scar: Your hero now has the Ugly Hindrance.

3-4 Blinded: An eye is damaged. Gain the One Eye Hindrance (or the Blind Hindrance if he only had one good eye).

5-6 Brain Damage: Massive trauma to the head. Smarts reduced one die type (min d4).

▶ **Bleeding Out:** The injured character must make a Vigor roll at the start of each round after the one in which he was injured and before Action Cards are dealt:

- **Success:** The victim must roll again next round, or every minute thereafter if not in combat.
- **Raise:** The victim stabilizes and no further rolls are required.
- **Failure:** The character dies from blood loss.

Other characters may stop a victim's bleeding by making a Healing roll. If successful, the victim stabilizes immediately and no further rolls are required. This use of the Healing skill just stops the bleeding. See page 87 for the use of the Healing skill to recover actual wounds.

Soak Rolls

A character may spend a Benny to make a "Soak" roll, which is a Vigor check. A success and each raise reduces the number of wounds suffered from that attack by one.

If the character Soaks *all* of the wounds from an attack, he removes his Shaken condition too (even from a previous source). Don't count the wound modifiers he's *about* to suffer when making this roll.

▶ **Timing:** A character may only make one Soak roll per attack. If a Soak roll eliminates 2 of 3 wounds, for instance, a hero can't make another Soak roll to eliminate the third wound. (The hero *could* spend a second Benny to reroll the Vigor roll as usual, however.)

▶ **Shaken:** A character can also spend a Benny to immediately eliminate a Shaken condition (and act if it's his action). This can be done at any time—even just after a failed Spirit roll to recover.

Below are a number of rules for special maneuvers characters might perform during furious combat.

Aim

A character who spends a full round aiming (no movement allowed) may add +2 to his Shooting or Throwing roll in the following round versus whatever he aimed at (a person, vehicle, etc.). Aiming for multiple rounds has no extra effect.

Area Effect Attacks

Grenades, spell effects, and other attacks that cover a large area are "area effect attacks." The three most common size attacks have been made into Small, Medium, and Large Burst Templates, found on page 180 and on our website.

To attack with an area effect weapon, the character places the template on the table (or picks where he wants the center of the blast to be) and makes a Shooting or Throwing roll. If the attack is successful, the blast is centered where desired. Everything under (or partially under) the template is affected, rolling damage separately for each Wild Card or group of Extras.

Failure means the blast deviates. Just how far depends on whether it was thrown or launched, and what range bracket the target was in (Short, Medium, or Long). Roll 1d6" for thrown weapons (such as grenades) and 1d10" for fired projectiles. Multiply by 1 for Short range, 2 for Medium, and 3 for Long.

Next roll a d12 and read it like a clock facing to determine the direction the missile deviates. A weapon can never deviate more than half the distance to the original target. That keeps things from going behind the thrower.

Targets use their lowest armor value against area effect damage—armor must cover the entire body without gaps to provide any protection at all.

▶ **Cover:** Targets who are prone or behind cover still get some protection from area effect attacks. In these cases, the modifier they would normally receive against ranged attacks acts as that many points of Armor instead. A character in major cover, like a foxhole, negates four points of damage from a blast if he's caught within it.

▶ **Diving for Cover:** Thrown weapons with a blast effect (such as grenades) and artillery allow potential targets a chance to move out of the area of effect. Give targets who saw the danger coming an Agility roll at −2 to jump out of the way and avoid the damage. If successful, move the character just outside the template (his choice exactly where). Grenades can be thrown back as well (see Grenades on page 57).

Automatic Fire

Automatic weapons (those with an RoF of 2 or higher) fire much faster—and inherently differently—than regular firearms.

To attack with a full-auto weapon, roll a number of Shooting dice equal to the weapon's Rate of Fire. Compare each die separately to the Target Number to see if it hit. If the weapon has a RoF of 3, for example, a Wild Card rolls three Shooting dice plus a Wild Die and uses the best three results.

Note that Wild Cards roll their Shooting dice plus a Wild Die. They still can't hit with more shots than the weapon's Rate of Fire, however.

▶ **Recoil:** Fully automatic fire is typically inaccurate because of the recoil between each shot. Subtract 2 from the Shooting roll when firing full-auto (ignore the penalty when firing a single shot with such a weapon).

▶ **Full-Auto and Ammo:** This system is somewhat abstract so that we don't have to roll dice for every single bullet (though we treat them as such for game purposes). This means that each die rolled on full-auto represents a number of bullets equal to the weapon's Rate of Fire when counting ammo, even though only one "bullet" can hit and cause damage from that die. Firing all three dice with a Thompson gun (Rate of Fire 3), for example, consumes 9 bullets.

Most automatic weapons can be set to fire full-auto or single shot. If a weapon has selectable automatic use (Auto), you can fire a single shot (and also ignore the full-auto penalty of −2).

▶ **Suppressive Fire:** Instead of attacking specific targets, characters with fully automatic weapons can "spray" an area with lead in hopes of killing or suppressing a larger number of victims. To suppress an area, the attacker places the Medium Burst Template on the battlefield, and makes a single Shooting roll (regardless of the weapon's Rate of Fire). Include the standard modifiers for range, the full-auto penalty, and any other miscellaneous factors, but ignore the target's modifiers if any (such as being prone or in cover—these come into play in another way as you'll see below). If the attack misses, the spray is off-target and has no effect.

If the attack is successful, all possible targets within the area make Spirit rolls, adding any cover modifiers they would normally have against ranged attacks to this roll. Those who fail are Shaken. Those who roll a 1 on their Spirit die (regardless of any Wild Dice) are actually hit by the attack and suffer damage normally.

Suppressive fire uses five times the weapon's Rate of Fire in bullets. A weapon with a Rate of Fire of 3, for example, uses 15 bullets for suppressive fire.

Example: Buck and Virginia, two pulp-era adventurers, are escaping from ancient ruins in a stolen biplane. Suddenly, they're swarmed by an evil alligator shaman and his brainwashed minions. Virginia spins the plane's Maxim gun around and fires. She uses suppressive fire to slow them down.

She places a Medium Burst Template 16" away—that's Medium Range for the Maxim—and rolls her Shooting. She gets a 13, −2 for full-auto, −2 for an unstable platform (the plane), and −2 for Medium range, for a total of 7. Success! The tribesmen in the template must roll their Spirit or be Shaken. Those who make it charge on through, but those who roll a 1 are hit!

Breaking Things

Occasionally a character may want to break something, such as a weapon, a lock, or a door. Use the Toughness values below for these kinds of objects. Use these rules for solid objects. Larger objects with many components (such as vehicles) take multiple hits as per the vehicle rules.

Most anything can be broken given enough time and effort, so use this system only when attempting to break things in a hurry (such as during combat rounds).

The Parry of an inanimate object is 2. The catch is that damage rolls against them don't count bonuses from raises on the attack roll, nor Aces. Unlike a person or even a vehicle, an attack cannot hit a "vital" area on a lock or a door and thus do more damage. If an attack can't do enough damage to destroy an object, it can't destroy it (at least not quickly). This keeps characters from shattering swords with a feather and a lucky Strength roll.

If the damage roll equals or exceeds the object's Toughness, it's broken, bent, shattered, or otherwise ruined. The GM decides the exact effects—such as whether a good strike opens a hole in a door or knocks it off its hinges.

See **Obstacles** to attack *through* objects.

▶ **Damage Types:** After the type of Object and its Toughness is the type of damage that can affect it. Swords do cutting or piercing damage, spears are piercing weapons, and so on. Bullets are considered piercing weapons, though shotguns do blunt damage at close range for the purpose of this table.

The type of damage is important for objects because shooting a single bullet through a door, for instance, may penetrate it, but won't destroy it. Only a blunt or cutting attack is likely to destroy a door in one shot.

Object Toughness

Object	Toughness	Damage Type
Light Door	8	Blunt, Cutting
Heavy Door	10	Blunt, Cutting
Lock	8	Blunt, Piercing
Handcuffs	12	Blunt, Piercing, Cutting
Knife, Sword	10	Blunt, Cutting
Rope	4	Cutting, Piercing
Small Shield	8	Blunt, Cutting
Medium Shield	10	Blunt, Cutting
Large Shield	12	Blunt, Cutting

Called Shots

Use the following modifiers and effects when characters wish to target specific locations:

- **Limb (–2):** An attack to a limb causes no additional damage but may ignore armor or have some other special effect (see the **Disarm** maneuver).
- **Head or Vitals (–4):** The attacker gains +4 damage from a successful attack to these critical areas. The target must actually have vital areas, and the attacker must know where they are to gain this advantage.
- **Small Target (–4):** Attacks against small targets such as the heart of a vampire or a missing scale on a large dragon's chest are made at –4. The effect of success depends on the situation—the vampire might die instantly, the missing scale may mean the dragon gets no armor, etc. If the GM has no particular effect in mind, it adds +4 damage just like a shot to the head or vitals.
- **Tiny Target (–6):** Particularly small or narrow targets, such as the eye-slit of a knight's helmet, carry a –6 modifier. The effects of a hit depend on the target. In the case of the knight, the blow ignores armor and inflicts +4 damage because it's a head shot (as above).

Defend

If a character's only regular action is to defend, his Parry is increased by +2 until his next action. The defender may move normally while performing this maneuver, but no running or other actions are allowed.

Disarm

A character can try to make an opponent drop a weapon (or other object) with either a close combat or a ranged attack. To cause a disarm check, the attacker must first hit the opponent's arm (–2, see **Called Shots**). The defender must then make a Strength roll. If the roll is less than the damage, he drops his weapon. The attacker may choose to make this a nonlethal attack with a melee weapon. Ranged attacks can be nonlethal if the attacker targets the weapon instead of the limb (generally –4 instead of –2).

Double Taps & Three Round Bursts

A character with a semi-automatic weapon (such as a Colt .45, an M1 Carbine, or even an M16) can fire two shots in one action by "double-tapping." Double tapping is a single Shooting roll that gives the user +1 to hit and damage but expends two rounds of ammunition.

Many modern automatic weapons, such as the M16A2, have a selector switch that allows the user to go from single shot, to burst fire, to fully-automatic as a free action. Burst fire, or a Three Round burst, gives the user +2 to hit and damage, and uses exactly three rounds of ammunition.

The Drop

Sometimes an attacker is able to catch a foe off-guard and gets "the drop" on him. This usually happens at a distance of only a few feet, but other situations may occur (a sniper on a nearby rooftop).

Only the GM can determine when one character has obtained this kind of advantage over another. Usually it's when the victim is in the classic hostage pose, is completely unaware of the danger, or has been caught unarmed by an armed foe. The attacker is considered on Hold and adds +4 to his attack and damage rolls should he decide to strike.

Finishing Move

A completely helpless victim (bound, unconscious, etc.) may be dispatched with a lethal weapon of some sort as an action. This is automatic unless the GM decides there's a special situation, such as a particularly tough or naturally armored victim, a chance for escape, and so on.

The killer must usually dispatch his foe up close and personal, but the GM may occasionally let finishing moves be performed at range.

Firing Into Melee

Occasionally heroes have to fire into the middle of hand-to-hand fights. The trouble is that even though we might see figures standing perfectly still on the table-top, in "reality," they're circling each other, wrestling back and forth, and moving erratically. For that reason, firing into a tangle of people, such as a melee, is quite dangerous. Use the **Innocent Bystander** rules when this occurs (see below).

Full Defense

In addition to the usual Defend option, a character can go for a full defensive action. He makes a Fighting roll at +2 and uses the result as his Parry until his next action. This is a trait test, so he gets to roll his Wild Die as well. And, of course, the dice can Ace, and you can choose to use Bennies on the roll if you want to.

Note that the character's Parry never gets worse as a result of the roll. If the roll is lower than the hero's Parry score, he keeps that instead (but gains no bonus from the full defense).

A hero using the full defense maneuver cannot move at all, however. He's doing everything he can to fend off whatever is attacking him. If he wants to move away as well, use the Defend maneuver instead.

Ganging Up

Ganging up on a foe allows attackers to flank, exploit openings, and generally harass their outnumbered opponent. Each additional adjacent foe adds +1 to all the attackers' Fighting rolls, up to a maximum of +4. If three warriors attack a single hero, for example, each of the three warriors gets a +2 bonus to their Fighting rolls.

Grappling

Sometimes it's best to restrain an opponent rather than beat him to a bloody pulp. That's where grappling comes in.

Grappling is an opposed Fighting roll that causes no damage. If the attacker wins, he's entangled his foe. With a raise, his foe is also Shaken.

Once entangled, the defender may attempt to break free on his next action. Both the defender and attacker pick either their Strength or Agility and then an opposed roll is made. If successful, the defender is free but the attempt consumes his action. If he does so with a raise, he's free and may act normally. Failure means he is still entangled. Instead of breaking free the defender may attempt a different action but at a –4 penalty.

After grappling, the attacker may attempt to damage his victim on subsequent rounds by making an opposed roll as above. On a success he does his Strength in damage (gaining the extra d6 for a raise as normal).

Improvised Weapons

Heroes often find themselves fighting with objects that aren't intended for use as weapons. Torches, vases, chairs, tankards, bottles, tools, and other mundane items are frequently pressed into service in combat. And sometimes characters find themselves using existing weapons in improvised ways, defending with a ranged weapon in melee or trying to throw a hand weapon not designed to be thrown.

Such improvised weapons cause the wielder to suffer a –1 Fighting or Throwing penalty, as well as –1 to Parry. The Game Master is the final judge of an improvised weapon's effectiveness.

- **Small Weapons:** Range 3/6/12, Damage Str+d4, RoF 1, Min Str d4, –1 attack and Parry
- **Medium Weapons:** Range 2/4/8, Damage Str+d6, RoF 1, Min Str d6, –1 attack and Parry
- **Large Weapons:** Range 1/2/4, Damage Str+d8, RoF 1, Min Str d8, –1 attack and Parry

Innocent Bystanders

When an attacker misses a Shooting or Throwing roll, it may sometimes be important to see if any other targets in the line of fire were hit. The GM should only use this rule when it's dramatically appropriate—not for every missed shot in a hail of gunfire.

Each miss that comes up a 1 on the Shooting die indicates a random adjacent character was hit. If the attacker was firing on full-auto or with a shotgun, a roll of 1 or 2 hits the bystander. Roll damage normally.

Horses and other animals are possible targets when firing on mounted characters as well.

It's sometimes easier to hit an adjacent victim than the original target using this quick system. That may not be entirely realistic, but it's fast and simple, it makes large groups of people vulnerable to missile fire, and best of all, increases the drama of firing at opponents locked in melee with the attacker's allies.

Mounted Combat

Characters fighting from horseback (or other strange beasts) have certain advantages and disadvantages in combat, as described below.

Mounts aren't dealt Action Cards—they act with their riders. Animals specifically noted as being trained to fight (such as warhorses) may attack any threat to their front during their riders' action. Untrained horses do not fight unless riderless, and even then usually only if cornered.

► **Horsemanship:** Characters who wish to fight from horseback must use the lowest of their Fighting or Riding skills. This makes it important for cavalrymen to actually be able to ride well!

► **Collisions:** If a mounted character runs into something solid—such as a wall—both he and the mount suffer Collision Damage as explained in the Vehicle Rules on page 115.

► **Running:** Riders suffer the usual running penalty (–2) to attacks if the animal runs.

► **Falling:** Anytime a character is Shaken or suffers a wound while on horseback he must make a Riding roll to stay horsed. If he fails, he falls. If the horse is moving, the rider suffers 2d6 damage (he's merely Fatigued for the rest of the fight if the horse was still).

► **Firing on Mounted Targets:** Shots directed at mounted characters use the Innocent Bystander rules to see if the horse was hit. Of course, an attacker can always aim for the horse instead.

► **Charging:** A rider on a charging horse adds +4 to his damage roll with a successful Fighting attack. To be considered charging, the rider must have moved at least 6" or more in a relatively straight line towards his foe.

► **Setting Weapons:** A weapon with a Reach of 1 or greater can be "set" against a cavalry attack. To do so, the attacker must be on Hold when he is attacked by a charging mount (see above).

If so, he rolls to interrupt as usual, but each combatant adds +2 to his Agility roll for each point of his weapon's reach. The winner attacks first, and adds the +4 charge bonus to his damage; the loser gains no bonus.

▶ **Wounded Mounts:** When an animal is Shaken or wounded, it rears or bucks. A rider must make a Riding roll to stay mounted, or suffer the consequences of falling (see above). Mounts which aren't trained in fighting flee in a random direction when Shaken, taking their riders with them.

Nonlethal Damage

A character who wants to beat someone up without killing them can choose to do nonlethal damage. This requires the attacker use only his fists or a blunt weapon of some sort. Edged weapons may be used if they have a flat side, but this subtracts −1 from the attacker's Fighting rolls.

Nonlethal damage causes wounds as usual, but if a character is rendered Incapacitated he's knocked out for 1d6 hours instead.

Nonlethal wounds are otherwise treated exactly as lethal wounds. This means it's much easier to render an Extra unconscious than a Wild Card. This is intentional, and should work well for most genres where heroes can take multiple punches before going down for the count, but most "mooks" go out with one or two good punches.

Example: Virginia is whacked on the head by a cultist. The villain gets lucky and does 4 wounds to our heroine. Virginia rolls her Vigor and gets a failure. Because he was doing nonlethal damage, Virginia is simply knocked out for 1d6 hours.

Obstacles

Sometimes characters have sufficient power to attack their foes *through* obstacles. (See the **Breaking Things** section to actually destroy intervening obstacles.) To do so, first decide if the attack hits. If it misses, there's no additional effect other than a small hole in the intervening obstacle.

If the attack would have hit without the cover modifier, the round is on target but the obstacle acts as armor for the target behind it. In the table below are the Armor bonuses for some obstacles commonly used as cover. This is added directly to the target's Toughness, including any actual armor he's wearing in the affected location. Subtract the weapon's Armor Piercing value from the total protection offered—not from *both* the obstacle and armor actually worn by the target.

Example: A soldier blasts an Axis abomination hiding behind a stone wall (Armor +10) with a bazooka. The bazooka ignores 9 points of Armor, so the wall only provides 1 point of protection.

Obstacle Toughness

Armor	Obstacle
+1	Glass, leather
+2	Plate glass window, shield
+3	Modern interior wall, sheet metal, car door
+4	Oak door, thick sheet metal
+6	Cinder block wall
+8	Brick wall
+10	Stone wall, bulletproof glass

Off-Hand Attacks

Characters are assumed to be right-handed unless the player decides otherwise. Actions that require precise eye-hand coordination, such as Fighting or Shooting, suffer a –2 penalty when done with the off-hand.

Prone

Smart heroes lie down when lead starts flying. They move, shoot, and then get prone behind cover before their action is over, forcing attackers to go on Hold to attack them. Prone gives them Medium Cover against most attacks. Ranged attacks within 3" ignore the modifier since the target is just as exposed as if he were standing next to these characters.

If a prone defender is caught in melee, his Parry is reduced by 2 and he must subtract 2 from his Fighting rolls. Getting up from prone costs 2" of movement.

Push

Sometimes characters may want to push a foe in hopes of knocking him out of position, prone, or even into a deadly hazard. This is called a Push.

To push a foe, the attacker and the target make opposed Strength rolls. If successful, the attacker has three choices. He can:

- **Bash:** Push the target 1" for a success and 2" on a raise on the Strength roll. If the defender hits an obstacle, he suffers 1d6 damage for every 1" he would have moved.

- **Shield Bash:** If the attacker has a shield, he can push the attacker as above, but also causes Str damage. Add +1 to the damage for a small shield, +2 for a medium shield, and +3 for a large shield.
- **Knock Prone:** The defender is knocked prone.

▶ **Running:** If the attacker ran at least 3" before the push, he adds +2 to his roll.
▶ **Hazards:** The Game Master must determine results from any other obstacles or hazards, such as a cliff edge, wall of fire, etc.

Ranged Weapons in Close Combat

No ranged weapon larger than a pistol may be fired at adjacent foes engaged in melee. Larger weapons may be used as clubs, however. Pistols can be fired in close combat, but since the defender is actively fighting back, the TN for the Shooting roll is his Parry rather than the standard TN of 4.

That means it's harder to hit someone who's wrestling with your character in melee than someone a few feet further away who isn't actively wrestling with your hero.

Rapid Attack

Sometimes an outnumbered fighter needs to sacrifice skill for blind luck. A rapid attack is a wild swing of the blade or a hasty spray of shots that favors fortune over expertise. Both the melee and ranged version inflict a –2 penalty to Parry.

In melee, the warrior can make up to three attacks as a single action. Roll a Fighting die for each, and subtract –4 for the totals (Wild Cards get a Wild Die as usual).

Ranged attackers with a semi-automatic weapon or revolver may fire up to six shots at a –4 penalty to each. Roll a Shooting die for each shot (along with the Wild Die if the attacker is a Wild Card). Single action revolvers refer to this maneuver as "fanning the hammer," and it requires two hands to perform.

Rapid attack cannot be combined with any other effect that allows attacking multiple foes in one action (Sweep, Frenzy, Autofire, Two Weapons, etc.), nor may it be used with a Double Tap or Three Round Burst.

The rapid attack must be taken all at once but the warrior can assign his skill dice to multiple targets if he chooses.

Tests of Will

Intimidation and Taunt allow a character to make a "Test of Wills" attack against an opponent. In combat situations or during competitive miniature battles, Tests of Will have objective effects, as seen below. More subjective effects are determined by the Game Master in roleplaying situations.

To make a Test of Wills, the character makes an opposed roll against his chosen target. The defender uses Smarts to resist Taunt, and Spirit to resist Intimidation.

The Game Master should modify both character's rolls depending on the situation. Waving a gun in someone's face isn't polite, but it's definitely worth a +2 bonus to Intimidation, for example (unless the target has an even bigger gun!).

A success means the attacker gets a +2 bonus to his next action against the defender during this combat. A raise on the roll gives the attacker the bonus and makes the defender Shaken as well. This can be a great setup for an attack, a trick, or even a second Test of Wills if the first one didn't get a Shaken result.

Test of Wills Table

"Attack" Skill		Resisted By…
Taunt	vs.	Smarts
Intimidation	vs.	Spirit

Example: *Buck Savage tries to Taunt a crocodile cultist by flipping his machete and grinning like a hyena. He rolls his Taunt and beats the warrior's Smarts with a raise. The cultist is Shaken and Buck adds +2 to his next action against the spearman.*

Touch Attack

A character who simply wants to touch a foe (usually to deliver a magical effect of some kind) may add +2 to his Fighting roll.

Tricks

Heroes often attempt fancy maneuvers or clever tricks to distract their foes and set them up for deadly follow-up attacks. This might include throwing sand in an opponent's eyes, ducking between a tall foe's legs to stab him in the back, and so on. Tricks do not include weapon feints—those are already "assumed" in a character's Fighting and Parry scores.

To perform the trick, the player must first describe exactly what his character is doing. Next he makes an opposed Agility or Smarts roll against his foe. The GM must determine which is more appropriate based on the player's description of the maneuver.

If the character is successful, his opponent is distracted and suffers −2 to his Parry until his next action. With a raise, the foe is distracted and Shaken as well.

These penalties do not stack. Tricking a foe twice has no additional effect.

Example: *Buck is backed into a corner by a very large and dangerous thug. Our hero pulls the oldest trick in the book. He says "Hi Virginia!" and pretends to smile at someone behind his less-than-brilliant foe. He and the thug both make Smarts rolls, and Buck wins with a raise. The thug swirls about, expecting an attack from behind, and is momentarily Shaken. The unfortunate goon also suffers −2 to his Parry until his next action, giving Buck time for a quick rabbit punch that just might put the big fellow down.*

Two Weapons

A character may attack with a weapon in each hand if he desires. This works just like any other multi-action, and inflicts a –2 penalty to each attack. (Note that the Two-Fisted Edge negates the multi-action penalty when attacking with two weapons.)

Unless your hero has the Ambidextrous Edge, subtract another 2 points from the off-handed attack (see Off-Hand Attacks). A hero with the Frenzy Edge adds the additional die with either melee attack of his choice.

Example: A warrior is backed into a corner by a pack of ravenous dire wolves. He has two short swords but isn't Ambidextrous. The first roll suffers a –2 penalty (for using two weapons), and the second suffers a –4 penalty (the multi-action penalty for two weapons plus the off-hand penalty). He makes his Fighting roll twice, and gets his Wild Die with each roll.

Unarmed Defender

If one character has a melee weapon and his foe doesn't, the opponent is considered unarmed and is very likely in a world of hurt. Since he can only dodge and evade rather than parry, any armed attacker trying to hit him may add +2 to his Fighting roll. Nearly all animals and monsters are considered armed due to natural weapons such as claws and teeth.

Unstable Platform

A character attempting to fire a ranged attack from the back of a horse or other mount, a moving vehicle, or other "unstable platform" suffers –2 to his Shooting roll.

Wild Attack

Sometimes a desperate character may want to throw caution to the wind and attack with everything he's got. This is called a "wild attack," and can be devastating if used correctly. If used recklessly, it can quickly get even a veteran character slaughtered.

Performing a wild attack adds +2 to the character's Fighting attack and resulting damage roll, but his Parry is reduced by 2 until his next action.

Wild attacks can be used with multiple attacks, such as from the Frenzy or Sweep Edges, or with two weapons.

Withdrawing From Close Combat

Inevitably, your hero will decide discretion is the better part of valor. Whenever a character retreats from melee, all adjacent non-Shaken opponents get an immediate free attack (but only one—no Frenzy or other Edges apply unless they specifically say otherwise).

A character may take the Defend option (+2 Parry) while retreating from combat, but won't be able to perform other actions that round besides movement and still suffers the free attack.

Example: Inspector Mars is attacked by three cultists in melee. He decides to run for it, giving each cultist a free Fighting roll against him. Mars wisely uses the Defend maneuver as well to increase his Parry by +2 until he can get away.

Healing

The Healing skill can be used to treat any wound suffered within the last hour. Each attempt takes 10 minutes.

A character may only attempt to heal fresh wounds on a given patient once within the hour they were sustained. A different character may attempt a Healing roll, but once attempted, that healer has done all he can for that particular patient.

A success on a Healing roll removes one wound, and a raise removes two. Further raises have no effect.

▶ **Modifiers:** The healer must subtract the patient's wound levels from his skill roll. A wounded character trying to heal his own injuries suffers from both effects (his wounds plus the wound penalty to the Healing roll).

Healing requires some basic supplies such as bandages and reasonably clean water. If these aren't available, the healer suffers a –2 penalty to his roll.

▶ **The Golden Hour:** After one hour, only natural healing or the *greater healing* power can help.

▶ **Incapacitated Patients:** If a victim is Incapacitated the healer must first make a Healing roll to remove that state, He may then attempt further Healing rolls to remove actual wounds.

Design Note - The Golden Hour

In the real world, paramedics have a term called "the Golden Hour." Patients who survive their initial trauma have about an hour to survive most life-threatening injuries. If they receive medical attention during that time, they can generally be saved. The longer the wait, however, the more likely the wounds are to be fatal.

In Savage Worlds, we extend this concept to healing in general. A medic who can treat a wound within the first hour can typically negate some of its ill effects. Besides reflecting the real-world concept, it also provides good game balance and drama. If the party could simply retry Healing rolls over and over at any time, their group would never experience the drama of being beaten up by the bad guys, then deciding whether or not to seek shelter and rest up, or striving on despite their gruesome wounds.

Natural Healing

Every five days, wounded or Incapacitated characters may make Vigor rolls. Wild Cards remove one wound level (or their Incapacitated status) with a success, or improve two steps with a raise. A critical failure on a natural healing roll increases a Wild Card's wound level by one. If the hero already has three wounds he becomes Incapacitated. Extras lose their Incapacitated status with a success and expire if they roll a 1 on their Vigor die.

Subtract wound penalties from these rolls as usual, as well as any of the modifiers below. These are cumulative, so rough traveling in intense cold with one wound is a total penalty of –5, for example.

Medical attention means that someone with the Healing skill is actively checking the patient's wounds, changing dressings, giving what medicines are available, and generally looking after the patient's well-being.

Natural Healing Modifiers

Modifier	Condition
–2	Rough traveling
–2	No medical attention
–2	Poor environmental conditions, such as intense cold, heat, or rain
—	Medical attention (1940 or earlier)
+1	Medical attention (1941 or better)
+2	Medical attention (2010 and beyond)

Aftermath

It's often important to know what happens to Extras who were Incapacitated during a fight. This creates interesting choices for the players after battle as they must decide what to do with their wounded companions and living captives. Do they leave their men behind? Do they slaughter their foes? These situations should present your group with chances to roleplay their characters, and challenges to their overall plans as they have to deal with prisoners or walking wounded.

After a fight, the players make Vigor rolls for all of their wounded allies and the GM rolls for wounded foes. With a success, the Extra is alive but Incapacitated (failure indicates death). With a raise, the wounds were only superficial and the character may function normally.

▶ **Walking Wounded:** If it becomes important to know which Incapacitated characters can walk and which cannot, make a second Vigor roll for each. Those who make it are "walking wounded"— they may shamble slowly but still cannot fight or perform other useful actions.

Those who don't make the roll can be moved but risk aggravating their injuries. They must make another Vigor roll for each and every hour of movement. Should they fail, they begin to die. They may be stabilized with a Healing roll at –2, but any further movement will no doubt be fatal.

Aim: +2 Shooting/Throwing if character does not move

Area Effect Attacks: Targets under template suffer damage, treat cover as armor; missed attack rolls cause 1d6" deviation for thrown weapons, 1d10" for launched weapons; x1 for Short, x2 for Medium, x3 for Long

Automatic Fire: See rules

Breaking Things: See Obstacle Toughness Table; Parry 2; No bonus damage or Aces

Called Shots: Limb –2; Head –4, +4 damage; Small target –4; Tiny target –6

Cover: Light –1; Medium –2; Heavy –4

Darkness: Dim –1; Dark –2, targets are not visible beyond 10"; For Pitch Darkness, targets must be detected to be attacked at –4

Defend: +2 Parry; character may take no other actions

Disarm: –2 attack; defender makes Str roll vs. damage or drops weapon

Double Tap/3 Rd Burst: +1 attack and damage/+2 attack and damage

The Drop: +4 attack and damage

Finishing Move: Instant kill to helpless foe with lethal weapon

Firing Into Melee: See Innocent Bystanders

Full Defense: Fighting roll at+2 replaces Parry if higher

Ganging Up: +1 Fighting per additional attacker; maximum of +4

Grappling: Opposed Fighting roll to grapple. Raise=opponent Shaken; Defender makes opposed Strength or Agility to break free (any other action made at –4); Attacker can make opposed Str or Agility to cause damage

Improvised Weapons: *Small Weapons:* Range 3/6/12, Damage Str+d4, RoF 1, Min Str d4, –1 attack and Parry; *Medium Weapons:* Range 2/4/8, Damage Str+d6, RoF 1, Min Str d6, –1 Attack and Parry; *Large Weapons:* Range 1/2/4, Damage Str+d8, RoF 1, Min Str d8, –1 attack and Parry

Innocent Bystanders: Missed Shooting or Throwing roll of 1 (1 or 2 with shotguns or autofire) hits random adjacent target

Nonlethal Damage: Characters are knocked out instead of potentially killed when Incapacitated

Obstacles: If attack hits by the concealment penalty, the obstacle acts as Armor

Off-Hand Attack: –2 to Fighting/Shooting with off-hand

Prone: As Medium cover; prone defenders are –2 Fighting, –2 Parry

Push: *Bash:* Push the target 1" for every success and raise on the Strength roll; *Shield Bash:* As above but causes Strength damage, +1 for a small shield, +2 for a medium shield, and +3 for a large shield; *Knock Prone:* The defender is knocked prone

Ranged Weapons in Close Combat: Pistols only; Target Number is defender's Parry

Rapid Attack: Make up to 3 Fighting attacks at –4 or fire up to 6 shots from a semi-automatic weapon or revolver at –4 penalty to each die; –2 Parry until next action

Suppressive Fire: With successful Shooting roll, targets in Med Burst Template make a Spirit roll or are Shaken; roll of 1 are hit for normal damage

Touch Attack: +2 Fighting

Tricks: Describe action; make opposed Agility or Smarts roll; opponent is –2 Parry until next action; with a raise, foe is –2 Parry and Shaken

Two Weapons: –2 attack; additional –2 for off-hand if not Ambidextrous

Unarmed Defender: Armed attackers gain +2 Fighting

Unstable Platform: –2 Shooting from a moving vehicle or animal

Wild Attack: +2 Fighting; +2 damage; –2 Parry until next action

Withdrawing from Close Combat: Adjacent foes get one free attack at retreating character

The heroes are two soldiers in a Weird Wars: Vietnam campaign—Lt. Griffith and Private Daniels. While on patrol, they're attacked by a pack of ravenous walking dead. The Game Master goes to combat rounds and deals out Action Cards. He draws a Ten of Clubs for the zombies. Lt. Griffith draws a Jack of Spades. Private Daniels has the Quick Edge and draws a Two of Clubs. That's too low so he draws again and gets a Joker!

Private Dan'– Joker

Dan whips out a grenade and places the Medium Burst Template directly over three of the zombies. They're in Short Range so there are no penalties to the roll. The Joker gives him a +2 and his Throwing is d6. He rolls a 6, which is an Ace. He rolls again and gets a 4. That's 6+4+2 for the Joker, or 12. He hits with a raise over the standard TN of 4. Grenades cause 3d6 damage, and 4d6 with the raise. After Acing and adding all the dice together, he gets a 23. That's far more than a raise over the zombies' Toughness 7, so that's a wound to each. They're Extras so that's all they can take and all three are wiped out.

Lt. Griffith – Jack of Spades

Lt. Griffith now fires full-auto and decides to split his shots between zombies G, F, and E. His Shooting is d6 and he has an M-16. He doesn't have the Rock n' Roll Edge so his shots are at −2. His TN at Short Range is 4, so with the −2 he needs to roll 6 or better on each of his dice.

The first two dice are misses. The third die is an Ace (6) so he rolls again and gets another Ace (6). He rolls once more and gets a 4 for a total of 16, minus two for full-auto is 14. A hit with a raise on Zombie E. The Lt.'s Wild Die also Aces and winds up with a grand total of 6. He chooses to use that on Zombie F.

Lt. Griffith rolls the hit on Zombie F first. Damage on an M-16 is 2d8. He rolls the dice together and gets a total of 9. That exceeds the zombie's Toughness of 7 but isn't a raise, so it's Shaken.

Now Lt. Griffith rolls the hit with the raise on Zombie E. The damage is 2d8 plus a d6 for the raise. Griffith rolls a 4, an 8, and a 6. He rolls both the 8 and the 6 again since those are both Aces and gets a 2 on both dice. That's (4+8+6+2+2=) 20! That's a raise over the zombie's Toughness so it's blasted to pieces.

The Zombies – Ten of Clubs

Now the zombies go. Zombie F is Shaken and makes a Spirit roll at +2 for being undead. It gets a total of 7, so it's unShaken but cannot act. It can move, however, so it shambles into contact with Private Dan.

Zombies D and G also move into contact with Private Dan. Since Zombie F is in contact, this gives them +2 on their Fighting rolls due to the Gang Up Bonus (page 73). Zombie D misses but G gets a total of 6 and Dan's Parry is 5, so that's a hit. It does Str+d4 with its claws. It's Strength is a d6, so the GM rolls a d6+d4 and gets a 5. Dan's Toughness is 5, so he's Shaken.

Round Two

The GM shuffles the deck because Dan got a Joker, then deals new Action Cards. Lt. Griffith gets a lousy Two of Clubs. The zombies get an Ace of Diamonds, and Dan gets an Ace of Clubs. Diamonds go before Clubs, so the zombies act first.

Zombies – Ace of Diamonds

All the zombies can now attack, and give each other +2 to their Fighting rolls since they're ganging up on the private. Zombie D misses with a 1. Zombie G gets a 5, +2 for ganging up for a total of 7. That's regular damage of Str+d4, and it gets a total of 6. Since Dan is already Shaken, that causes a wound and he remains Shaken.

Zombie F now gets really lucky. It hits with a combat and rolls 15 damage. Every raise over Dan's Toughness is a wound, so that's two wounds. He already has one from Zombie G, so that brings him to three wounds total. He's already Shaken so that doesn't change.

Private Dan — Ace of Clubs

Dan fails his Spirit roll and can't act. He doesn't move out of combat either or the zombies will get free attacks on him (page 76).

Lt. Griffith — Two of Clubs

It's all up to Lt. Griffith. He fires on full-auto again and puts a die into each zombie. He misses Zombie D but hits with a raise on Zombie G—it goes down with a damage total of 13 (a raise over its Toughness).

Unfortunately, the shot at Zombie F comes up a 2. The Innocent Bystander rules kick in (page 73) and Private Dan is hit for 2d8 damage! The Lt. grimaces, rolls, and causes 12 damage. Dan is already at 3 wounds and this causes more, so he's Incapacitated. He makes a Vigor roll at −3 for his wounds and gets a total of 2. He rolls on the Injury Table and is Bleeding Out (page 69). He'll have to make Vigor rolls each round to keep from dying unless Lt. Griffith can finish the zombies and heal him.

But the GM asks Lt. Griffith to make a Fear check as he sees his trooper fall to the gruesome monsters. He fails.

The last thing Private Dan sees is his commanding officer run screaming into the night.

War is Hell.

Chapter Four: Situational Rules

The following chapter contains rules you need only in particular situations—such as handling large groups of allies, chases, or dealing with hazards such as fire, drowning, or radiation.

If this is your first time through the book, skim over the various sections so you know what's in here, then come back and check them out in detail when you need them.

Allies: Whether they're sturdy men-at-arms, a hardy pirate crew, or soldiers under the heroes' command, Allies are often a big part of *Savage Worlds.* Here you'll find statistics for common henchmen, how to use them, and how to increase the experience of those who survive your warriors' adventures.

Chases: Fast-paced chases between hunter and prey are the subject of this section. Run anything from cat-and-mouse car chases through busy cities to massive dogfights with this simple system. For those who played previous versions of *Savage Worlds,* this is all new and greatly simplified.

Dramatic Tasks: Defusing a bomb, performing an ancient ritual, or hacking a computer are all Dramatic Tasks. These rules turn what would otherwise be simple skill rolls into a tense and exciting encounter.

Fear: This is the section to turn to when your hero faces Things Man Was Not Meant to Know. Fear tests and the grim consequences of failing them are found within.

Hazards: Hazards include the rules for Fatigue, plus Bumps and Bruises, Cold, Disease, Drowning, Falling, Fire, Heat, Hunger, Poison, Radiation, Sleep, and Thirst.

Interludes: Books, movies, and real life provide heroes with many opportunities to share something of their personality or their past with their companions. This often gets overlooked in roleplaying games where the narrative is focused on action and mysteries. Interludes address this by giving some form and function to small talk, and rewarding those players who get into character and roleplay a dramatic tale of their adventurer's backstory.

Mass Battles: Many Savage Settings feature massive wars, bloody battles, and terrible conflicts. This system gives the Game Master and the player characters a way to game out any size battle quickly and dramatically. It also provides a way for the heroes to get in on the action and influence the final results.

Setting Rules: The standard rules are a foundation for your campaign. Setting Rules help one world stand out from another. Here you'll find rules like Blood & Guts—which allows players to spend Bennies on damage rolls! Or No Power Points, which trades the Power Point system for a faster but riskier method. These Setting Rules are referenced in the One Sheet adventures at the end of this book at the start of each tale.

Social Conflicts: How do you handle a court case? What do you do if your heroes petition the king for aid—while a rival actively works against them? This section presents a simple and dramatic system for social conflicts based on Persuasion and how successful—or unsuccessful—the petitioner is.

Travel: Here you'll find guidelines for travel times and how to stage encounters along the way.

Vehicles: Vehicular battles are a staple of post-apocalyptic fiction, World War II adventures, and other technological settings. This section covers how to move vehicles on the table-top, handle attacks between them, and what happens when they go out of control.

Allies

Allies play a big part in many *Savage Worlds* games. They serve as troops under your hero's command in *Weird War* games, loyal retainers in fantasy settings, or fellow fighters in glorious rebellions against oppression.

Keeping up with allies in *Savage Worlds* is simple. Just download the Ally Sheet from our website and fill in the blanks.

Allied Personalities

You can add a little flavor to your allies by rolling on the Personality Table. Jot down the keyword on the Ally Sheet so that you and your Game Master can have a little insight into each particular ally's character.

For the most part, you should consider these general impressions with no particular game effect. What they can do is help both the players and the GM decide just how an ally might react in a given situation. In a *Weird War Two* game, for instance, a player with a young lieutenant character could look over his list and choose the "Observant" character to pull guard duty. If he has to go with the "Lazy" soldier for some reason, there's a good chance the GM will rule he falls asleep sometime during his watch.

Personality Table

d20	Personality	d20	Personality
1	Young	11	Crude
2	Cruel	12	Agile
3	Old	13	Observant
4	Happy	14	Clueless
5	Experienced	15	Mysterious
6	Gung Ho	16	Creative
7	Lazy	17	Artistic
8	Sneaky	18	Fearless
9	Bright	19	Cowardly
10	Dumb	20	Heroic

Allies & Experience

Allies who take part in battle with their more heroic employers gain experience as well—but not as quickly as player characters. Don't keep track of their experience points—just roll randomly to see if they've "leveled."

At the end of a game session in which the allies had a significant role (usually by participating in combat), roll a d6 for each group of identical troops. On a roll of 5-6, the survivors level up just like player characters and get one Advance. On a failure, they don't.

Ammo

Keeping track of ammo for all your firearm-bearing allies can be a real pain. Here's an easy and dramatic way to handle this problem.

The ammo level of each group of allied Extras starts at Very High, High (the usual level), Low, or Out, as determined by the GM. A dot for each of these ammunition states can be found on the Ally Sheet.

After each fight, the ammo drops a level (unless the GM feels the allies didn't really use much in that scene). In combat, if the allies are dealt a Two, their ammo level drops a level *after* that round. This makes for dramatic situations and realistic logistical problems while eliminating a major bookkeeping chore.

Typical Allies

Here are a few typical soldier archetypes you might use for your own *Savage Worlds* games. Fill in any additional skills or Edges as you see fit. A group of rangers, for example, should have the Tracking skill, while cavalrymen should have the Riding skill, and so on.

Soldier

Attributes: Agility d6, Smarts d4, Spirit d6, Strength d6, Vigor d6
Skills: Fighting d6, Notice d6, Shooting d6, Stealth d4
Charisma: —; **Pace:** 6; **Parry:** 5; **Toughness:** 5

Experienced Soldier

Attributes: Agility d6, Smarts d6, Spirit d6, Strength d8, Vigor d8
Skills: Fighting d8, Notice d8, Shooting d8, Stealth d6
Charisma: —; **Pace:** 6; **Parry:** 6; **Toughness:** 6
Edges: Any two combat Edges.

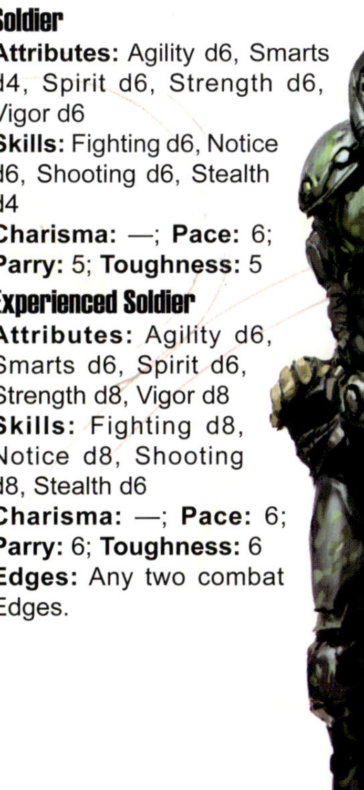

Chases

The Vehicle Rules on page 113 handle fast-paced action on the table-top. This is impractical for chases that take place over longer distances such as city streets or the open ocean, so use the Chase rules instead. It's built for situations when the heroes must catch someone or something—or escape from it!

Chase Length

First determine the length of the Chase:

- **Standard:** Five rounds, used for most chases and usually simulates less than a minute of action per turn.
- **Extended:** 10 rounds, used for long pursuits such as those that take place between ships, and may be measured in minutes, hours, or even days.
- **Dogfight:** The "chase" is actually a battle with highly mobile participants. It ends only when one side or the other withdraws or accomplishes its objectives.

At the end of the last round, any prey who haven't been otherwise stopped or captured escape and the pursuit ends.

Chase Cards

Rather than dealing Action Card as usual, have everyone roll the appropriate "maneuvering Trait" as listed below:

- **Agility:** Foot chase
- **Boating:** Watercraft
- **Driving:** Vehicular chase
- **Piloting:** Air or spacecraft
- **Riding:** Mounted animals

Participants draw a card for each success and raise on the maneuvering Trait roll, and keep one (usually the highest) as their Action Card. This determines not only their initiative but how well they managed to "maneuver" that particular round.

Characters who don't score at least a single success remain in the chase but get no Action Card that round.

Making a maneuvering Trait roll does not count as an action.

▶ **Advantage:** A character with a higher card than a foe is said to have "advantage" over him. This is abstract so it may mean the character is ahead, behind, or even parallel to his foe. The important thing is that he has somehow maneuvered in such a way as to gain a superior position, and can bring his weapons to bear (if he has any and is inclined to use them). See **Attacks** for further information on using the Advantage.

▶ **Speed:** A character may add +2 to his roll if he or his vehicle has a higher top speed than the fastest opponent; or +4 if his top speed is twice as fast as his opponent's. (Use Pace plus the character's maximum possible running value if on foot or mounted.)

▶ **Edges:** Level Headed and the Quick Edge don't apply to maneuvering Trait rolls in Chases.

▶ **Terrain:** If the Chase takes place primarily over difficult terrain, the GM should inflict a –2 penalty to all participants' Trait rolls.

▶ **Climb:** If an aircraft has a better Climb than his foe, he may also add +2 to the roll.

▶ **Passengers:** Those riding in a vehicle have a choice. If they want to help the pilot or driver maneuver, and it makes sense in the context of the situation, they may make a cooperative maneuvering Trait roll. They draw no cards themselves but may add to the driver's total as usual.

The GM must decide what makes sense here. A passenger in a car might help navigate and make a cooperative roll—but a second passenger probably could not. On a sailing ship, the crew could make a group cooperative Boating roll to help the captain's total.

A passenger who makes a cooperative roll and wants to act would suffer the usual multi-action penalty. Passengers act on the driver's Action Card.

Attacks

Characters act on their Action Card as usual. Since distance is abstract, the value of their Action Card determines any penalties to the roll due to Range and whether or not a melee attack is possible (in chases where it's even a possibility).

A character must have Advantage (an equal or higher Action Card) than his target to attack it. A character with an Action Card of 7, for example, can only attack targets with Action Cards of 7 or lower. A target with a higher card has outmaneuvered the attacker this round and cannot be targeted.

▶ **Groups:** Extras roll as distinct groups and act on the same Action Card as usual. Divide each group's attacks up proportionately among the opposition, losing attacks against heroes who have Advantage over them. For example, nine wolves act on Seven and there are five player characters, so each hero is assigned two wolves. Any heroes who have higher cards than the wolves aren't attacked that round. (This keeps characters with low cards from getting attacked by every enemy in the chase.)

The opposite is not true. The player characters may always attack any foe or group of foes they have Advantage over.

▶ **Force:** A driver with advantage may attempt to distract or even ram another vehicle in the chase as a normal action. The "trappings" may vary, but it is treated as an opposed maneuvering Trait roll modified by range. (Cooperative rolls may be allowed as usual.) On a success, the target suffers a –2 to his next maneuvering Trait roll. On a raise, the target is affected as if they hit an obstacle (see Complications).

▶ **Shaken Characters:** If a character driving or piloting a vehicle is Shaken, he must make an Out of Control roll (see page 115). If the vehicle suffers damage, calculate it at half the vehicle's Top Speed (see page 113).

Characters who are Shaken at the start of a turn make their maneuvering Trait roll at –2. They attempt to become un-Shaken on their Action Card as usual.

Attack Range and Complication Table

Card	Range	Complication Table
Two	Out of Range. The enemy is out of range or blocked and no attack is possible this round	**Disaster:** Make a Trait roll at –4. If the roll is failed, the character suffers a disaster of some sort—a car hits a solid obstacle at its top speed, a runner falls off a ledge, etc. Where this isn't possible, the runner gives out, the vehicle stops, etc. In any event, this participant is out of the chase.
3-10	Long Range (–4)	**Major Obstacle:** Objects of some sort get in the way. Make a Trait roll at –2 to avoid them or suffer damage appropriate to half top speed if in a vehicle, or a Fatigue level (Bumps and Bruises, see page 86) if on foot.
Jack— Queen	Medium Range (–2)	**Minor Obstacle:** Objects of some sort get in the way. Make a Trait roll to avoid them or suffer damage appropriate to half top speed if in a vehicle, or a Fatigue level (Bumps and Bruises, see page 86) if on foot.
King— Joker	Short (no penalty), and melee attacks are possible	**Distraction:** Something obscures the character's vision or path. He cannot attack this round.

Complications

If a character's Action Card is a Club, he faces some sort of Complication on his action. Check the Complications Table.

Players who rolled high enough to get multiple cards may choose to take a lower card to avoid a Complication. After the Complication is dealt with, the character may continue his action as usual—assuming he survived.

Example: Knights & Bandits

The heroes are a knight and a squire chasing three bandits through the woods. The knights are on horseback while the bandits are on foot.

The three bandits make a group Agility roll (as they're on foot) and get a 5. That's one success so they draw a single card—a lowly Three.

The squire's Riding roll is 7 after adding +2 for being faster than the bandits. That's one success so he draws one Action Card—a Jack of Clubs. Clubs signals a Complication, and the Jack indicates a Minor Obstacle (the GM decides he must avoid low-hanging branches). The Squire fails and is hit by the heavy limbs for Fatigue from Bumps and Bruises.

The knight's Riding total is 13. He draws three cards and chooses the best—a Joker. Since he's ahead of the bandits and has a King or higher he can make a melee attack. He levels his lance and one less rogue plagues the King's Road.

Example: Road Warriors

Abel drives a rig through the wasteland. Big Ben rides shotgun beside him, while Cale mans the turret on the back of the fuel tanker. Dala trails behind on a motorcycle.

Chasing them are five gangers on motorbikes. They make a group Driving roll of 7, draw a single card, and get an Eight.

Abel makes a Driving roll and gets a 7. Big Ben decides to "navigate," pointing out the debris in the road ahead, and makes a cooperative Driving roll. He's successful and adds +2 to Abel's total, making it 9. That's a success and a raise, so Abel draws two cards and takes the highest—a Ten. He's faster than the gangers, so they can't attack him this round.

Cale mans a crossbow turret on the back of the rig. He acts on Abel's card of Ten, meaning he's at Long Range (–4). He fires and a scores a kill—a ganger bites the radioactive dust.

Dala is on a motorcycle and rolls a 4. She gets one card—a Four of Clubs. That's a Major Obstacle Complication so she has to make a Driving roll at –2 or suffer a nasty wipeout. She barely makes it, the GM describing her skidding around an outcropping of rocks.

The gangers are on Eight so they can only attack Dala (on a Four). Since there are five of them and four targets, the GM divides them up proportionately and decides only two are in position to attack. One ganger misses but the other scores a hit and wounds Dala, meaning she has to make another Driving roll or go Out of Control.

Dramatic Tasks

Heroes often find themselves in dramatic situations such as defusing a bomb or hacking a computer with a definite—and often deadly—time limit. The system below simulates these events and helps the Game Master throw some monkey wrenches and drama into what would otherwise be simple skill rolls.

To start, first determine the skill to be used, such as Knowledge (Demolitions) to defuse a bomb, Knowledge (Occult) to complete a ritual, Knowledge (Electronics) to hack a computer, and so on.

A standard Dramatic Task takes five "actions," and requires the same number of successes (see below). Actions here may mean combat rounds or they may mean "attempts." That's entirely up to the Game Master and the situation.

Performing a Dramatic Task

Each action, the hero draws an Action Card (even if not in combat) and acts on that card. Edges such as Level Headed or Quick work as usual.

If the character nets five successes with the required Trait before time runs out, he's accomplished his goal. It's best to keep track of these successes with tokens of some sort so you don't forget from round to round—and to give the player a visible measure of his success.

If time runs out and the hero has not acquired five successes, the bomb detonates, the ritual fails, the computer shuts down, an alarm sounds, or the action otherwise fails. It's up to the Game Master whether it may be attempted again, but since this was a Dramatic Task, it should normally have resulted in something very bad, or at least require an entirely new approach to attempt again.

▶ **Difficulty:** Most Dramatic Tasks should have at least a –2 modifier. This reflects any safeguards on a bomb, the complexity of a ritual, security on a computer, etc. These are *dramatic* tasks, and by their very nature should be fairly difficult.

▶ **Cooperative Rolls:** Other characters may assist the acting hero as usual, using the Cooperative Rolls rule on page 71.

Complications

If the acting character's Action Card is a Club, something has gone horribly wrong. He must make his roll this turn at −2 (in addition to any other modifiers). If failed, the worst possible resolution to the task occurs—the target escapes, the argument ends violently, the bomb explodes, or the battle is lost.

> *Example: Ian "Haxxor" McTavish is trying to hack into a high-security mainframe at the corporate headquarters of Genesis, Inc. He draws a Three of Clubs and must make his Knowledge (Computers) roll this round at −2. If he fails, Genesis security system detects the intrusion. In this high-tech world of netrunners, the Game Master decides Ian doesn't just fail—a powerful jolt of electricity is sent through the cables for 2d6 damage!*

Example: Defusing a Bomb

The heroes are counter-terrorist operatives holding off waves of suicidal attackers while their demolitions expert, John, attempts to defuse a nuclear weapon. The Game Master decides the skill required is Knowledge (Demolitions), and all rolls suffer a −2 penalty due to the bomb's inherent complexity.

On the first round, the rest of the heroes attack the terrorists while John tries to defuse the bomb. His Action Card is a Six of Clubs—a Complication! The Game Master tells John the bomb was booby-trapped. John puts everything he has into the roll this turn and asks for help from one of his teammates who also has Knowledge (Demolitions).

The companion makes a cooperative roll and adds +2 to John's total. John starts by rolling a pathetic 3. He spends a Benny and rolls a 7. The −2 for the task makes it 5 and the −2 for the Complication makes it a 3. The companion's cooperative roll brings it back up to 5—and saves the day!

John now needs four more successes to defuse the bomb. This round he draws a Joker—breakthrough! "I've figured out the bomb-maker's pattern," he says confidently and gets a raise on his Knowledge (Demolitions) roll. Now he has three total successes.

In the third round, John gets a Nine but fails his roll. He starts to sweat.

Round four. John manages one success for a running total of four. "I don't know if I'm going to make it!" he yells to the team. Soon after, John takes a wound from one of the terrorists' rifles, leaving him Shaken and wounded!

It's the fifth round. The terrorists are closing in. John gets an Ace for his Action Card but fails his Spirit roll to recover from being Shaken! He spends his last Benny to eliminate the Shaken result, calls for help from his friend again, and makes his Knowledge (Demolitions) roll. If he makes it, the nuke is defused. If he doesn't—it's time to start a new campaign!

Example: The Ritual

The heroes are five investigators trying to stop an ancient and terrifying creature from entering our world. Four of the team battle the cultists who summoned it in their underground lair. The fifth, Professor Carter, begins to read a magical incantation he believes will close the gate and send the thing back to whatever hell it came from.

In the first two rounds, the confident Dr. Carter gets four total successes. In the third, things go awry. He draws the unfortunate Seven of Clubs. The Game Master describes a sudden surge of tentacles and amorphous yet angular ooze seeping into our world.

Professor Carter rolls at −2 and fails. "All hail our new masters," says the doctor just before the Thing from another world devours him and begins a reign of terror that lasts a thousand years.

Not every story has a happy ending. These are *savage* worlds, after all…

Fear

Certain creatures and horrific scenes may challenge a character's resolve and cause them to make a Fear check (a Spirit roll) when they see them. A success on the Spirit roll means the character manages to overcome the situation and carry on. A failed Fear roll depends on whether the cause of the roll was grotesque or terrifying in nature.

- **Fear/Nausea:** If the scene was grotesque or horrific, such as a grisly discovery or learning a secret "Man Was Not Meant to Know," the character is Shaken and must make a Vigor roll or suffer severe nausea/mental shock that causes a level of Fatigue for the remainder of the encounter. A natural 1 on the Spirit die (regardless of the Wild Die) causes the victim to roll on the Fright Table as well.

- **Terror:** A terrifying trigger, such as a monstrous creature or unknowable evil, is much more intense, and can rattle even the most stout-hearted hero. Extras are typically Panicked. Wild Cards must roll on the Fright Table should they fail their Fear check. Roll 1d20 and add the monster's Fear penalty, if any, to the roll (a −2 adds +2 to the roll, for example).

▶ **Becoming Jaded:** After encountering a particular type of creature, the character shouldn't have to make Fear checks every time he sees another one in that particular scenario. If the party clears out a dungeon full of zombies, for example, they should only have to roll the first time they encounter them—not in every room. The Game Master might require a roll if the heroes encounter zombies in a particularly different or frightening situation, however, such as if they fall into a pit full of the ravenous creatures.

Fright Table

1d20*	Effect
1-4	**Adrenaline Surge:** The hero's "fight" response takes over. He adds +2 to all Trait and damage rolls on his next action.
5-8	**Shaken:** The character is Shaken.
9-12	**Panicked:** The character immediately moves his full Pace plus running die away from the danger and is Shaken.
13-16	**Minor Phobia:** The character gains a Minor Phobia Hindrance somehow associated with the trauma.
17-18	**Major Phobia:** The character gains a Major Phobia Hindrance.
19-20	**The Mark of Fear:** The hero is Shaken and also suffers some cosmetic physical alteration—a white streak forms in the hero's hair, his eyes twitch constantly, or some other minor physical alteration. This reduces his Charisma by 1.
21+	**Heart Attack:** The hero is so overwhelmed with fear that his heart stutters. He becomes Incapacitated and must make a Vigor roll at −2. If successful, he's Shaken and can't attempt to recover for 1d4 rounds. If he fails, he dies in 2d6 rounds. A Healing roll at −4 saves the victim's life, but he remains Incapacitated.

Add the creature's Fear penalty as a positive number to this roll.

Hazards

Heat, cold, hunger, thirst, lack of sleep, and other hazards can wear down even the hardiest heroes, sending them into a downward spiral that can lead to death if he can't improve his situation. Drowning, fire, and falling are much more immediate dangers, while others are more insidious—such as poison and disease.

On the following pages are the most common hazards, with details on when a character must roll, any important modifiers, and how one recovers from any effects he's suffered from it. Use these hazards mostly for dramatic purposes. A quick trip to the outhouse through a blizzard isn't worth keeping up with, but a long trek through the Mountains of Dread certainly is, especially if it heightens the drama and makes the party think about things they might otherwise ignore, such as shelter, warm clothing, or eating their mounts to stay alive.

Fatigue

Some hazards cause direct damage, but most cause Fatigue—stress or weakness that makes a victim less effective and can eventually lead to Incapacitation or even death.

A character who falls victim to Fatigue passes through several declining states before finally succumbing to his stress. Each of these states and the penalties they incur are described below.

- **Fatigued:** The hero is tiring quickly. All of his Trait checks suffer a −1 modifier. If he suffers Fatigue again, he becomes Exhausted.
- **Exhausted:** The hero is fading fast. He suffers −2 to all Trait rolls. If he suffers Fatigue again, he's Incapacitated unless the hazard description says otherwise.
- **Incapacitated:** The victim collapses and is Incapacitated. See Incapacitation Effects under each Hazard for what happens next.

▶ **Recovery:** Recovering from Fatigue varies depending on its source. Severe hunger requires food, cold requires warmth, and so on. Exactly how Fatigue is relieved depends on how it was acquired. This is explained under each Hazard.

▶ **Multiple Hazards:** It doesn't matter what the source of Fatigue is. If a hero who's already Exhausted from hunger then suffers a level of Fatigue from cold, he becomes Incapacitated. A character suffering from multiple sources of Fatigue must address *both* to recover.

Bumps and Bruises

Characters who suffer minor but troubling injuries, such as stumbling down a slope or running through a cavern in the dark, can suffer from Fatigue rather than suffering actual wounds. This is the hazard to use when characters should be beat up a bit but not truly wounded.

When a character suffers injuries like these he must make a Vigor roll. Those who fail gain a Fatigue level from bumps, bruises, cuts, and scrapes. The Game Master may occasionally allow sure-footed characters to make Agility rolls to avoid this damage instead. Fatigue gained in this way can lead to Exhaustion, but not to being Incapacitated.

- **Recovery:** Fatigue levels from Bumps and Bruises automatically improve one step 24 hours after the original injuries were suffered.
- **Incapacitation Effects:** None. A victim cannot be Incapacitated from Bumps and Bruises.

Example: Two heroes race down a steep slope to escape the clutches of some angry crocodile cultists. The Game Master decides they trip and suffer Bumps and Bruises if they don't make Agility rolls. The first succeeds but the second fails and suffers Fatigue for the next 24 hours.

Cold

Trudging through deep snow for hours on end, or facing biting, bitter winds, can dehydrate and fatigue a character as quickly as blazing deserts. Every four hours spent in weather below freezing (32° F), a character must make a Vigor roll. Failure means the victim gains a Fatigue level. Subtract 1 from the victim's Vigor roll for every 20 degrees below freezing to a maximum of −3.

The roll assumes the character is wearing warm clothing. If not, subtract 2 from the total. Modern winter gear adds +2, and advanced gear (arctic suits) add at least +4 or more depending on the setting.

- **Recovery:** Warmth and shelter from the elements allows a hero to recover a Fatigue level every 30 minutes.
- **Incapacitation Effects:** Make a Vigor roll every hour or perish.

Disease

Diseases cover a wide range of maladies, from long-term debilitating illnesses to those which might cause immediate spasms or death. To handle such a diverse range of diseases, we've broken them down into those most likely to come into play in a typical game or campaign session. If you're trying to model a specific disease, you'll want to adjust the rules to better reflect that illness' symptoms.

- **Recovery:** Unless the disease description says otherwise, it can only be treated with specific medicines or very powerful magic. If the proper medicine is available, all the victim's ailments vanish in 2d6 days minus half his Vigor die type, to a minimum of one day. If not, healers can make the victim more comfortable but have no further effect on his condition. For magical healing, see page 133.
- **Incapacitation Effects:** Typically death unless the text details a different result.

Contracting Diseases

Diseases may be acquired in one of the following ways:

- **Airborne:** The toxin is in the air. If a character is aware of the toxin he can hold his breath for a number of rounds equal to 2 plus his Vigor die, or half that if he wasn't prepared. After that he must breathe and automatically contracts the disease. If the victim is surprised by the release of the disease (such as a creature with exploding spores), he must make a Smarts roll to hold his breath before the tainted air enters his lungs.
- **Touch:** The victim must make a Vigor roll immediately on being touched. If successful, the disease didn't manage to "take" and there is no effect. Failure means the disease takes immediate effect as described below.
- **Induction:** The disease must enter the bloodstream, most typically by an animal's bite, or a cut by an infected weapon. In these cases, if a victim is Shaken or wounded by such an attack, he must make a Vigor roll. If failed, he contracts the disease. If successful, the disease didn't manage to get into the bloodstream and there is no further effect.

Disease Types

- **Long-Term Chronic, Majorly Debilitating:** These diseases cause constant irritation and exhaustion and eventually end in death. Leprosy, untreated tuberculosis, and similar fatal diseases fall into this category. Victims have frequent spasms and coughing fits and so are always Exhausted. If they suffer an additional Fatigue level, they are Incapacitated but do not die. At the start of every game session, the character must make a Vigor roll. If his total is ever a 1 or less, he's going to pass away before the end of that session. The Game Master is encouraged to let the hero go out with style if possible, but he will perish before the game ends this time.
- **Long-Term Chronic, Minorly Debilitating:** This works exactly as above except the unfortunate hero is constantly Fatigued rather than Exhausted. Examples of this kind of disease include malaria, fantasy diseases such as the touch of certain undead, or living in a foreign and slightly toxic environment.
- **Short Term, Debilitating:** These are extremely rare in the real world but are very appropriate for fantasy or science-fiction settings. They are typically acquired from the scratch of a creature or breathing air laden with toxins (see Airborne and Induction, above). A victim who fails his Vigor roll and contracts the disease suffers Fatigue and is Shaken as he begins to cough and wretch uncontrollably. Once he recovers from being Shaken he may act normally but the Fatigue level (and thus the disease) remains for 2d6 days while the sickness works itself out.
- **Short Term, Lethal:** Even more rare are diseases that can kill in seconds. Treat this exactly as Lethal Poison (see Poison). If a character survives but suffers Fatigue from the poison, it lasts 2d6 hours.

Drowning

Water is deadly to those who aren't prepared for it. Here are some standard water hazards and how often a character must make a Swimming roll, with each failure adding a Fatigue level.

- A character with at least a d4 in Swimming does not have to roll when in calm water.
- In rough water, all characters must make a Swimming roll every minute.
- In white water, the hero is swept into eddies and whirlpools (hydraulics) and rolls every round.
- A hero forced to tread water for long periods without a flotation device must roll once every hour.

▶ **Modifiers:** Subtract −2 from a hero's Swimming rolls if he is trying to hold something up, including another character. Add 2 to the roll if he's wearing a life vest.

- **Recovery:** Once a character is out of the water, he recovers one Fatigue level every five minutes.

- **Incapacitation Effects:** Death in a number of rounds equal to half the victim's Vigor die. If someone can get to the victim within five minutes of "death," he can be resuscitated with a Healing roll at –4.

Falling

Falling damage is 1d6+1 per 10 feet fallen (round up), to a maximum of 10d6+10. If you're playing on the table-top, treat every 2" as 10' for simplicity.

▶ **Snow:** Particularly soft ground, such as deep snow, acts as a cushion. Every foot of soft snow reduces damage by one point.

▶ **Water:** A fall into water reduces the number of dice rolled by half (rounded down), and an Agility roll means the character dives and takes no damage at all, though he is automatically Shaken if he dives from a height of greater than 50'. A fall over 15" (30 yards) requires an Agility roll at –2 to avoid damage.

Fire

Even giants impervious to the puny weapons of sword-slingers are often afraid of flame and fire. Roll the damage listed below when a character is first burned and at the beginning of each round until he is free of the flame. Only sealed, fireproof armor adds to a character's Toughness when resisting the effects of fire.

Fire Damage

Damage	Description
+2	Burning weapon
1d10	"Spot fire," such as a burning arm or leg
2d10	Flamethrower
3d10	Lava

▶ **Spreading:** Anytime something flammable is hit by fire, roll 1d6. On a 6, the target catches fire. Very flammable targets, such as a scarecrow, catch fire on a 4-6. Volatile targets, such as a person soaked in gasoline, catch fire on anything *but* a 1.

Each round after a victim catches fire (at the beginning of his action), roll as if checking to see if the victim catches fire again. If he does, the fire grows in intensity and does the damage listed above each round.

▶ **Smoke Inhalation:** Fires in confined areas produce deadly smoke. Every round a character is in such an environment, he must make a Vigor roll. A wet cloth over the face adds +2 to the roll, and a gas mask negates the need for the roll entirely. If the roll is failed, the character gains a Fatigue level.

Heat

Intense heat, typically that over 90 degrees Fahrenheit, can cause heat exhaustion and heat stroke, both of which are very dangerous. The actual danger is from dehydration, so well-supplied and conscientious characters can greatly improve their chances in extreme heat simply by carrying a good amount of water and drinking frequently.

When the temperature reaches 90 degrees or more, the GM should pay attention to how much water characters are able to drink. If they are able to drink at least four quarts of water a day, they may be tired and sunburned, but are in no immediate danger.

If that amount of water isn't available, characters must make Vigor rolls every four hours. Subtract two from the roll if the hero has half the water he needs, and subtract 4 if he has less than half. Failure means the character gains one level of Fatigue.

- Subtract 1 from the roll for each additional 5 degrees above 90 degrees Fahrenheit.
- Add +1 if the hero stops all physical activity.
- Add +1 to the roll if the character has substantial shade.
- **Recovery:** A victim who receives sufficient water recovers one Fatigue level every hour.

- **Incapacitation Effects:** An Incapacitated character suffers heat stroke and may suffer brain damage. Make a Vigor roll. If the roll is failed, the victim's Smarts and Strength decrease by one step permanently (to a minimum of d4).

Hunger

Humans need approximately one pound of food every 24 hours. If sufficient sustenance isn't available, a character begins to suffer from severe hunger.

Starting the first day after the meal was missed, the character must make a Vigor roll. Subtract 2 if the hero has less than half the required amount of food. Failure means the character gains a Fatigue level.

After the first day, the character must roll for hunger every 12 hours, and thirst every 6 hours.

▶ **The Survival Skill:** A successful Survival roll each day provides enough food and water for one person, or enough for five with a raise.

- **Recovery:** At least a pound of decent food allows a character to recover a Fatigue level every hour, or every 12 hours if he reached Incapacitated.
- **Incapacitation Effects:** A character Incapacitated by hunger dies 3d6 hours later.

Poison

Poisons can be delivered many ways. If ingested, its effects occur automatically. If a victim is Shaken or wounded by a bite or weapon coated in poison, he must make an immediate Vigor roll against the type of poison listed on the Poison Effects Table below. If the poison has a modifier associated with it (such as Venomous [–2]), the victim's Vigor roll is modified appropriately.

The Game Master must decide which category is appropriate based on the poison. Most real-world animals are Venomous with only a few falling in the Lethal category. Ghouls might have paralyzing poison in their claws, while spies might use Knockout poison in drinks or gases.

Characters who suffer Paralysis or a Knockout are Incapacitated until they recover.

▶ **Treatment:** To treat a poisoned victim, the healer can try a Healing roll minus the strength of the poison itself (found in the poison's description). If successful, the victim's life is saved and the poison no longer has any effect—paralyzed victims can move and those rendered unconscious wake.

Each character may only attempt one Healing roll per incident to cure the poison, but another character with Healing may make a second attempt, and so on.

- **Recovery:** Fatigue leves from poison recover in 24 hours.
- **Incapacitation:** Characters Incapacitated by accrued Fatigue recover as above. Other effects from the table below are handled separately.

Poison Effects Table

- **Lethal Poison:** Failure results in death in 2d6 rounds. Success results in 1 wound and Exhaustion.
- **Venomous Poison:** Failure causes death in 2d6 minutes. Success causes 1 wound and Exhaustion.
- **Paralysis Poison:** Paralyzed for 2d6 minutes if failed, or 2d6 rounds with success.
- **Knockout Poison:** Knocked out for 2d6 hours with failure, or 2d6 minutes with success.

Radiation

Characters in a radioactive environment must make a Vigor roll every hour spent in low radiation, and every minute in high radiation. Each failure results in a Fatigue level.

- **Recovery:** Fatigue from radiation fades at the rate of one level every 24 hours, or half that if the victim can shower or scrub away lingering dust and other contaminants.
- **Incapacitation Effects:** The victim contracts radiation sickness, a Long-Term Chronic, Minorly Debilitating disease, as explained under **Disease**.

Sleep

Most people need a minimum of six hours sleep out of every 24. A character who goes without this amount of sleep must make a Vigor roll at a cumulative –2 every 12 hours thereafter (maximum penalty of –6). A large amount of coffee, soda, or other stimulant adds +2 to the roll.

- **Recovery:** Every four hours of restful sleep removes a level of Fatigue.
- **Incapacitation Effects:** A character who suffers this much Fatigue simply falls into a deep sleep for 2d10 hours.

Thirst

An average-sized man requires two quarts of water a day. This requirement is doubled in both very dry conditions (such as the desert) or areas of high humidity (the jungle) as the character perspires constantly and begins to dehydrate.

If enough water isn't available, the hero begins to suffer from dehydration. Starting the first day after the water runs out, he must make a Vigor roll. Subtract 2 if the hero has less than half the required amount. Failure means the character gains a Fatigue level. After the first day, the character must make the required Vigor roll every 6 hours.

▶ **The Survival Skill:** A successful Survival roll each day provides enough water (and food) for one person, or enough for five with a raise.

- **Recovery:** Two quarts of water allows a character to recover a Fatigue level every hour.
- **Incapacitation Effects:** Death in 2d6 hours.

LUFTVERKEHRGESE
KARL HAUSHO
OOI - ZYL

In most heroic tales, characters engage in small talk that reveals something about their past or further develops their personality. Such "Interludes" are rare in roleplaying games where we focus primarily on action and the next encounter.

The system below formulizes these scenes and rewards players for roleplaying their character and revealing their backstory to the rest of the group.

Running an Interlude

The Game Master should run an Interlude during natural down-time such as when healing up after a fight, performing research, or between legs of a long trip.

To start, pick a player and have her draw a card. The Suit determines the general topic as shown on the Interlude Table below. Each entry requires the player to tell a story in the voice of her character. The tale should be substantial enough to take a few minutes and may draw in other characters' participation as well.

The next time the Game Master feels an Interlude is appropriate, he should pick a different player so that everyone has a chance to participate and reap the rewards.

▶ **Rewards:** After a player completes her tale, award her a Benny or an Adventure Card—her choice.

Interlude Table

- **Clubs—Tragedy:** Describe a tale of tragedy or misfortune from your hero's past, featuring one of his Hindrances if possible. If the teller has a dark secret of some kind, hint strongly at it, drop clues, or otherwise give the rest of the group a glimpse into your hero's dark side during your narrative.
- **Spades—Victory:** Tell the group about a great victory or personal triumph in your adventurer's past. How did it affect him afterward? Was there a reward?
- **Hearts—Love:** Speak fondly of the character's greatest love—lost, found, or waiting on him back home. What is her name? Where does she live? Why is the traveler not with her now?
- **Diamonds—Desire:** Tell a tale about something your hero wants (or already has). It might be a material possession, recognition, a political goal, or even a trip he wishes to take to some amazing destination.

Example: Crossing Mars

Colonel Green of the Martian 24th Highlanders, his guide Sanjay of the Gurkhas, Lady Emily, and big game hunter extraordinaire Sir John Hobbsworth cross the vast Martian desert. They face sandstorms, intense heat by day, and bone-numbing cold at night.

The Game Master decides to call for an Interlude after each encounter along the way.

Colonel Green goes first and draws a Spade. He describes with great vigor his travails against the wild Martians at Zimkangaroon and the tense battle he fought there. "It's how I got this injury," he says as he points to his Lame leg.

Later, after surviving a terrible sandstorm, Lady Emily draws a Heart. "I will withstand any trauma," she begins, "if only it will help me discover what happened to my beloved Nathaniel, lost in the mountains I have asked you all to escort me to." She then goes on about how she and Nathaniel met, traveled to Mars, and began a new life far away from the grime and corruption of New York City.

A day later, the party is ambushed by Martian raiders. Sanjay draws the next card—a Diamond. "See this bandit blade?" he says proudly. "It is a poor substitute for my kukri, awarded ten years ago when I joined the regiment." Sanjay goes on to describe his training and some of the terrible battles he fought in the 6th Gurkha regiment before volunteering for service on faraway Mars.

Sir Hobbsworth is next, with a Club. "I have hunted every creature on earth. Now I've come to Mars to bag the biggest, most ferocious beast on all the known worlds—the crask. I'll kill the thing and mount its head on my wall. And *nothing* will stop me." Hobbsworth then hints that he hopes the monster slays him as he slays it— revealing his Death Wish and the chronic disease he picked up during the campaign in the process.

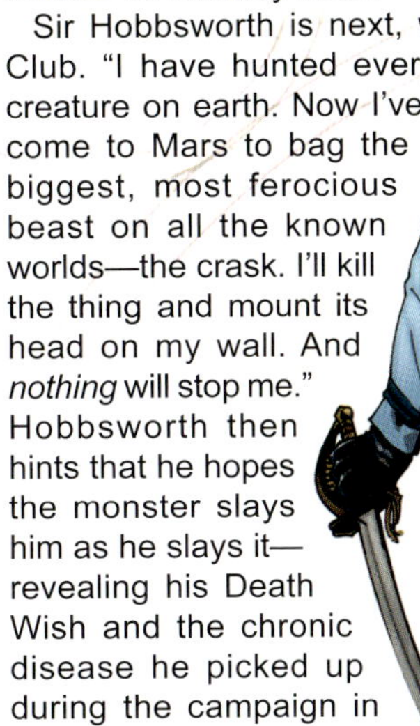

Mass Battles

Truly savage worlds often feature wars with massive and bloody battles. The system below rewards players who not only take part in these battles, but are instrumental in gathering political support, recruiting troops, and deciding strategies that win them.

These rules allow the Game Master to handle everything from a small warband holding a fort against an undead horde to full divisions of troops fighting a massive field battle or a planetary assault from a space-based invasion fleet. It's abstract, but provides a narrative base for heroes to plan, get involved, and even become involved in the fight themselves.

Setup

To start, give the larger or more powerful army 10 tokens. Give the opposing army a proportional number of tokens. If one army has 10,000 men, for example, and the other has 7,000, give the smaller army seven tokens.

The Game Master will need to adjust for special or elite troops, better equipment, and so on. It's not important to count every point of armor and damage point—just get close enough to give a reasonable approximation of strength, adjust where needed, and trust in the dice and the player's actions to handle the rest.

Knowledge (Battle)

Once the odds are determined, both sides make opposed Knowledge (Battle) rolls, modified by any of the circumstances below:

Battle Modifiers

Modifier	Circumstance
+1	The side with more tokens adds +1 for every token it has more than the foe each round

Artillery or Air Support

+1	Light
+2	Medium
+3	Heavy

Terrain

−1	Foe has slight advantage
−2	Foe has minor advantage
−3	Foe has major advantage

Battle Plan—GM's Call determined each round

+/−?	The army gains a penalty or a bonus

depending on the tactical decisions made by the leader each round. Springing a hidden flank attack, sending reserves to a crucial front, and so on, all add to the Battle roll.

▶ **Casualties:** Each success and raise causes the other side to lose one token. Casualties are generally distributed evenly throughout the force.

▶ **Morale:** Each round in which an army loses a token, its leader must check morale. This is a Spirit roll modified by the circumstances below. With a success, the army fights on and both sides make another Knowledge (Battle) roll as described above.

Failure means the army is defeated but the troops conduct an orderly retreat. Make one more Battle Roll and then end the fight. (A leader may voluntarily choose this option as well.)

On a result of 1 or less, the troops rout and the battle is over immediately.

Morale Modifiers

Mod	Situation
−1	For each token lost in battle so far
+2	The army is made up predominantly (75% or more) of undead or other fearless drones
+2	The army is within major fortifications, such as a fortress or prepared positions
+2	The army cannot retreat

Characters in Mass Battles

The heroes of your campaign aren't likely to sit idly by while war rages around them. Fighters may want to charge the gates, wizards unleash fireballs into the masses, and a gallant knight may ride his trusty warhorse directly into the enemy formations.

Those who want to get involved can dramatically affect the results of the battle. Have each character make a Fighting, Shooting, or arcane skill roll (their choice) each action and consult the Character Results below.

▶ **Modifiers:** Add or subtract the number of tokens difference between the heroes' side and their opponent. If the enemy has 8 tokens and the heroes have 5, for example, the heroes must subtract −3 from their attack rolls.

Also add +1 to the roll for each Rank a hero has above Novice to account for his various Edges and abilities that aren't reflected in a straight skill roll.

Character Battle Results

- **Failure:** The hero is stopped by overwhelming numbers, an unfortunate tactical development, or bad fortune. He suffers 4d6 damage.
- **Success:** The hero fights well and adds +1 to his side's Battle Roll, though he suffers 3d6 damage.

- **Raise:** The hero wreaks havoc, slaying enemy leaders and destroying important assets. He suffers 2d6 damage, but adds +2 to his side's Battle Roll.
- **Two Raises:** The warrior covers himself in glory! Scores of foes fall before him and his success inspires his allies to fight like demons. His efforts add +2 to his side's Battle Roll and he emerges from the fight unscathed.

▶ **Ammo:** If it's important to track, each round a hero enters the fray and uses his Shooting or an arcane skill (such as Spellcasting), he expends some of his ammunition or Power Points.

Arcane types use 2d6 Power Points per round. Characters with ranged weapons use 3d6 shots for ranged weapons (triple that for weapons that usually fire bursts or full-auto). If the hero winds up without any ammo or Power Points she'll have to change tactics for the next round.

Battle Aftermath

When one side routs, retreats, or runs out of tokens, the battle ends and casualties are removed. Some of the troops lost in the battle can be recovered as they regroup or receive first aid.

If it's important to know how things stand after the fight, roll 1d6 for each token lost. The victor recovers a lost token on a roll of 4-6. The loser recovers a lost token on a roll of 5-6. A routed army recovers tokens only on a roll of 6.

After the battle and once both sides have figured out how many tokens they lost, remove the actual casualties from their armies. The side that started with the larger force simply multiplies the number of tokens lost by 10%. Losing four tokens, for example, means the entire army suffered 40% casualties. The side with the smaller force must figure out what percentage of his men are left. If he started with 8 tokens and ends up with only 2, for example, he's lost 75% of his force.

Once you've figured the total percentage of casualties to your army, distribute the losses among specific units as evenly as possible.

Example: The Invasion of Earth

The insectoid Gorram Empire is conducting a planetary assault of Earth. The Gorram have 10 tokens that represent their massive invasion fleet and armored walkers with fiery death rays. Earth has all the world's militaries at their disposal. Given the superiority of Gorram technology and greater numbers, the GM decides the Earth Defense Force (EDF) gets 8 tokens.

Both sides have heavy artillery and air support (+3 to both sides), but there are no terrain advantages since it's a world-wide battle.

The Gorram Empire makes a Knowledge (Battle) roll and gets a 13. The player characters load up in stratospheric fighters and lend a hand. Collectively, they suffer some damage but also add a grand total of +3 to the roll. The EDF's Knowledge (Battle) final total is 17—Earth wins by 4. That destroys two of the invaders' tokens and 20% of their force.

The Game Master describes the first few hours of the invasion and a spirited defense by earth's militaries. The evil insectoids are dealt heavy losses, but are far from defeated, and the battle goes on.

Setting Rules

There are many Savage Worlds with settings ranging from dark and gritty detective tales to cinematic epics to political thrillers. These rules provide a great framework for anything you want to do but adding the right setting rules really bring the world and the action to life.

Blood & Guts

Characters can spend Bennies on damage rolls! Use this rule when you really want to up the carnage.

Born A Hero

During character creation, heroes may ignore the Rank qualifications for Edges. They must still have any other requirements as usual. The usual rules for Rank requirements apply after the character is created.

Critical Failures

This rule works well for very dark or very humorous games. When a character rolls double 1's on a Trait roll, he can't spend a Benny—he's stuck with the critical failure.

Fanatics

Use this rule in pulp-style games where villains are larger than life. When a Wild Card enemy character is hit by a successful attack, any of his henchmen, goons, or other allies jumps in front of his master and suffers the attack instead.

Gritty Damage

This variation on damage works well for settings such as gritty detective scenarios or "realistic" military adventures. It can be very lethal so use it cautiously.

Treat Extras' wounds normally.

For Wild Cards, count wounds as usual and go through the normal steps for Incapacitation should he accumulate more than three wounds.

In addition, every time the hero suffers a wound, roll on the Injury Table and apply the results immediately (but roll only once per incident regardless of how many wounds are actually caused). A hero who takes 2 wounds from an attack, for example, still only suffers one roll on the Injury Table.

Injuries sustained in this way are cured when the wound is healed. (Injuries sustained via Incapacitation may be temporary or permanent as usual.)

A Shaken character who's Shaken a second time from a damaging attack receives a wound as usual but does *not* have to roll on the Injury Table.

Example: Sergeant Trotter is a hero in *Weird Wars.* He takes a wound from a German sniper, doesn't Soak it, and so has to roll on the Injury Table. He rolls a 10—Leg. The GM rolls a die and decides it's the left leg. Trotter is now Lame. If he takes another wound to that leg, he'd have the One Leg Hindrance. Further wounds to the same leg add to his wound total as usual but have no further effect as there's nothing beyond the One Leg Hindrance.

Later, the unfortunate Sarge takes two wounds to the Guts. The Game Master rolls once and gets the Battered result, reducing the Sarge's Vigor from d8 to d6. Note that while the attack caused two wounds, the Game Master only rolled once on the Injury Table since it was one attack.

Heroes Never Die

Heroes in movies very rarely die. And when they do, they go down fighting or perform one last, epic act of heroism. With this rule in play, heroes who would normally die are simply knocked out for a dramatically appropriate time instead. Only if the situation is particularly heroic, or if it serves as a major story point can characters actually die.

An adventurer who falls into a volcano, for example, might land on a floating piece of rock and leapfrog to safety. Conversely, if a hero confronts a massive demon on a crumbling bridge and suffers what would normally be a mortal wound, perhaps he does perish but the Game Master decides with his final blow he takes the demon into the boiling lava with him, allowing his companions to escape.

▶ **Villains:** Of course the reverse of this rule is also true—villains never die either! The Game Master will need to explain the spirit of these rules to the group so their characters don't take advantage of it by doing something gruesome and fatal to a fallen villain. In Heroes Never Die, the party is assumed to capture their rivals and turn them over to the authorities—where of course they eventually escape to return again.

High Adventure

Characters can spend a Benny to gain a one-time use of a Combat Edge. Player Characters have to meet the Rank and any Edge requirements, but can ignore Trait requirements for this one-time use. Multiple bennies can be spent in one round for multiple Edges, either for different effects or in order to meet a needed requirement to gain another Edge.

Joker's Wild

This is a great rule to add to your game if you're the kind of Game Master who's a little stingy in awarding Bennies. It slightly ups the heroics and is a lot of fun for the group.

When a player character draws a Joker during combat, he receives his normal +2 bonus to Trait and damage rolls. In addition, all player characters receive a Benny!

Multiple Languages

Some settings feature characters and cultures who typically speak many different languages. If this Setting Rule is in play, your hero knows his cultural or national language plus an additional number of languages equal to half his Smarts die. An elf with a d8 Smarts in a swords & sorcery campaign, for example, knows Elvish and four other languages—perhaps human, dwarven, and two others of her choosing.

No Power Points

Instead of using Power Points, characters with Arcane Backgrounds simply choose the power they want to activate and make an arcane skill roll. The penalty to the roll is half the power's usual Power Point cost (rounded down). Casting the *armor* power, for example, which costs 2 Power Points, is an arcane skill roll at –1.

Once cast, check the results below:

- **Success:** The power activates as usual.
- **Raise:** A raise on the roll grants any additional bonuses to the power stated in its description. *Armor,* for example, grants a +4 bonus to Toughness with a raise.
- **Failure:** All currently maintained powers are cancelled and the caster is Shaken.

▶ **Backlash:** Channeling magic, spiritual, or psionic energy, tinkering with unstable technology, and even using superpowers all come with certain risks.

If a caster rolls a 1 on the arcane skill die when using one of his powers it automatically fails and he suffers 2d6 damage.

Replace each Arcane Background's specialized backlash rules with these:

- **Magic:** Use the above Backlash results.
- **Miracles:** As above, but the damage is reduced by half the priest's Faith skill.
- **Psionics:** Use the above Backlash rules, but the damage is applied to all sentient creatures within a Large Burst Template centered on the psionicist.

- **Super Powers:** The hero does not suffer damage, but cannot use the power for the rest of this encounter or until he spends a Benny to negate the Backlash.
- **Weird Science:** As above and the "device" is destroyed and must be rebuilt. This typically takes 1d3+1 hours, minus one hour for every success and raise on the Repair roll.

▶ **Maintaining Powers:** Characters can maintain powers as long as desired, but each power maintained inflicts a –1 to cast any new powers. Thus an invisible mage can keep the power going indefinitely, but suffers a –1 penalty if he then attempts to hurl a *bolt*.

▶ **Interrupting Powers:** If a character with an activated power is Shaken or suffers a wound or Fatigue level, he must make a Smarts roll to maintain all his powers. If the roll is failed, all powers are instantly dropped. A wizard with *armor* who suffers a Shaken result, for example, must make a Smarts roll. If the wizard suffers two wounds from an attack, he must make a Smarts roll at –2.

Powers shut down automatically if the caster sleeps or is rendered unconscious.

▶ **Power Preparation:** A caster may prepare a spell by concentrating for a round (no movement or other actions and avoid interruption, as described above). If successful, he ignores 2 points of penalties on all powers cast with his next action. If he does not enact any powers on his next action, the preparation is lost.

Skill Specialization

Savage Worlds skills are intended to be broad, allowing characters to focus primarily on Edges for customization rather than multiple iterations of something like Fighting for edged weapons, Fighting for blunt weapons, etc.

If it's important to your setting to have more detail, a character uses his normal skill for one device of choice. When using any other variation he suffers a –2 penalty.

Gaining an additional specialization counts as raising a skill below its linked Attribute. So a character can gain two new specializations with an Advance, or gain a specialization and increase a skill below its linked Attribute.

Below are skills appropriate for this extra detail and some example specializations:

- **Boating:** Powered, Sailed, Steam
- **Driving:** Hover, Tracked, Wheeled
- **Fighting:** Axe, Blunt Weapon, Exotic (such as nunchaku; each is separate), Long blade, Pole arm, Short blade.
- **Piloting:** Fixed Wing, Rotary, Space
- **Riding:** Camel, Horse, etc.
- **Shooting:** Bow, Crossbow, Pistol, Rifle, Shotgun, etc.
- **Survival:** Arctic, Desert, Temperate

Social Conflict

Not every conflict is won by the blade. Successful oratory can topple nations.

The following system works well for protracted and dramatic negotiations, such as convincing a council to send troops to a noble's lands, winning a court case, or tricking a guard into opening the gates to the space station.

The conflict is broken down into three rounds of conversation, each focusing on one particular point (or a few highly connected points). Further rounds represent the turn of conversation to additional points.

Each round, the player character roleplays his argument and makes a Persuasion roll (or an opposed Persuasion roll if a rival is arguing against him).

A speaker accumulates a success for each success and raise on the Persuasion roll (it's best to keep track of this with tokens).

At the end of the third round of conflict, the side with the most successes "wins" the argument. The more successes, the more convinced the target to be persuaded is, as shown on the Social Conflict Table below.

► **Modifiers:** The Game Master should grant a +2 bonus to a side that makes a particularly brilliant or undeniable point; or a −2 penalty if the speaker commits a faux pas, such as making a provably untrue statement or insulting the audience he hopes to convince.

► **Knowledge Is Power:** If the characters are arguing technical points, such as a legal battle or the best plan for a kingdom's defense, the character must roll the lowest of his Persuasion or appropriate Knowledge roll. So for example a lawyer with a Persuasion of d10 and Knowledge (Law) of d4, would roll d4. It always pays to know what you're talking about.

Social Conflict Results

Margin of Victory	Result
Tie	The issue is unsettled and no action is taken until new and more compelling evidence can be presented to reopen the negotiation. In a court case, the defense would win as the burden of proof is on the prosecution.
1-2	The target isn't truly convinced but decides it's better to be safe than sorry. He provides the minimum amount of support possible. In a court case, the jury barely finds reasonable doubt if the defense wins, or assigns minimal sentencing if the prosecution wins.
3-4	The target is reasonably convinced. He grants the help requested, more or less, but may have conditions or ask favors in return. In a court case, the judge invokes severe sentencing if the prosecution wins. If the defense wins the defendant is cleared of all charges.
5+	The target is sure of his decision. He provides more support than requested. If the prosecution wins in a court case, the defendant receives the maximum penalty.

Example: To Arms!

Orcs have invaded multiple baronies across the kingdom. The hero is a young noble attempting to convince the king to send royal troops to his aid. The king is disinclined to send his troops as a rebellion is also near-at-hand.

The young noble begins by telling the king of his own battles against the orcs and the depredations they have committed across the kingdom. He makes his Persuasion roll and gets a 7. One success.

The noble next presents his scouts who tell the king which baronies the orcs have been spotted in. The noble rolls again and gets a 9 for a total of three successes.

Finally, the young warrior reminds the king that it was his family that supported his coronation, subtly implying that a debt is owed. This time, the noble fails.

With three total successes, the king agrees to send a token force of infantry, but will not send his more loyal mounted knights. One of the infantry commanders, an old friend of noble's family, is likely to rebel in the coming revolt, so the king not only sends him to the noble's aid but also instructs an assassin to ensure he doesn't return! The Game Master now has a new subplot to work into his adventure as the heroes try to prevent the assassination of their friend—and the commander of their allied troops.

Travel

Most epic tales feature trips across great expanses—whether it's the Hobbits' quest to Mordor in *The Lord of the Rings* books or warping across space in a hard science-fiction tale. This section helps you figure out how long these journeys might take and what might dramatic events might happen along the way.

Time and Distance

Land Travel by Foot or Mount

A creature or character's Base Speed is half its Pace in miles per hour, with a minimum of ½ mile per hour. A human with a Pace of 6, for example, walks about 3 miles per hour.

Groups move at the speed of their slowest member. Fatigue and Encumbrance penalties don't normally modify Pace, but the Game Master may choose to apply them when calculating overland movement rates if it's dramatically appropriate.

► **Flying Speeds:** Travelers with the luxury of flying mounts or some other means of leaving the ground behind may ignore the modifiers below and may be able to take shorter routes than the land-bound. Game Masters may adjust airspeeds for headwinds, thin air, smoke, or other aeronautical phenomena.

Overland Speed Modifiers

Ground	Speed	Terrain Type
Easy	−0 mph	Plains, road
Average	−1 mph	Rocky desert, light forest, low hills
Hard	−2 mph	Steep hills, sand, medium forest
Difficult	−3 mph	Mountains, heavy forest, marsh

Vehicular Travel

For reasonably paced travel over the course of one or more days, just use the vehicle's Top Speed as its average miles per hour.

Multiply Top Speed by the number of hours traveled (eight per day being typical) to see how far a vehicle can travel in one day. For example, a vehicle with a Top Speed of 40 could travel 320 miles in 8 hours.

Multiply the mileage by 1.5 for interstate or autobahn travel, or by .5 if traveling over difficult terrain such as clogged highways in a post-apocalyptic aftermath, lack of roads, etc.

Sailing Ships

Powered vessels use the same system as Vehicles, above. Sailing ships require more work on the part of the crew. Each day, the ship's captain makes a Boating roll, plus or minus any modifiers the Game Master feels are appropriate for strong or weak winds, currents, traveling

upriver, and so on. These rates are based on eight-hour stretches, but sailing ships with enough crew don't usually stop, so multiply the results by three if the vessel sails the entire 24-hour period.

- **Total of 1 or Less:** The craft is becalmed, goes in circles, or is effectively lost. It makes no progress that day and must make a Knowledge (Navigation) roll the following day or sail in a direction other than intended.
- **Failure:** 3 x Top Speed in miles traveled
- **Success:** 10 x Top Speed in miles traveled
- **Raise:** 15 x Top Speed in miles traveled

Encounters

Unless the area traveled is patrolled, draw a card from the Action Deck once per day (or whatever period the Game Master feels is dramatically appropriate for the current scene). A face card or higher represents an encounter, and the card suit can be used to determine the type.

Game Masters are highly encouraged to customize encounters based on their setting.

Encounter Table

- **Clubs—Obstacle:** The heroes encounter an obstacle of some kind and must figure out how to circumvent it. Some examples are a flooded river, minefields, a decaying rope bridge, whirlpool, etc. The obstacle might also be defended by creatures or enemies as well.
- **Hearts—NPCs:** The group comes upon neutral or friendly nonplayer characters such as merchants, lost travelers, a guide, or even other adventurers.
- **Diamonds—Fortune:** Somewhere along the way is something of value—the hulk of a spaceship full of supplies, a small treasure cache, a vein of useful or valuable minerals, or a minor magic item in the clutches of some unfortunate corpse.
- **Spades—Enemies:** Monsters, enemies, or hostile beasts bar the way. Perhaps they lie in ambush if it's known the heroes are coming this way.

From armored combat in World War II to ship-to-ship battles on the high seas, vehicles often play a key role in the furious action of our Savage Settings. The following section contains rules for handling vehicle combat on the table-top. For more abstract Chases that take place over larger areas, see page 94.

Movement

A vehicle's Acceleration value is how many inches per turn it can increase its current speed. A pickup with an Acceleration of 5, for instance, can increase its movement by 5" every action, up to its Top Speed. A vehicle can decrease its speed by twice its Acceleration (or more in a Hard Brake—see Maneuvers).

The player controlling the vehicle decides his speed at the beginning of his action, and moves it that many inches. The vehicle remains at that speed until the driver's next action, so record the current speed somewhere for the next round and in case it hits something.

Vehicles have some restrictions on maneuvering, particularly in how they turn. Use the Turning Template for normal turns, or perform a maneuver (see below) for tighter moves.

▶ **Action Cards:** Vehicles move on their driver's Action Card. Driving is a free action unless the driver attempts a maneuver. Passengers act on their own initiative as usual.

▶ **Speed Kills:** It's much easier to maneuver a vehicle slowly than it is at high speed. A vehicle moving over 15" a round on the tabletop inflicts a –2 handling penalty on its driver. A vehicle moving over 30" inflicts a –4 penalty.

▶ **Difficult Ground:** Slippery gravel, uneven ground, and mud are all difficult ground and work just as for characters on foot. Count each inch moved through such rough terrain as two, and apply a –2 penalty to all Driving rolls made while in rough terrain. Driving through rough terrain at over half of Top Speed requires a Driving roll every round.

▶ **Reverse:** A vehicle can move up to half its Top Speed in reverse. Driving rolls made while in reverse suffer a –2 modifier.

▶ **Aircraft:** Aircraft ignore terrain. Unless the aircraft has the ability to hover, it must move at least half its Top Speed each action. Climb isn't used in table-top battles—only in Chases.

▶ **Animals and Conveyances:** Animals don't have to worry about Acceleration or Top Speed—they simply move their Pace (plus any running roll) each round. Animal-drawn transportation has an Acceleration equal to half the animal's basic Pace. Carts and wagons don't have a Top Speed because the animal simply moves its Pace as usual (plus a running die if it runs).

Maneuvers

Below are some common maneuvers with any penalty to the Driving roll listed in parentheses. If the maneuver is failed, move the vehicle to the point of the maneuver, then roll on the Out of Control Table to see where it actually ends up.

- **Bootlegger Reverse (−4):** The vehicle moves forward at half its current speed and then turns between 90 and 180 degrees (player's choice). The vehicle instantly decelerates to a complete stop and cannot move further this round.

- **Hard Brake (0):** The driver decelerates up to three times the vehicle's Acceleration.

- **Jump (0):** With a ramp, ground and water vehicles can jump a distance equal to one-quarter of their current speed, plus 1d10" with a raise on the Driving roll. They descend one inch for every two inches jumped forward, so a vehicle jumping 20" falls 10" by the end of its jump.

- **Maneuver (−1 to −4):** This one covers most everything else a driver, rider, or pilot might try to do, such as riding a horse down a steep or slippery hill, avoiding a manhole cover or other obstacle, or driving through an oil slick at high speed. The GM sets the modifier. If the roll is failed, the driver goes out of control as usual.

- **Obstacle (−2 or more):** Driving through a really tight obstacle looks easy enough on the tabletop since a vehicle is simply moved however the player wants. But in "reality," the car is shifting around and is much more difficult to hold steady than the table-top shows. For this reason, drivers trying to pass through tight obstacles—narrow alleys, other cars, flying under power lines—must make Driving rolls.

Turning

To perform turns when using miniatures on the table-top, use the Turning Template found at the back of this book. Simply line your vehicle up with the template and move it along the outside, as shown in the Turning diagram. Vehicles can perform tighter turns as a Maneuver (see Maneuvers).

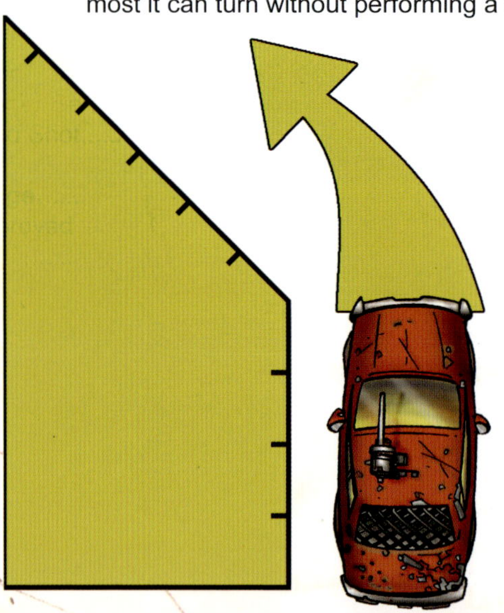

The car here is performing a turn to the left. This is the most it can turn without performing a maneuver.

The car has moved 5". This is its position at the end of its move.

The standard difficulty is –2, but really tight spots might call for a –4 or greater penalty. If the roll is failed, the vehicle hits the obstacle and suffers collision damage as usual.

- **Ram (Opposed):** Though we have to move vehicles in turns on the table-top, they're actually moving simultaneously in the "real world." For that reason, when one car rams another, we give the defender a chance to get out of the way—even if it's not his turn. When this happens, the two drivers make opposed Driving rolls. If the attacker wins, he's managed to ram his foe and damage is calculated normally. If the defender wins, he must move his vehicle just out of the way, whether backwards, forwards, or sideways. Sometimes cars run into people as well. In this case, the driver makes an opposed roll against the target's Agility instead.
- **Tight Turn (0):** The vehicle can turn up to 90 degrees.
- **Two Wheels (–4):** Sometimes a character needs to put a wheeled vehicle on its side, maybe to squeeze through a narrow alley or avoid running over some deadly obstacle. Turning a vehicle up on two wheels requires a ramp of some kind—even an embankment can do the trick. The effect is to decrease the width of the car—usually by about 25%. The driver must make a Driving roll at the beginning of each turn he wants to keep the car up on two wheels.

Collisions

Collisions are very deadly in *Savage Worlds*. The damage to the vehicle and its passengers is 1d6 for every 5" of its current speed (round normally). If a motorcycle moving at 16" per turn hits a tree, for instance, it suffers 3d6 damage, as does its rider and anything it rams into.

▶ **Relative Speeds:** Increase the damage if a vehicle hits another object moving toward it. This is called "relative speed." If two tanks ram into each other at a speed of 12, for instance, their relative speed is actually 24 and each tank suffers 4d6 damage. Similarly, a vehicle moving away from an attacker subtracts its speed from the ramming vehicle's.

▶ **Vehicular Armor:** Vehicles with Heavy Armor add their Armor rating as an AP value to their damage.

▶ **Safety Harnesses:** A seat belt protects anyone wearing it. Roll half the normal damage dice (round down) for these characters. Do the same for air bags, but subtract one additional die of damage as well.

▶ **Soft Obstacles:** The collision rules assume the vehicle has hit something hard, like another vehicle, rock, wall, and so on. If the obstacle was soft, like a person, the damage is halved for the vehicle. The person takes damage normally, of course.

▶ **Falling or Jumping From Vehicles:** Characters who fall from a moving vehicle suffer damage just as if they were in a collision. Characters who jump and make an Agility roll suffer half the usual damage dice (round down). If a character jumps out of a boat, treat this as nonlethal damage.

Losing Control

Failing a Driving roll causes a vehicle to go "out of control." When this happens, roll 2d6 on the Out of Control Table. Resolve any additional movement (such as slips or flips) immediately. Anything in the way gets smashed—check out the collision rules above if that happens.

Vehicular Attacks

Combat between vehicles and their crews works just like regular combat but with two additional modifiers.

Attack Modifiers

Penalty	Situation
–2	Unstable Platform
–1 per 10" of Speed	Fast Targets

▶ **Unstable Platform:** Any character on an unstable platform, including a moving vehicle, suffers a –2 penalty to any "fine" physical skills such as Fighting and Shooting. This applies to characters who are firing vehicular weapons as well. Note that the Steady Hands Edge eliminates this penalty.

▶ **Fast Target:** A fast-moving vehicle is more difficult to hit, and subtracts 1 from any attacks directed at it for every full 10" of its speed. This is relative, so a vehicle heading directly toward a character doesn't get the modifier, nor does the modifier apply if the hero is shooting at a vehicle driving parallel to his own.

Damage

Damage that equals or exceeds the vehicle's Toughness forces the driver to make a Driving roll or go Out of Control (roll on the Out of Control Table).

Each raise on the damage roll also inflicts a "wound." Each wound caused to the vehicle inflicts a +1 penalty to the driver's Driving skill rolls until someone repairs the damage. The attacker also scores a critical hit for each wound inflicted, and rolls on the Critical Hit Table to find out exactly what happened.

When a vehicle takes its fourth wound, it is automatically wrecked and the driver must make a Driving roll or go out of control.

A wrecked vehicle won't run anymore, though its weapons may still be able to fire if they aren't powered by the vehicle's propulsion system.

▶ **Wrecked Aircraft:** If an aircraft goes Out of Control, don't use the usual table. Instead, the pilot makes a Piloting roll. If he fails, the aircraft crashes and is destroyed. If the pilot can eject, he gets one chance to do so by making an Agility roll.

▶ **Wrecked Watercraft:** Unless the vessel is cracked open and sinks instantly, a wrecked boat sinks at the following rate:

- Small craft (rowboats, canoes) sink at the end of the round in which they're wrecked.
- Medium craft, such as a fishing boat, sink in 1d6 minutes.
- Large craft, such as a private yacht, sink in 4d6 minutes.
- Ships, such as oil tankers, cruise ships, or naval vessels, sink in 2d6 hours.
- A wrecked boat that hasn't sunk drifts with the current (if any). This is typically 2d6" per round for fast-moving rivers, and 1d6" for most other rivers or in strong seas. In the ocean, the GM can roll 1d12 to determine which direction a vessel drifts.

Repairs

Characters may repair vehicles given sufficient time and at least some basic tools. This requires a Repair roll that takes two hours per wound the vehicle has (regardless of how many are actually repaired). Attempting to fix up a tank that has suffered two wounds, for example, takes four hours regardless of the result of the Repair roll.

Field work requires at least a toolbox and basic supplies, and subtracts 2 from the Repair roll. An average garage negates this penalty, and an excellent or dedicated facility adds +2.

Each success and raise on the Repair roll fixes one of the vehicle's wounds. With an additional raise above and beyond that required to fix all its wounds, the repair time is halved.

▶ **Wrecks:** Wrecked vehicles can also be repaired, but it takes much more time and decent spare parts. The time is equal to 1d6 x 10 hours per wound level repaired.

Example: Corporal Tunny has been tasked with patching the holes in a B-17 bomber with two wounds. He's at the airbase with a dedicated garage and thus adds +2 to his rolls. Each attempt takes four hours, and each success and raise removes one wound.

2d6	Effect
2	**Roll Over:** The vehicle performs a Slip and rolls over 1d6 times in that direction. Roll collision damage for the vehicle and everyone inside. Any exterior-mounted weapons or accessories are ruined.
3–4	**Spin:** Move the vehicle 1d6" in the direction of the maneuver, or 1d6" away from a damaging blow. Roll a d12, read it like a clock facing, and point the vehicle in that direction.
5-9	**Skid:** Move the vehicle 1d4" left or right (in the direction of a failed maneuver, or away from a damaging attack).
10–11	**Slip:** Move the vehicle 1d6" left or right (in the direction of a failed maneuver, or away from a damaging attack).
12	**Flip:** The vehicle flips end over end 1d4 times. Move it forward that many increments of its own length. Roll collision damage for the vehicle, its passengers, and anything it hits. Slow and heavy vehicles such as tanks (GM's discretion) don't flip but suffer a Slip or Skid instead.

Critical Hits

2d6	Effect
2	**Scratch and Dent:** The attack merely scratches the paint. There's no permanent damage.
3	**Engine:** The engine is hit. Oil leaks, pistons misfire, etc. Acceleration is halved (round down). This does not affect deceleration, however.
4	**Locomotion:** The wheels, tracks, or whatever have been hit. Halve the vehicle's Top Speed immediately. If the vehicle is pulled by animals, the shot hits one of them instead.
5	**Controls:** The control system is hit. Until a Repair roll is made, the vehicle can only perform turns to one side (1–3 left, 4–6 right). This may prohibit certain maneuvers as well.
6–8	**Chassis:** The vehicle suffers a hit in the body with no special effects.
9–10	**Crew:** A random crew member is hit. The damage from the attack is rerolled. If the character is inside the vehicle, subtract the vehicle's Armor from the damage. Damage caused by an explosion affects all passengers in the vehicle.
11	**Weapon:** A random weapon on the side of the vehicle that was hit is destroyed and may no longer be used. If there is no weapon, this is a Chassis hit instead.
12	**Wrecked:** The vehicle is wrecked and automatically goes Out of Control.

Most roleplaying games feature "magic" in one form or another. Whether it's hidden occult lore practiced only by dark cultists, voodoo rituals, the eldritch sorcery of powerful wizards, weird gadgets created by mad scientists, superpowers, or the psionic powers of the mind, these rules handle it all in one simple system.

For ease of use, we call all of these effects "powers." Best of all, powers work the same from game to game, but the particular use and Trappings give the same powers endless variations. That means you can create wizards, mad scientists, superheroes, and even creatures with one simple set of easy-to-remember rules.

Making Arcane Characters

Before we go any further, you need to make sure your GM will allow arcane characters in his game. You can't make a wizard in a realistic military campaign, and mad scientists might not fit in every fantasy setting.

Now that that's out of the way, you need to buy the Arcane Background Edge and choose which type of supernatural power your hero is blessed with.

Five different types of powers are presented in this rulebook: Magic, Miracles, Psionics, Super Powers, and Weird Science. All types of powers use the same basic mechanics but with a few important differences in the details.

Let's talk about what's similar before we get into what's different.

Arcane Skill

Each type of power has a particular arcane skill: Faith for miracles, Psionics for psionics, Spellcasting for magic, and Weird Science for weird science. Super powers use skills a little differently, as you'll see on the following pages.

You need to take the listed skill for your character's particular Arcane Background and put points into it as usual. You'll find the attribute the skill is linked to in parentheses beside the skill itself.

Power Points

Arcane characters energize their powers with "Power Points." As soon as you buy an Arcane Background Edge, your hero gets the listed number of Power Points.

Using a power requires that you spend a number of these points. Some powers allow you to pay additional points for better effects, and some allow you to maintain the effect by spending Power Points each round.

Heroes recover 1 Power Point per hour.

Starting Powers

Arcane characters start with a number of powers dictated by their particular Arcane Background. See the Arcane Background list for specifics.

Learning New Powers

An arcane character can learn a new power by selecting the New Power Edge. As soon as he levels up and chooses this Edge, he can instantly begin using whichever power he chooses.

Using Powers

As an action, a character may use a single power by declaring the power he's using, spending the desired number of Power Points, and making an arcane skill roll.

If the roll is failed, there's no effect but the Power Points are lost. If successful, consult the particular power to determine the results.

Some powers have variable effects depending on how many Power Points are used to cast them. The player must spend the desired Power Points *before* rolling his character's arcane skill to see if he's successful.

Maintaining Powers

Some powers may be maintained, as listed in the power's Duration description. This is a free action. The number following the duration is the cost in Power Points to keep the power going. No new skill roll is needed to maintain a power.

For each power currently being maintained, the

caster suffers a –1 to future arcane skill rolls (but not other Trait tests). A wizard maintaining *armor* and *charm*, for example, suffers a –2 penalty to his Spellcasting rolls until he allows those powers to lapse. He does *not* suffer penalties to his Fighting (or other) rolls while these spells are being maintained.

Disruption

A character who is actively maintaining a power may be disrupted if he suffers damage. To maintain concentration for *all* of his powers, the hero makes one opposed arcane skill roll versus the damage he suffered. If his roll is higher, he maintains all of his spells. If he fails, he instantly drops all of his powers *after* the attack that caused the disruption is resolved.

A character who is Shaken by non-damaging means (such as a Test of Wills) must make a simple Smarts roll to maintain his powers.

Arcane Backgrounds

Below are the five different types of Arcane Backgrounds. Each type describes the Arcane Skill a character with that background uses, his starting Power Points, the number of powers he starts play with, and any potential drawbacks to the power (such as Backlash or Malfunctions).

Arcane Background (Magic)

Arcane Skill: Spellcasting (Smarts)
Starting Power Points: 10
Starting Powers: 3

Magicians range from powerful wizards to vile cultists. They draw on raw supernatural energy to fuel their eldritch fires. This energy often infuses the worlds in which they live, and is drawn forth with elaborate rituals, words of power, runes, or perhaps even dark sacrifices.

Wizards are often quite weak early in their careers, but are forces to be reckoned with as they become powerful sorcerers.

► **Backlash:** When a wizard rolls a 1 on his Spellcasting die (regardless of his Wild Die), he is automatically Shaken. This can cause a wound.

Arcane Background (Miracles)

Arcane Skill: Faith (Spirit)
Starting Power Points: 10
Starting Powers: 2

Those who draw on miracles are priestly types or holy champions. Their power comes from a divine presence of some sort, including gods, nature, or spirits. Their powers are usually invoked with a few words of prayer or by performing established rituals.

► **Protector:** Those who cast miracles are champions of their particular religions. Good priests vow to protect the innocent, fight evil, and obey all other tenets of their particular religion. Evil priests typically vow to defeat those who oppose their religion, or simply to cause as much misery and strife as possible. The player and Game Master should come up with a simple list of what is important to the character's religion and use this as a guide.

Champions who violate their beliefs are temporarily or permanently forsaken by their chosen deity. Minor sins give the character a –2 to his Faith rolls for one week. Major sins rob him of all arcane powers for one week. Mortal sins cause the character to be forsaken until the penitent hero completes some great quest or task of atonement to regain his lost powers.

Arcane Background (Psionics)

Arcane Skill: Psionics (Smarts)
Starting Power Points: 10
Starting Powers: 3

Psionicists have discovered how to tap into their own psychic powers. They can manipulate matter, create fire, or control their own bodies with but a thought.

► **Brainburn:** When a psionic character rolls a 1 on his Psionics die (regardless of his Wild Die), he is automatically Shaken. On a critical failure, the psi lets out a psychic scream that causes him to be Shaken along with all allies in a Large Burst Template who fail a Spirit roll. This can cause a wound.

Arcane Background (Super Powers)

Arcane Skill: Special (None)
Starting Power Points: 20
Starting Powers: 1

Characters with super powers gain their abilities through strange circumstances, such as being bitten by irradiated creatures, exposure to strange chemicals, or perhaps by finding alien artifacts. This particular level of power is intended for relatively low-level "pulp" heroes. More powerful super types are dealt with in specific Savage Settings, and you'll find an alternate and far more detailed system in our *Super Powers Companion*.

Super powers work a little differently from most

other Arcane Backgrounds—each power is its own skill and has no linked attribute (and thus counts as "lower" than its linked Attribute for purposes of Advancement). A hero with the *armor* and *bolt* powers, for example, also has an Armor and a Bolt skill he uses to enable it. It's more expensive for a character to improve his powers, but he starts with more Power Points than other arcane types so he can use his abilities more often.

Best of all, there are no drawbacks for super powers as there are with other types of arcane powers—the power either works or it doesn't.

Arcane Background (Weird Science)

Arcane Skill: Weird Science (Smarts—see below)

Starting Power Points: 10 (but see below)

Starting Powers: 1

Weird Science is the creation of strange and powerful devices. It differs from regular science in that some element of the arcane is involved. Maybe it's just generic "super-science," or perhaps it's divinely (or demonically) inspired. Maybe the science itself is relatively sound, but it derives power from an arcane source, such as ghost rock in *Deadlands*, or some other magical mineral or essence in a steampunk fantasy game.

Weird Science is different in that each new power is actually a new "gizmo." The player must write down exactly what the device is when he gains the power. An inventor with the *invisibility* power, for instance, actually has an *invisibility* belt, cloak, etc. Players are encouraged to give their devices pseudo-scientific names as well ("Dr. Zee's Chromatic Disfibulating Device!").

Weird Science is the skill an inventor uses when activating most devices, and raises increase the effects of the power as usual. If a device uses a different skill, such as Driving, Fighting, or Shooting, the inventor uses that instead. A ray gun, for example, uses the Shooting skill, while a "vibroknife" (a knife with the *smite* power) uses Fighting.

Powers that require an opposed roll, such as *puppet,* also use the scientist's Weird Science skill.

Each device comes with its own Power Points equal to the inventor's Power Points. An inventor with the *bolt* power and 10 Power Points, for example, could make a ray gun that fires electrical beams. The gun has 10 Power Points it can use to fire the beams just like a wizard would cast the *bolt* spell.

▶ **Malfunction:** Weird science devices are never perfect technology. They often suffer from spectacular and deadly malfunctions. If a gadgeteer uses a device and rolls a 1 on the skill die used to activate the gizmo, it has malfunctioned in some way and does not work. Draw a card and consult the Malfunction Table below:

Weird Science Malfunction Table

- **Clubs—Catastrophic Malfunction:** The device explodes for 2d6 damage in a Large Burst Template.
- **Hearts—Major Malfunction:** The device breaks down. The gadgeteer may not use it again until it's repaired, which requires a Repair roll and 2d6 hours of work.
- **Diamonds—Minor Malfunction:** The device suffers a minor hang-up. It can be fixed with a Repair roll at −2.
- **Spades—Glitch:** The gizmo activates but does the reverse of its intent. An *invisibility* belt makes the caster glow brightly, a weapon fires at a random target, and so on. If a reverse effect makes no sense, treat it as a Major Malfunction instead.

▶ **New Powers:** Each time a Weird Scientist takes the New Power Edge, he has invented a new gadget. He simply chooses a power and decides what kind of gizmo it's contained in as usual. He can also repeat a power he's already taken. A mad scientist might want to create two ray-guns, for example, so that he can use one and give one to a companion.

▶ **Maintaining Powers:** Because weird scientists use inventions rather than cast spells, they don't suffer any penalties for maintaining powers, but their devices still pay the maintenance costs in Power Points as usual.

▶ **Recharging:** Devices regain Power Points just like a character, at the rate of one point per hour. Recharging may represent the device being plugged into an outlet, gathering solar rays, or even fritzing out for a while until it miraculously just starts working again. Regardless of the description, however, it regains Power Points at the rate of one per hour just like other power types.

The Power Edges Rapid Recharge and Improved Rapid Recharge apply to all of the inventor's devices rather than the inventor himself.

More on Weird Science

Weird Science is a little more complicated than other Arcane Backgrounds and requires a bit more explanation. First off, it's important to understand

Weird Science isn't used to make mundane devices, even if they are extraordinary. As long as they're possible and aren't too far above the given tech level of the world, they're just "high-tech." Only actual weird science, inspired by, created by, or powered by some sort of supernatural force qualifies.

It's also important to remember that Weird Science doesn't allow a character to make anything he wants. He can only make a device that utilizes one of the powers in this book (or an appropriate Savage Setting).

► **Sharing:** An inventor can hand his device over to a companion to use. The device works the same for the companion as it does for the owner. If the Weird Science skill is required, the companion must make a default roll as usual. That means gizmos are typically more effective when used by weird scientists than in the hands of others.

► **Soul Drain:** Weird Scientists cannot take the Soul Drain Edge.

► **More Power Points:** When an inventor gains more Power Points, he's assumed to tinker with his existing devices and upgrade them as well. This means *all* of his devices gain the additional Power Points. In effect, if an inventor has 20 Power Points, each of his devices have 20 Power Points as well.

► **Losing Devices:** If an inventor's gizmo is taken away, lost, or destroyed, he can make another in 2d6 hours as long as he has access to a workshop and some basic components. This requires a Repair roll. A raise halves the time needed to create the device.

If the original should somehow be returned, it no longer functions (the character doesn't get a "free" duplicate in this way).

> *Example: Doctor Gold starts play with a vibroknife (a knife with the* smite *power) and 10 Power Points. Later on, he levels up and chooses the New Power Edge. With that he invents a ray-gun with the* bolt *power. Both devices have 10 Power Points.*

> *In a fight, Doctor Gold first "turns on" his vibroknife by making a Weird Science roll. He gets a raise so the knife does +4 damage for its duration. The ray-gun doesn't have to be activated. The Doc simply makes a Shooting roll whenever he fires it (just like a mage would make a Spellcasting roll).*

Trappings are the heart and soul of the powers system. With just a few simple twists, a *bolt* power can represent rays of ice, streaks of light, or swarms of stinging bees.

The powers themselves are designed to be as simple to use and remember as possible. This helps the Game Master remember what all the powers do, and helps players remember the rules for common powers even between different settings. But just because these powers work the same from setting to setting doesn't mean they have to look the same, have the same names (to the characters in that world), or even have the *exact* same effects—that's where Trappings come in.

For the most part, Trappings should be merely cosmetic. But sometimes it makes sense for there to be additional effects. A heat ray should have a chance of catching combustible objects on fire, for example, and an electric blast should do slightly more damage to targets in full metal armor.

Below are examples of effects players and Game Masters can use for common Trappings.

Acid

Acid is most commonly an attack Trapping, but could be used defensively against those who touch it (such as *armor* that corrodes anyone who touches it).

- **Corrosion:** If the subject with an acidic Trapping is touched the victim must make a Vigor roll or suffer Fatigue (the equivalent of Bumps and Bruises). If the ability is a damaging attack that results in a Shaken or higher result, roll a d6. On a 6, any material the acid hit is ruined (armor loses a point of protection instead).
- **Burn:** A power that does fixed damage reduces its die type by one, but does one less die of damage on the caster's next action unless counteracted in some way (taking an action to wash it off or stripping off the acid-covered item). For instance, a 2 PP acid *bolt* causes 3d4 when it hits and 2d4 on the caster's action as well (unless the target neutralizes it with liquid).

Cold/Ice

Cold and ice cause freezing effects, and can be both positive and negative.

- **Armor:** Beneficial powers provide +2 Armor versus cold, ice, fire, and heat, but fire and heat attacks count as a *dispel* against them.

- **Fatigue:** Harmful powers require a Vigor roll (at −2 on a raise) to avoid cold-based Fatigue, but the power's range is reduced to half (non-ranged powers have their Power Point cost doubled).
- **Skate:** A success on a beneficial power (like *armor*) results in ice not counting as Difficult Ground as ice spikes or skates form on the target's feet.
- **Slow:** A raise with a detrimental power (like *stun*) results in the target's movement counting as Difficult Ground while the power is active (or his next movement for Instant powers) due to the slick ice frozen on him.

Darkness

Darkness is frequently tied to another trapping such as cold or necromantic, so those options can apply as well.

- **Darkening:** Targets suffer a penalty to oppose the power equal to the current darkness penalty. The caster suffers a −2 penalty in normal light, and the *light* power works as *dispel* against the power.
- **Shroud:** The target is momentarily shrouded in tendrils of darkness. Targets of negative powers suffer a −1 penalty to all vision-based trait rolls while the power is active or on their next action for Instant powers. Positive effects slightly obscure the character, making him −1 to be hit by ranged attacks.
- **Stealth:** For beneficial powers, adding +1 Power Point to the cost causes the darkness to cling to the target and increases Stealth by one die type, or two on a raise.

Electricity

Electricity has a strong impact on the body's nervous and muscular systems.

- **Armor Piercing:** The electricity arcs to a foe's exposed areas, ignoring some armor (AP 2) at a cost of +1 Power Point.
- **Conduction:** Damaging powers reduce damage by one die type, but add an additional die of damage to targets in the following situations: carrying more than 10 pounds of conductive metal, contacting a source of water, or otherwise touching an electrical conductor of some kind. For instance, an electrical *blast* at maximum effect does 3d4 damage in a Large Burst Template, but if the targets are standing in water, they take 4d4 damage.
- **Jazz:** Beneficial powers "jazz" the target. They cost +1 Power Point to cast, but on a success add +2 to Pace and on a raise increase Agility

one die type for the duration of the power.

- **Jolt:** Helpful powers shock a target out of their distraction on a raise, providing an immediate free roll to recover from being Shaken.
- **Spasms:** Harmful powers cause temporary muscle contraction if cast with a raise; the target has to make a Vigor roll or be at −2 Parry until his next action.

Fire/Heat

Fire is a very common trapping for attack powers with heat having similar but less combustible effects.

- **Armor Piercing:** Fire and heat bypass cracks in armor. A damaging power gains AP 2 by increasing the base cost by +1 Power Point.
- **Aura:** Beneficial powers surround a subject with a hot or fiery aura, and as a replacement for their normal benefit on a raise, the target gains the effect of the *damage field* power that causes 2d4 damage.
- **Fatigue:** A heat trapping on an attack forces the victim to make a Vigor roll or suffer Fatigue.
- **Flammable:** With a hit by a fire power, roll for any potentially flammable objects to catch fire (see page 101). For a heat trapping, liquids on the target (water, potions, etc.) evaporate on a 6 on a d6 with a success or a 4–6 on a raise.

Light

Light typically represents goodness, sunshine, or holiness.

- **Beam:** Light-based damaging attacks are like a focused laser, providing armor piercing capability. Reduce the damage by one die type, but add AP 4 to the effect.
- **Enhance:** This trapping applies directly to the *light* power. Reduce it to a Medium Burst Template and extend the duration to 1 hour (1/ hour) or give it a range of Smarts x 2 affecting animate targets as well (an unwilling target gets an opposed Agility roll to avoid). Reduce *light* to a Small Burst Template and give it both abilities.
- **Glow:** Subjects affected with a raise glow for the duration, creating light in a Small Burst Template centered on them. This can give them light, but also make them targets. An Instant power with that effect allows a character on Hold or with the Joker to make an attack for the split second the subject is illuminated (avoiding any darkness penalties to hit them). The character must take his action immediately after the caster's turn to gain the benefit.
- **Sunlight:** In a setting with vampires and other such creatures, *light* is equivalent to natural sunlight.

Necromantic

Necromantic trappings may involve a "negative energy" opposed to life or symbols of death like bones and skulls.

- **Fear:** All Undead (depending on their prevalence) are considered to have a level of Arcane Resistance versus the power, and the living must make Fear checks when hit with it.
- **Feign Undeath:** A raise on the roll provides a −1 to be hit by Undead as they see the subject as one of their own.
- **Shards:** Ranged attacks splinter on impact, creating shrapnel that does +1 damage versus unarmored targets but −1 damage versus foes with Armor.

Sound

Sound is a common trapping for sonic or music-based spellcasters. Sound-based powers should never work in a vacuum!

- **Absorbtion:** Beneficial powers absorb the subject's sound, so Stealth is increased a die type, but they have to yell to be heard normally and speaking becomes a normal action instead of a free one.
- **Aquatic Boom:** Sound travels better in water than in air. Underwater, an attack power causes +2 damage. In air, however, it causes −2 damage.
- **Deafen:** A raise with the power (or a Shaken or better from damage) results in a −2 penalty to hearing-based Notice rolls for the target until the power ends or they recover from being Shaken.

Design Note - The Power of Names

What really makes powers stand out in a setting are their names, particularly if they're spells or miracles. Nickodemus' Necrotic Surge sounds much more frightening than bolt.

It's important for official Savage Worlds books to use the simpler nomenclature for ease of reference. We don't want you to have to look up every power listed under a spellcaster's repertoire after you've become familiar with the standard powers. You should encourage your players, however, to use more descriptive names.

If the group in a modern-day horror game finds a scroll of armor, that's probably much more rare and exciting than it would be in a fantasy game. Give it a name like Blessing of the Faithful and then tell them it works "just like the armor spell." They'll get the idea and the extremely functional and flexible powers system will convey much more flavor and excitement.

Powers

Listed below are a number of powers available in most Savage Settings. Each power has the following statistics:

► **Rank:** This is the Rank a character must be in order to learn this power: Novice, Seasoned, Veteran, Heroic, or Legendary.

► **Power Points:** The number of points it costs to use the power. Some powers allow the character to pay additional points for additional effects. This is always determined—and paid for—before the dice are rolled.

► **Range:** The maximum distance the target of the power can be from the user when the power is first activated (it remains in effect even if the target moves out of Range as long as it's maintained). A Range of Smarts, for example, means 10" for a character with a Smarts of d10. If a power lists three Ranges, such as 12/24/48, these are read just like missile weapon Ranges, and subtract the standard penalties for each Range bracket (0/–2/–4). The arcane character's skill roll acts as both his "casting" and attack total for these type powers (Weird Scientists use Fighting or Shooting as usual instead).

► **Duration:** How long the power lasts in rounds. A power with a Duration of 1 lasts until the heroes' next action. A Duration of 2 means it lasts for two actions, and so on.

If the Duration of a power has a second entry in parentheses, such as 3 (1/round), it means the power has a Duration of 3 rounds and may then be maintained from round to round by spending the listed number of Power Points (1 in this case). Each power maintained subtracts 1 from future uses of the hero's arcane skill.

► **Trappings:** Listed here are some ideas for what the power might look like in different types of settings. In a science fiction game, *armor* might represent the psyker's telekinetic force pushing attacks away from him. The same power used by a superhero might be a force field, or a body of flame that melts incoming projectiles.

> ***Example:*** *Greywald the Melodious is a bard in a high-fantasy setting. In battle, he strums his lyre or sings songs to enable his powers.*
>
> *His* burst *is a sonic cone that rattles nerves and shatters eardrums. He calls this one "The Battle Cry of Evanier." Greywald's* slumber *is*

> *"Lullaby of the Fallen," a sad mournful tune that puts his enemies to sleep even in the heat of battle.*
>
> *Greywald's player has decided for himself that he won't take powers that don't work well within his theme—such as* disguise *or* elemental manipulation.

Armor

Rank: Novice
Power Points: 2
Range: Touch
Duration: 3 (1/round)
Trappings: A mystical glow, hardened skin, ethereal armor, a mass of insects or worms.

Armor creates a field of magical protection around a character or an actual shell of some sort, effectively giving the target Armor. Success grants the recipient 2 points of Armor. A raise grants 4 points of Armor.

Whether the *armor* is visible or not depends largely on the trapping.

Banish

Rank: Veteran
Power Points: 3
Range: Smarts
Duration: Instant
Trappings: Holy items, arcane symbols, handful of salt.

Whether ghosts, elementals, or demons, *banish* removes them all. This power can affect any creature that is not native to the current plane of existence (GM's determination).

This spell is an opposed roll of the caster's arcane skill versus the target's Spirit. On a success, the target is Shaken. On a raise, it is sent to its proper plane of existence.

If the target is a Wild Card, each casting of *banish* causes a wound instead. If the target already has three wounds, it is then banished to its native plane—but it is not slain.

Barrier

Rank: Seasoned
Power Points: 1/section
Range: Smarts
Duration: 3 (1 per section, per round)
Trappings: Fire, ice, thorns, force, bones.

Barrier creates a solid, immobile wall to protect the user against attack or to entrap an opponent.

Regardless of what the *barrier* is made of (ice, thorns, stone, energy, etc.), it has a Toughness of 10. Every Power Point spent creates a 1" wide section of wall. The *barrier* ranges in thickness from a few "real world" inches for stone or other hard materials up to a foot for things like bones or ice. (If you're using a gridded mat to play, draw the *barrier* between the squares directly along the grid-lines.) The exact placement of each section is defined by the caster, but each section must be connected to at least one other section after the first.

When the spell expires or a section is broken, it crumbles to dust or dissipates. Trappings are never left behind.

Each section of the *barrier* may be destroyed by an attack that equals its Toughness of 10. Physical walls are treated exactly like inanimate objects; they are considered to have a Parry of 2 (ranged attacks work as normal), but raises on the attack roll do not grant bonus damage nor do damage dice Ace. Opponents may climb the *barrier* at −2 to their Climbing roll if it is made of something solid. Fiery versions of the barrier cause 2d4 damage to anyone who wishes to leap through instead.

Beast Friend

Rank: Novice
Power Points: Special
Range: Smarts x 100 yards
Duration: 10 minutes
Trappings: The mage concentrates and gestures with his hands.

This spell allows mages to speak with and guide the actions of nature's beasts. It works only on creatures with animal intelligence, not humanoids. Nor does it work on conjured, magical, or otherwise "unnatural" animals.

The target must be within the sorcerer's range—it is not conjured.

The cost to control a creature depends on its Size. The base cost is 3, plus twice its Size for creatures with a Size greater than 0. A great white shark (Size +4) costs 3 plus 8 (2x4), or 11 points. A roc (Size +8) costs 19 Power Points to control.

Swarms may also be controlled. Small swarms cost 3, Mediums 5, and Large 8. Thus a single rat costs 3 to control, as does a small swarm of the creatures.

Blast

Rank: Seasoned
Power Points: 2–6
Range: 24/48/96
Duration: Instant
Trappings: Balls of fire, ice, light, darkness, colored bolts, swarm of insects.

Blast is an area effect power that can put down many opponents at once. The caster first picks where he wants to center the *blast*, then makes the appropriate skill roll. Normal ranged attack modifiers apply.

The area of effect is a Medium Burst Template. If the roll is failed, the *blast* deviates as a launched projectile.

Targets within the blast suffer 2d6 damage. *Blast* counts as a Heavy Weapon.

▶ **Additional Effects:** For double the Power Points, the blast does 3d6 damage, *or* the size is increased to a Large Burst Template. For triple the points, it does both.

Blind

Rank: Novice
Power Points: 2–6
Range: 12/24/48
Duration: Instant
Trappings: Bright flash of light, sand in eyes, sticky shadows.

This power temporarily blinds a target or targets. Those affected must make an Agility roll at −2 to avert their gaze and avoid the effect (at −4 if the caster got a raise on the attack roll). On a failure, victims are Shaken and −2 to Parry until their next action. If the target rolls a 1 on his Agility die (regardless of the Wild Die), he's Shaken and fully blind until he recovers from being Shaken. Blinded victims suffer a −6 penalty to all Trait rolls that require vision and have their Parry reduced to 2.

▶ **Additional Effects:** For 2 Power Points, the power affects a single target. For 4 Power Points, the power affects everyone in a Medium Burst Template. For 6 points, it affects everyone in a Large Burst Template.

Bolt

Rank: Novice
Power Points: 1 per missile
Range: 12/24/48
Duration: Instant
Trappings: Fire, ice, light, darkness, colored bolts, insects.

Bolt is a standard attack power of wizards, and can also be used for ray guns, bursts of energy, streaks of holy light, and other ranged attacks. The damage of the *bolt* is 2d6.

▶ **Additional Bolts:** The character may cast up to 3 *bolts* by spending a like amount of Power Points. The *bolts* may be spread among targets as the character chooses. This is rolled just like fully-automatic weapons fire but without the full-auto penalty—the character rolls a spellcasting die for each *bolt* and compares each to the Target Number separately. If the caster is a Wild Card, he also rolls a Wild Die, which may replace any of the casting dice.

▶ **Additional Damage:** The caster may instead cast a single 3d6 *bolt* for 2 Power Points. He may not cast multiple *bolts* when using this ability.

Boost/Lower Trait

Rank: Novice
Power Points: 2
Range: Smarts
Duration: 3 (1/round)
Trappings: Physical change, glowing aura, potions.

This power allows a character to increase any of a target's Traits by one die type for a standard success, or by two with a raise. The affected Trait can exceed d12. Each step over d12 adds +1 to his Trait total. For example, a raise on someone who already has a d12 in the affected Trait grants him d12+2 for the duration of the power.

The power can also be used to lower an opponent's Trait. This is an opposed roll against the victim's Spirit. Success lowers any Trait of the caster's choice one step, a raise lowers it two steps. A Trait cannot be lowered below a d4. Multiple castings stack, though the caster must keep track of when each casting expires as usual.

▶ **Additional Targets:** The power may affect an additional target for every additional Power Point spent, up to a maximum of five targets. All targets share the same effect and Trait affected.

Burrow

Rank: Novice
Power Points: 3
Range: Smarts x 2
Duration: 3 (2/round)
Trappings: Dissolving into the earth and appearing elsewhere.

Burrow allows a mage standing on raw earth to meld into it. He can remain underground if he wants in a sort of "limbo" or *burrow* to anywhere with a Pace equal to the power's Range. A mage with a Smarts of d8 could therefore move up to 16" (32 yards) on the first round, then maintain the spell and stay submerged for the second and move another 16".

A *burrowing* earth mage can attempt to surprise a foe (even one who saw him *burrow*) by making an opposed Stealth versus Notice roll. If the mage wins, he gains +2 to attack and damage that round, or +4 with a raise. Targets on Hold may attempt to interrupt the attack as usual.

▶ **Additional Targets:** The power may affect an additional target for every additional Power Point spent, up to a maximum of five targets.

Burst

Rank: Novice
Power Points: 2
Range: Cone Template
Duration: Instant
Trappings: A shower of flames, light, or other energy.

Burst produces a large fan of energy that bathes its targets in red-hot fire or other damaging energy.

When cast, place the thin end of the Cone Template at the character's front. Targets within the template may make Agility rolls versus the caster's arcane skill roll to avoid the blaze. Those who fail suffer 2d10 damage. This counts as a Heavy Weapon.

Confusion

Rank: Novice
Power Points: 1
Range: Smarts x 2
Duration: Instant
Trappings: Hypnotic lights, brief illusions, loud noises.

Instilling confusion in enemies is a powerful aid in combat, and this power provides that ability. On a success, a target must make a Smarts roll at –2 or be Shaken, and on a raise, the roll is made at –4.

▶ **Additional Targets:** The character may affect up to five targets by spending a like amount of additional Power Points.

Damage Field

Rank: Seasoned
Power Points: 4
Range: Touch
Duration: 3 (2/round)
Trappings: Fiery aura, spikes, electrical field.

Damage field creates an effect around a character that deals damage to anyone who contacts them in close combat. The damage affects any adjacent character who makes a successful attack roll against the subject. It has no effect on non-adjacent attackers (for example, Reach or ranged attacks).

If a character with a *damage field* strikes someone in unarmed combat, the target takes the field's damage plus the character's Strength die (Str+2d6). The character may also simply touch the opponent (+2 to Fighting) and do the field's damage only. A target who is grappled suffers the field's damage each round on the attacker's action; if the attacker chooses on following rounds to actively damage the target, he adds his Strength die to the damage roll as above and may get a bonus die for a raise.

With a success, the power does 2d6 damage. With a raise, *damage field* causes 2d8 damage.

Darksight

Rank: Novice
Power Points: 1
Range: Touch
Duration: 1 hour (1/hour)
Trappings: Glowing eyes, dilated pupils, sonic sight.

Whereas *light* creates a source of illumination usable by others, *darksight* affects only a single person and can be much more clandestine.

On a success, this spell halves any darkness penalty for the subject (round down). For example, a character in Dim (–1) lighting would suffer no penalty, and one in Pitch Darkness (–4) would only suffer a –2. On a raise, the spell negates all darkness penalties up to the maximum of –6.

▶ **Additional Targets:** The character may affect up to five targets by spending a like amount of additional Power Points.

Deflection

Rank: Novice
Power Points: 2
Range: Touch
Duration: 3 (1/round)
Trappings: Mystical shield, gust of wind, phantom servant that intercepts the missiles.

Deflection powers work in a variety of ways. Some actually deflect incoming attacks, others blur the target's form or produce other illusionary effects. The end result is always the same however—to misdirect incoming melee and missile attacks from the user.

With a standard success, attackers must subtract 2 from any Fighting, Shooting, or other attack rolls directed at the user. A raise increases the penalty to –4. This also acts as Armor against area effect weapons.

Detect/Conceal Arcana

Rank: Novice
Power Points: 2
Range: Sight
Duration: 3 (1/round) or 1 hour (1/hour)
Trappings: Waving hands, whispered words.

Detect/conceal arcana allows a character to sense supernatural persons, objects, or effects within sight. This includes invisible foes, enchantments on people or items, mad science devices, and so on.

The power can also be reversed to conceal a single supernatural item, being, or effect. This has the same cost, but the duration is much longer—1 hour with a maintenance cost of 1 per hour. When used in this way, those who wish to see through the ruse with *detect arcana* use their arcane skill roll as an opposed roll against the concealer's skill (rolled anew each time *detect arcana* is cast). The detecting character may only attempt to see through concealed powers once per fresh casting.

Disguise

Rank: Seasoned
Power Points: 3–5
Range: Touch
Duration: 10 minutes (1/10 minutes)
Trappings: Malleable features, illusionary appearance, hair of new form.

Disguise allows the character to assume the appearance (but none of the abilities) of another person. The base cost is 3 Power Points, plus 1 point per level of Size difference between the character and the person she is impersonating. The character cannot emulate someone more than 2 Size levels different from themselves. It requires a Notice roll at –2 to see through *disguise* if someone is familiar with the specific person mimicked; the penalty increases to –4 with a raise. If unfamiliar, the penalties are –4 and –6 respectively.

Dispel

Rank: Seasoned
Power Points: 3
Range: Smarts
Duration: Instant
Trappings: Waving hands, whispered words.

Dispel allows a hero to negate enemy spells, miracles, mad science, or super powers. It has no effect on innate powers, such as a dragon's breath or a banshee's scream. Neither does *dispel* work on magic items or permanent enchantments unless the specific item or enchantment says otherwise.

Dispel can be used on a power already in effect or to counter an enemy power as it's being used. The latter requires the countering mage to be on Hold and interrupt his foe's action as usual.

In either case, *dispelling* the opponent's power is an opposed roll of arcane skills. The *dispelling* character suffers a –2 modifier if the target power is of another type (magic vs. miracles, superpowers vs. mad science, etc).

Divination

Rank: Heroic
Power Points: 5
Range: Self
Duration: 1 minute
Trappings: Contact spirits of dead, commune with deity, demonic interrogation.

This power allows the caster to contact an otherworldly being to gain information. Due to the extraplanar nature of this power, it is very draining to the caster.

On a success, the caster may ask one question that can be answered by "Yes," "No," or "Possibly" (if there is no absolute answer). On a raise, the question may be answered in five words or less (the GM may allow a longer, more detailed answer in cryptic form).

The spell's duration is one minute, during which the caster may take no other actions or movement. If the caster is Shaken during that time, he must make a Smarts roll or the power is disrupted.

If the question relates to a living being (including beings who may "live" by mystical means such as undead, constructs, elementals, etc.), then the arcane skill roll is opposed by their Spirit. *Divination* is also opposed by *conceal arcana*. In the case of *conceal arcana* on a being, the *divination* must first beat the *conceal arcana*, and then if successful, the subject may roll Spirit against the *divination* result.

Drain Power Points

Rank: Heroic
Power Points: 3
Range: Smarts
Duration: Instant
Trappings: Prayer, whispered words, gestures.

This spell removes a spellcaster's source of power, limiting his ability to cast magic.

The caster picks a single target within range and makes an opposed arcane skill roll. The caster suffers a –2 modifier if the target power is of another type (magic vs. miracles, superpowers vs. mad science, for example).

With a success, he drains 1d6+1 Power Points from the victim. On a raise, the victim loses 1d8+2 Power Points. These rolls don't Ace. Targets with Arcane Background: Weird Science lose the Power Points from all "gizmos" on their person equally.

The victim cannot be reduced below zero Power Points. Drained Power Points are not taken by the caster—they are simply lost to the victim. Drained Power Points recharge as normal. The spell works only on creatures with an Arcane Background—it has no effect on magic items except those created through Arcane Background: Weird Science as noted above.

Elemental Manipulation

Rank: Novice
Power Points: 1
Range: Smarts x 2
Duration: 3 (1/round)
Trappings: A few simple gestures.

A character who chooses this power can perform basic "tricks" using the four elements: air, earth, fire, and water (these elements may vary depending on the setting). The GM is the final arbiter on what effects can be performed (nothing that mimics another power), but some examples are listed below.

► **Air:** The caster can create lesser air currents to blow out a candle, fan a flame, lift a skirt, or cool his body in oppressive heat (+1 to a single Fatigue roll caused by heat).

► **Earth:** A wave of the hand can open a one-foot square hole in soft earth (or half that in stone), or cause a spray of sand that might blind an opponent (+1 to a Trick roll).

► **Fire:** The caster can snap his fingers to create a small flame (about the size of a hot match). With existing fire, he can urge it to spread (+1 to see if a fire spreads), cause it to flare (perhaps as part of a Trick maneuver), or slowly light an object over the course of a few rounds (as if holding a match to it).

► **Water:** The caster can conjure up to a pint of water somewhere within his sight (not "inside" objects or people). A wave of his hand also purifies one gallon of water, whether it be poisoned or simply salt-water. Those who have been poisoned within the last minute also get a second chance to resist any remaining effects.

Entangle

Rank: Novice
Power Points: 2–4
Range: Smarts
Duration: Special
Trappings: Glue bomb, vines, handcuffs, webs.

This power allows the character to restrain a target with snaking vines, lengths of hair, spider webs, or some other vine-like trapping.

The arcane skill roll is opposed by the target's Agility. Success indicates partial restraint so that the target suffers a –2 penalty to Pace and skills linked to Agility and Strength. A raise restrains the target fully. He cannot move or use any skills linked to Agility or Strength.

Each following action, an *entangled* target may make a Strength or Agility roll to break free. Other characters may also attempt to free the ensnared person by making a Strength roll at –2.

For 2 Power Points *entangle* targets a single opponent. For 4 points it affects everyone in a Medium Burst Template.

Environmental Protection

Rank: Novice
Power Points: 2
Range: Touch
Duration: 1 hour (1/hour)
Trappings: A mark on the forehead, potions, gills.

Adventurers sometimes travel beneath the waves, in space, or other hazardous environments. This power protects them from the crushing depths or blazing sun as they do.

This power allows the target to breathe, speak, and move at his normal Pace while in one normally harmful environment, such as underwater, a zero-G vacuum, the lava of a volcano, or even the heat of the sun. Pressure, atmosphere, air, etc, are all provided for.

The power does not protect against attacks with similar trappings though. A fire attack still causes normal damage, for example. With a raise on the casting roll, maintaining the power becomes 1 Power Point per two hours.

▶ **Additional Targets:** The character may affect up to five targets by spending a like amount of additional Power Points.

Farsight

Rank: Seasoned
Power Points: 3
Range: Touch
Duration: 3 (1/round)
Trappings: Invisibly marked targets, guiding winds, eagle eyes.

This spell endows the recipient to see over great distances. With a success, ranged penalties are halved for the subject (–1 at Medium and –2 at Long). If a raise is achieved, all range increments for the subject are doubled in addition (12/24/48 becomes 24/48/96).

Fear

Rank: Novice
Power Points: 2
Range: Smarts x 2
Duration: Instant
Trappings: Gestures, eldritch energy, cold chills.

This power causes the target overwhelming dread and horror. The area of effect is the Large Burst Template. Every creature beneath the template must make a Fear check, at –2 if the caster got a raise. Wild Cards who fail roll on the Fear Table. Extras are Panicked instead.

Fly

Rank: Veteran
Power Points: 3/6
Range: Touch
Duration: 3 (1/round)
Trappings: Gusty winds, wings, broomsticks.

Fly allows a character to fly at his basic Pace with a Climb of 0. He may double his Pace by spending twice the number of Power Points.

▶ **Additional Targets:** The character may affect up to five targets by spending a like amount of additional Power Points.

Greater Healing

Rank: Veteran
Power Points: 10/20
Range: Touch

Duration: Instant
Trappings: Laying on hands, touching the victim with a holy symbol, praying, giving a drink of water.

Greater healing restores wounds more than one hour old. This use of the power requires 10 Power Points and otherwise works exactly like the *healing* power. It can also be used to neutralize any poison, disease, or sickness.

Greater healing can also heal Permanent Crippling Injuries. This requires an arcane skill roll at −4, 1d6 hours of time, and 20 Power Points. Only one casting is permitted per injury—if it fails, the injury really is permanent.

Growth/Shrink

Rank: Seasoned
Power Points: 2+
Range: Smarts
Duration: 3 (2/round)
Trappings: Gestures, words of power, potions.

Growth doubles the overall size of the target. The subject gains +1 Size for each 2 Power Points invested when the spell is cast. Each step of Size grants the target a one-step increase to Strength and a point of Toughness. This spell may be cast multiple times on the same target, though the caster must track each casting separately.

Shrink reduces the Size of the subject by one step for each 2 Power Points, down to a minimum of Size −2 (approximately the size of a rat). Each level of Size reduction reduces the target's Strength by one die type (minimum of d4) and his Toughness by 1 (minimum of 2).

Subjects from Size +4 to +7 have the Large ability and fill a 2" square on the table-top. From Size +8 to +10, they are Huge and occupy an area 3" square. If the target is +11 or more, he is considered Gargantuan and occupies a 4" square area. Creatures of Size −2 have the Small ability.

For unwilling targets, the caster's arcane skill roll is opposed by their Spirit.

Havoc

Rank: Seasoned
Power Points: 2−4
Range: Smarts x 2
Duration: Instant
Trappings: Whirlwind, chaotic poltergeists, repulsion field.

While unpredictable, this spell allows a wizard to change the field of battle in an instant as targets are thrown in every direction.

With a success, the caster places a Medium Burst Template anywhere within range. Any character touched by the template must make a Strength roll (at −2 if the caster gets a raise). Any target that fails is knocked 2d6" in a random direction (roll a d12 and read the result as a clock facing) and becomes prone. If the target strikes an inanimate object, he is Shaken as well. Targets with cover may subtract the cover modifier from the total distance moved (to a minimum of 0), and flying targets suffer an additional –2 to their Strength roll. Additionally, roll a d6 to see if the flyer is moved toward the ground (1–2), stays level (3–4), or is moved away from the ground (5–6).

▶ **Additional Effects:** For double the Power Points, *havoc* affects a Large Burst Template.

Healing

Rank: Novice
Power Points: 3
Range: Touch
Duration: Instant
Trappings: Laying on hands, touching the victim with a holy symbol, prayer.

Healing repairs recent bodily damage. It must be used within the "Golden Hour," though, for it has no effect on wounds more than one hour old.

For Wild Cards, each use of the *healing* spell removes a wound with a success, two with a raise. The roll suffers a penalty equal to the victim's wounds (in addition to any the caster might be suffering himself).

For Extras, the GM must first determine if the ally is dead (see Aftermath on page 88). If so, no healing may be attempted. If not, a successful arcane skill roll returns the ally to the game Shaken.

Healing can also cure poison and disease if used within 10 minutes of the event.

Intangibility

Rank: Heroic
Power Points: 5
Range: Touch
Duration: 3 (2/round)
Trappings: Ghost form, body of shadow, gaseous transformation.

With a successful arcane skill roll, the user becomes incorporeal. He is unable to affect the physical world, and it in turn cannot affect him. He can travel through walls, and non-magical weapons pass straight through him. Any items carried at the time of casting are also incorporeal.

While incorporeal, the mage may affect other incorporeal beings (including himself), and he is still susceptible to magic attacks, including physical powers, such as *bolt*, and magic items.

The character may not become corporeal while within someone or something. If that occurs, the caster is instantly shunted to the nearest open space, and he is Shaken.

Invisibility

Rank: Seasoned
Power Points: 5
Range: Self
Duration: 3 (1/round)
Trappings: Powder, potion, iridescent lights.

Being invisible is a powerful aid in combat and useful for spying on maidens' changing rooms as well.

With a success, the character is transparent, but a vague outline is visible. A character may detect the invisible presence if he has a reason to look and makes a Notice roll at –4. Once detected, he may attack the foe at –4 as well. With a raise, the character is completely invisible. The penalty to Notice or hit him is –6.

In either case, the power affects the character and his personal items. Anything picked up after the power was cast remains visible.

▶ **Additional Targets:** The character may affect up to five targets by spending a like amount of additional Power Points.

Light/Obscure

Rank: Novice
Power Points: 2
Range: Smarts
Duration: 30 minutes (1/10 minutes) or 3 (1/round)
Trappings: Illusionary torch, sunlight, darkness, thick fogs.

The ability to affect visibility (create or remove obscurement) is a pretty simple but very effective power.

Light/obscure can be cast on an inanimate object, but if the item is in an opponent's possession, the arcane skill roll is opposed by Agility.

Light negates any darkness/obscurement penalty up to –6 in an area equal to a Large Burst Template for 30 minutes (1/10 minutes). The reverse of the power, *obscure*, creates a –6 obscurement penalty of the same size lasting for 3 (1/round).

Mind Reading

Rank: Novice
Power Points: 3
Range: Smarts
Duration: 1
Trappings: Psionic invasion, soulsight.

Mind reading allows a character to read another's thoughts. This is an opposed roll versus the target's Smarts. A success allows the character to gain one truthful answer from the subject. The target is aware of the mental intrusion unless the mind reader gets a raise. The GM may apply modifiers based on the subject's mental Hindrances or current state of mind.

Pummel

Rank: Seasoned
Power Points: 2
Range: Cone Template
Duration: Instant
Trappings: Rippling earth, buffeting winds, rushing waters.

Pummel allows a character to knock down multiple foes. The caster makes an arcane skill roll and then places a Cone Template in front of him. Any friend or foe touched by the template must make a Strength roll (at –2 if the caster gets a raise). Any target that fails is knocked back 2d6" and becomes prone. If the target strikes an inanimate object, he is Shaken as well. Targets with cover may subtract the cover modifier from the total distance moved (to a minimum of 0), and flying targets suffer an additional –2 to their Strength roll.

Puppet

Rank: Veteran
Power Points: 3
Range: Smarts
Duration: 3 (1/round)
Trappings: Glowing eyes, trance-like state, a swinging pocket watch, voodoo dolls.

Sometimes it pays to persuade others to do your fighting for you. Some do this by blatant mind control, others do it by manufacturing visual and auditory illusions. *Puppet* is an opposed roll of the character's arcane skill versus the target's Spirit. The user must score a success and beat the target's roll to gain complete control. The victim will attack friends and even commit suicide, though such acts allow the victim another opposed Spirit roll to break the spell.

Quickness

Rank: Seasoned
Power Points: 4
Range: Touch
Duration: 3 (2/round)
Trappings: Blurred motion, hyperactivity.

This power grants incredible swiftness to the recipient. With success the target has two separate turns per round on his action card instead of the usual one. Each turn is handled independently with its own actions, but the character must resolve one turn entirely before beginning the second. With a raise, the recipient can redraw any initiative cards lower than Eight each round.

Shape Change

Rank: Special
Power Points: Special
Range: Self
Duration: 1 minute (1/minute)
Trappings: "Morphing," talismans, tattoos.

Many cultures have legends of shamans or wizards who take on the shape of animals. This power does just that. This version of the power only allows a user to transform into mundane animals, but more bizarre transmutations may be found.

A character may learn this spell while of Novice Rank but cannot transform into the more powerful creatures until he attains the appropriate Rank. The cost in Power Points depends on the type of creature the character wishes to change into. Use the Shape Change table as a guideline for unlisted creatures.

Weapons and other personal effects are assumed into the animal's form and reappear when the power ends, but other objects are dropped.

While transformed, the character retains his own Smarts, Spirit, and linked skills (though he may not be able to use them since he cannot speak). He gains the animal's Agility, Strength, and linked skills and cannot use most devices. He has no capacity for speech and cannot use powers, though he may continue to maintain powers previously activated. Vigor is the higher of the caster's or the creature's.

The GM has final say on what an animal can and cannot do. A shaman in dog-form might be able to pull the trigger on a shotgun, for instance, but would use a default skill roll of d4–2 as the animal has no Shooting score of its own. The shaman's Persuasion functions normally, but might suffer a –4 or worse penalty without speech, depending on what he tries to accomplish.

Shape Change

Cost	Rank	Animal Types
3	Novice	Hawk, rabbit, cat
4	Seasoned	Dog, wolf, deer
5	Veteran	Lion, tiger
6	Heroic	Bear, shark
7	Legendary	Great white shark
10	Legendary	Dragon

Slow

Rank: Seasoned
Power Points: 1
Range: Smarts x 2
Duration: 3 (2/round)

Trappings: Tying a knot in a piece of string, slowing time, distracting invisible ghost monkey.

Skilled fighters and monsters with fast reflexes can strike before lesser beings have time to blink. Slowing their reflexes reduces their advantage.

The caster makes an arcane skill roll opposed by the target's Spirit. With a success, movement becomes an action, giving the target a multi-action penalty if he wants to move and act in the same round. With a raise, the target must redraw initiative cards above 10, except Jokers.

A victim who usually draws multiple initiative cards discards only those with a value higher than the spell allows.

▶ **Additional Targets:** The character may affect up to five targets by spending a like amount of additional Power Points.

Slumber

Rank: Seasoned
Power Points: 2
Range: Smarts x 2
Duration: 1 minute (1/minute)

Trappings: A lullaby, blowing powder or sand at targets.

Blasting a hoard of enemies into tiny pieces may be popular with some mages, but those who favor stealth or have a pacifistic bent are drawn to this spell.

The caster picks where he wants to center the spell and places a Medium Burst Template. He then makes an arcane skill roll. Any living creature (not undead or constructs) within the area must make a Spirit roll, at −2 if the caster scored a raise. Those who fail fall asleep.

Loud noises awaken the sleepers as if they were a normal sleeper (Notice roll). When the duration expires, the sleepers naturally wake up.

Smite

Rank: Novice
Power Points: 2
Range: Touch
Duration: 3 (1/round)

Trappings: A colored glow, runes, sigils, crackling energy, barbs grow from the blade.

This power is cast on a weapon of some sort. If it's a ranged weapon, it affects one entire magazine, 20 bolts, shells, or arrows, or one full "load" of

ammunition (the GM may have to determine the exact quantity for unusual weapons). While the spell is in effect, the weapon's damage is increased by +2 or +4 with a raise.

▶ **Additional Targets:** The character may affect up to five targets by spending a like amount of additional Power Points.

Speak Language
Rank: Novice
Power Points: 1
Range: Touch
Duration: 10 minutes (1/10 minutes)
Trappings: Words, pictures, hand motions.

This power allows a character to speak, read, and write a language other than his own. The language must be of an advanced form—not animalistic. A raise on the arcane skill roll allows the user to project a particular dialect as well.

Speed
Rank: Novice
Power Points: 1
Range: Touch
Duration: 3 (1/round)
Trappings: Blurred motion, "floating," acrobatics.

Warriors who need to close with their foes quickly often use this power, as do those who sometimes need to outrun things Man Was Not Meant to Know. *Speed* allows the target of the power to move faster than usual. With a success, the recipient's basic Pace is doubled. With a raise, running becomes a free action, so he may ignore the usual −2 running penalty.

Stun
Rank: Novice
Power Points: 2
Range: 12/24/48
Duration: Special
Trappings: Bolts of energy, stun bombs, sonic booms, burst of blinding light.

Stun shocks those within a Medium Burst Template with concussive force, sound, light, magical energy, or the like.

If the arcane character scores a success, targets within the area of effect must make Vigor rolls or be Shaken. With a raise, victims must make Vigor rolls at −2.

Succor
Rank: Novice
Power Points: 1
Range: Touch
Duration: Instant
Trappings: Prayer, laying on hands, curative tonic.

Succor removes one Fatigue level, two with a raise. It can also remove a character's Shaken status.

Succor may be used to restore consciousness to those who have been Incapacitated due to wounds as well, though the wounds remain. It does not stop bleeding or otherwise stop mortal wounds from worsening, however.

Summon Ally

Rank: Novice
Power Points: 3+
Range: Smarts
Duration: 3 (1/round)
Trappings: Call elemental, ghostly dog, dimensional double.

This power allows the character to summon a loyal and obedient servant. On a success, the ally is placed at any point within the range of the power. On a raise, the ally is more durable and gains the Hardy ability. A summoned ally acts on the initiative card of the caster and gets an immediate action as soon as it is summoned.

All Allies are Extras, even Mirror Selves (see below).

A character may learn this spell while of Novice Rank, but he cannot summon more powerful allies until he attains the appropriate Rank. The cost in Power Points depends on the type of ally the character wishes to summon. Use the Summon Ally table as a guideline for unlisted creatures.

A caster of sufficient Rank to summon more powerful allies may instead choose to summon additional lower Rank allies instead at the same cost. For each decrease in Rank, he gains one additional ally. For example, a Veteran caster could spend 5 Power Points to summon one Veteran-Rank-allowed ally, two Seasoned-Rank-allowed allies, or three Novice-Rank-allowed allies. Allies summoned by a single casting must all be of the same type.

See the Bestiary for statistics of some of the creatures listed below.

Summon Ally

Cost	Rank	Ally Types
3	Novice	Bodyguard, experienced soldier
4	Seasoned	Dire wolf, ogre
5	Veteran	Elemental (any kind)
6	Heroic	Sentinel
7	Legendary	Mirror self

Bodyguard

A bodyguard is a humanoid soldier made of stone (or equally tough material).
Attributes: Agility d6, Smarts d6, Spirit d6, Strength d8, Vigor d8
Skills: Fighting d6, Notice d6
Pace: 6; **Parry:** 5; **Toughness:** 10 (4)
Gear: Long sword (Str+d8)
Special Abilities:

- **Armor +4:** Stone skin.
- **Construct:** +2 to recover from being Shaken; no additional damage from called shots; constructs do not suffer from poison or disease.
- **Fearless:** Bodyguards are immune to fear and Intimidation.

Sentinel

A sentinel is a larger and more powerful version of a bodyguard.
Attributes: Agility d6, Smarts d6, Spirit d8, Strength d12+3, Vigor d10
Skills: Fighting d10, Intimidation d10, Notice d8
Pace: 8; **Parry:** 6; **Toughness:** 14 (4)
Gear: Great sword (Str+d10; Parry −1)
Special Abilities:

- **Arcane Bond:** Sentinels count as having Arcane Resistance for anyone other than their summoner.
- **Armor +4:** Stone skin.
- **Construct:** +2 to recover from being Shaken; no additional damage from called shots; constructs do not suffer from poison or disease.
- **Fearless:** Sentinels are immune to fear and Intimidation.
- **Improved Sweep:** Sentinels may attack everyone adjacent to them as a single action.
- **Size +3:** Sentinels are 8–9 feet tall and very dense.

Mirror Self

This is an ally that appears identical to the caster but with the following differences. The ally is an Extra as normal for the power. The duplicate has half the total Power Points of the caster, and all of the duplicate's Traits are one die type less than the caster's Traits (to a minimum of d4). The duplicate has identical mundane equipment, but none of it has any magical qualities.

Telekinesis

Rank: Seasoned
Power Points: 5

Range: Smarts
Duration: 3 (1/round)
Trappings: A wave of the hand, magic wand, steely gaze.

Telekinesis is the ability to move a single object or creature (including one's self) with arcane will. The weight a caster can lift is equal to 10 pounds times his Spirit die type, 50 pounds times his Spirit with a raise.

▶ **Lifting Creatures:** Living targets may resist with an opposed Spirit roll. If the roll is greater than the caster's skill total, the victim is unaffected. If the creature loses, however, it is lifted as usual and does not get another attempt to break free.

Occasionally a victim might manage to grab onto something solid to prevent itself from being lifted. When this happens, the victim may make an opposed Strength roll versus the caster's arcane skill. If the victim is successful, he manages to grab onto whatever was available and is not moved, bashed, or otherwise affected that round.

▶ **Telekinetic Weapons:** A caster can use *telekinesis* to wield a weapon. When this occurs, the weapon's Fighting is equal to his arcane skill, and its damage is based on the caster's Spirit instead of his Strength. A sword that does Strength+d6 damage, for example, does Spirit+d6 when wielded by *telekinesis*. The weapon otherwise functions normally, including granting bonus damage when it strikes with a raise.

▶ **Dropping Things:** Particularly ruthless characters often use *telekinesis* to drop their foes or bash them into walls and the like. A creature affected by this power can be moved up to the caster's Smarts in inches per turn in any direction. Dropped creatures suffer falling damage as usual.

Victims who are bashed into walls or other solid objects suffer the caster's Spirit+d6 as damage. If a caster with a d12 Spirit smashes an orc into a wall, for example, the orc suffers d12+d6 damage.

Teleport

Rank: Seasoned
Power Points: 3+
Range: Special
Duration: Instant
Trappings: A cloud of smoke, "phasing" out, change into a bolt of lightning.

Teleport allows a character to disappear and instantly reappear up to 10" distant for each 3 Power Points spent, or 15" with a raise. This counts as his movement for the round. Adjacent opponents do not get a free attack against the teleporting character. If the hero wishes to *teleport* somewhere he can't see, he must make a Smarts roll at −2. If it is an unknown area he has never seen, the roll is at a −4 penalty.

Failure of either roll means the teleporter hit an object of some sort. He returns where he came from and is Shaken. A roll of 1 on the casting die (regardless of the Wild Die) indicates a more serious disaster—in addition to being Shaken he also suffers 2d6 damage.

The teleporter can never enter a solid space even if he tries. The power instantly returns him to his starting location as above.

▶ **Carrying Others:** The hero can carry other beings with him at the cost of a level of Fatigue per additional "rider." More than two may be carried at once, but causes instant Incapacitation. One Fatigue level is regained for each full hour of rest.

Wall Walker

Rank: Novice
Power Points: 2
Range: Touch
Duration: 3 (1/round)
Trappings: A crushed spider, bit of web, piece of tentacle.

Spellcasters are frequently targeted in combat because of their arcane prowess and high-utility spells such as this are great for getting the caster safely out of harm's way. Of course, it has countless other uses too.

Wall walker allows the recipient to function much like a human spider. He can stick to any surface, allowing him to climb walls and even hang from the ceiling. With a success, the character can move along such surfaces at half his normal Pace. With a raise, he may move at full Pace and even run.

▶ **Additional Targets:** The character may affect up to five targets by spending a like amount of additional Power Points.

Warrior's Gift

Rank: Seasoned
Power Points: 4
Range: Touch
Duration: 3 (1/round)
Trappings: Gestures, prayer, whispered words, concentration.

Even combat mages cannot afford to spend all their time learning new combat maneuvers and martial skills. For those who enjoy the thrill of melee or want to improve their companions' skills, this spell provides a quick solution to a lack of training.

With a successful arcane skill roll, the recipient gains the benefits of a single Combat Edge chosen by the caster. The caster (not the recipient) must be one Rank higher than the Rank requirement of the Edge but ignores other requirements, even those requiring other Edges. For the duration of the spell, the recipient gains all the benefits of the Edge.

Edges gained through this power provide no additional benefit if the character already has the Edge.

Zombie

Rank: Veteran
Power Points: 3/corpse
Range: Smarts
Duration: Special
Trappings: Carving symbols on corpses, throwing bones, graveyards, "leather" books.

This power is considered evil in most settings, and so is typically used only by villainous nonplayer characters such as necromancers, evil scientists, dark cultists, and the like.

When cast, *zombie* raises a number of dead specified by the character when he spent his Power Points. The undead are immediately obedient, though perhaps a bit mischievous and literal-minded in their duties.

Corpses aren't summoned by this ability, so there must actually be a supply of bodies available for the power to have any effect. The bodies don't have to be fresh—*zombie* can raise servants that have been waiting patiently for centuries. Graveyards, morgues, and battlefields can all serve this purpose.

With a success, the dead remain animated for 1 hour. With a raise, they remain animated for 1d6 hours. With two raises, they remain animated for an entire day.

Certain powerful necromancers may have improved versions of this power that are cheaper to cast and create permanent undead.

Zombie

These walking dead are typical groaning fiends looking for fresh meat.
Attributes: Agility d6, Smarts d4, Spirit d4, Strength d6, Vigor d6
Skills: Fighting d6, Intimidation d6, Notice d4, Shooting d6
Pace: 4; **Parry:** 5; **Toughness:** 7
Special Abilities

- **Claws:** Str.
- **Fearless:** Zombies are immune to Fear and Intimidation.
- **Undead:** +2 Toughness; +2 to recover from being Shaken; called shots do no extra damage (except to the head).
- **Weakness (Head):** Shots to a zombie's head are +2 damage.

A group of heroes emarks upon an epic quest. Terrible monsters and bitter rivals oppose them. The elements are against them. Mysteries must be solved, artifacts found, innocents saved.

It's your job as Game Master to bring all these fantastic elements to life, to challenge your players with adventure beyond their wildest imaginations, and provide a framework to find out if they succeed in their ultimate goal—or fail.

This is the fun and excitement of being a Game Master—of creating, managing, and presenting an entire world of excitement and adventure to your closest friends. It can be one of the most satisfying entertainment experiences there is, and *Savage Worlds* is designed to help you wring every tension-filled moment and gut-busting laugh from it.

You've read the rules and probably have more ideas for a new campaign than you know what to do with. Before you do, let's take a moment to talk about the art of being a good Game Master, creating worlds, and putting together memorable and exciting adventures.

Learning the Rules

You need to know how to make Trait rolls, use Wild Dice, resolve attacks, and handle wounds. Everything else in this book, from combat maneuvers to Interludes, can be ignored until you need it.

A great way to do this is to run a very simple fight on your own first. Put a Wild Card fighter and three orcs on the table in front of you and have at it. Your only goal is to get a feel for rolling the dice, figuring totals from Aces and modifiers, rolling and applying damage, Soaking wounds. If you can handle that, you can run a game.

Your Game

You might think that the first step in starting a new game is finding a group of people to play with. That is important, but that's your next step. Your first step is to get *yourself* excited. Do that and you'll likely get all your friends excited as well.

Start by figuring out what kind of setting you want to run. What kind of characters might people play? What might a typical adventure be like? Jot down a few notes about what makes your game cool, who the bad guys are, what kinds of magic or other supernatural aspects are present, and what your basic storyline is. If you have these elements, you've got enough information to "sell" your game to your friends and get them to play.

Game Night

Now it's time to recruit. You've got a great campaign idea and enough information about it to explain it to your friends. The next step is to find out who wants to play, and when they can do it.

When you're finding out who wants to play, first ask *when* each person can make it. It's very important that you set both a time and a regular day to play. If you rely on a fluctuating week-to-week schedule, you're almost certainly doomed to failure. People have busy lives, and as much as everyone involved might love to play, they've still got to study for classes, take care of their children, and otherwise live their lives. If you have a set night every week, it's much easier for your friends to schedule most of their activities around game night. It also helps you know when you've got to be ready to run.

Don't rule out playing on weeknights. Friday and Saturday are great if you're single or in college, but difficult for players who need weekend nights to be with their families. If you start at 6 p.m., your players have time to get off work, grab some food (or share pizza with the group), and get deep into the game by 7 or so.

For most groups, you should wrap things up by 11 p.m. or so. Most people tend to get a little tired by then and you don't want game night to be a stressful experience. Talk it over with the group and see what works for them. Setting some basic rules will help everyone schedule and makes it far more likely everyone will show up week after week.

A wise Game Master tries to end each night with a bit of a cliffhanger as well. If your players are talking during the week about what's going to happen next, you've done your job well.

Character Types

Once you've got a few friends interested, it's great if you can give them a little primer information and find out what kind of characters they want to play. You don't need everyone to make characters at this point—character creation is fast enough that they can do it at your first session if you want. But if some of your friends have neat ideas as to their background or basic type (fighter, investigator, etc.), you can start doing more detail work on your story. If you're going to run *Evernight*, for example, and all your friends make combat types, you know they're looking for a high-action, "hack and slash" type game. That doesn't mean you can't mix in lots of other elements—exploration, horror, deep roleplaying, and so on—but every now and then you'll want to have a big nasty combat as well.

Getting the Party Together

The first thing you need to do in any new adventure or campaign is figure out why the characters are together. There are two common ways to handle this.

The Mission

The most common way of building a party is for an employer to offer a reward for adventurers to complete some task. Perhaps they answer a want ad, are hired in a smoky tavern, or are called on by connections or friends. Either way, the heroes are then thrown together by fate and must learn to work as a team.

There's a problem that sometimes arises from this approach. Say you're running a fantasy campaign and the mission is to deliver a message to a distant city. But one of the characters in your group is a witch hunter. His player is all excited about making such a unique character, but you need him (and the others) to be a courier for now and accept the assignment to kick off your campaign.

Fortunately, there's an easy way to fix this. Instead of arguing with the player about his character's motivations, let the *player* figure it out. Be honest and tell him that this is what you need to get things started. Maybe the witch hunter is simply between jobs. Or maybe he's working under cover to root out some evil sorceress, or needs to earn some gold to buy better arms and equipment for his task. Or maybe the employer or the recipient is an old friend (or enemy).

This approach not only helps get things moving, but may establish an entirely new and interesting subplot for your campaign!

Former Acquaintances

You can also start a campaign with all the characters already knowing each other. This works great for getting the game moving, and is very appropriate for certain campaign types. *Weird Wars* games in particular, for example, are often best run where the soldiers have served together for a bit and know at least the basic faults and vices of their companions. This is also a great way to kick off a convention game where your group only has a few hours to play.

The downside of starting a campaign like this is that some players may feel cheated if they put a lot of work into their characters' backgrounds. Players often come up with deep backstories for their heroes. This shows great imagination and enthusiasm for your game and should be encouraged.

Unfortunately, unless you've set the character up as an important person in your setting and his background figures prominently in the events that are to come, it's very likely all that work will never come to light. The reason why is that individual backgrounds likely aren't part of your overall plot, and characters don't engage in revealing small talk like real people do. (But see Interludes on page 105!)

Staying Together

After the first adventure, the players may wonder exactly why their characters might stay together. This is easy if they're employed by a common benefactor, or if similar groups are common to the setting (adventuring crews, military teams, and so on).

Staying together might be more difficult if the campaign goal isn't very clear, or if some of the characters don't get along that well. How to fix this depends a lot on the type of game you're running. If there's a clear, overall objective or over-arching storyline, the party might stay together to defeat the greater evil, even if they aren't the best of friends.

If the campaign goal is more ambiguous, the best answer may be to *not* force the heroes to stay together. Consider a modern horror game. The players are thrust together in a haunted mansion for a weekend. Terrible things occur, but eventually at least some of the player characters survive and stagger back into daylight. Why would they then go out hunting vampires or searching for zombies the following week just because they had one incredible encounter?

Maybe they don't. Maybe they all go home and try to forget what happened just like normal folks. Let a few days or weeks of nothing happen (narratively, of course). Later on though, one of the characters gets involved in another creepy encounter. This time out, however, he knows at least a few other people who won't laugh at him or throw him in the loony bin, so *he* calls and asks the other player characters for help.

Friction

So what happens if your group doesn't get along? That depends on whether it's the players or the characters who are arguing.

We won't give you advice on how to handle conflicts with your friends. You know them best, and will have to figure out if there are certain friends who just don't fit in your campaign. Remember though that friends are more important than games—even ours. If you and the rest of the group can't talk out your differences, find something else to do for a while that doesn't cause such friction. Maybe you can come back to the game once you've worked things out.

Friction between characters, on the other hand, is not only fine, it's actually encouraged to some degree. Any interesting group of personalities squabble and argue on occasion. As long as this is done in character, it adds to the roleplaying experience and the depth of your campaign. Quiet fights between the heroes can often take on a life of their own, encouraging players to take you, the Game Master, aside or write you private notes about actions their heroes perform away from the prying eyes of others.

Campaign Types

Different groups like different types of games. Some like lots of combat, others prefer to run fast and loose with more roleplaying and less "hack and slash." Most people mix all these elements together. When you cut to the chase, there are basically three campaign types: Hack and Slash, Roleplaying, and Exploration.

Hack and Slash

A Hack and Slash game features lots of combat. With *Savage Worlds,* you can do more than pit your five player characters against a couple of orcs and an ogre. You can throw a whole horde at your heroes, and give them a few staunch allies or henchmen to help as well!

The best part is that players who just want to wade into the forces of darkness with two blades

slashing can do it. More tactically-minded players can load up on Leadership Edges and direct the actions of hirelings and allies.

Players who like to think on their feet can take advantage of acrobatic maneuvers and the like to describe their heroes' actions down to the most minute details.

Exploration

Exploring lost cities, finding forgotten treasures, or reclaiming fallen civilizations is always exciting for the players. The Great Unknown lurks behind every pile of toppled columns, and Incredible Treasures await those brave enough to take them from their mysterious guardians.

The trouble with exploration games is that they're often difficult for you, the Game Master, to create. All those incredible surprises, fearsome beasts, and awesome treasures have to be created by you. Fortunately, *Savage Worlds* makes it easy to quickly create just about any creature, magic item, or other surprise you can dream up.

One important tip here. The players don't have access to your creatures' statistics unless you give it to them. If you describe mysterious creatures of different shapes and sizes, don't kill yourself trying to make their statistics vastly different.

Roleplaying

Perhaps the trickiest type of campaign to run is one that involves deep roleplaying. It's very easy to handle rules-wise—there likely won't be much die rolling besides a few Persuasion rolls here and there. The tricky part is handling all the different Extras and interacting with the player characters. Again, being able to create characters on the fly helps tremendously here. You can jot down a few notes about a character's most important skills and then move on. That way you can concentrate on giving your Extras more personality and worry less about how good they are at obscure skills.

Another thing to be careful of when running a game that's heavy on roleplaying is making sure there are at least a few events scheduled to give the group something to talk about. If the majority of your adventure is a bunch of people standing in a room, you're likely in for a slow night. If they're in a room trying to find out which one of them is a murderer, the action will likely be quite exciting. And if the lights occasionally go out and another victim turns up dead, the interaction between characters can easily get as exciting as the most knock-down, drag-out dungeon crawl.

Horror

Most every game has an element of horror to it. New Game Masters often ask how to handle horror in their games. They have visions in their heads of their friends sitting around shivering in utter terror as gruesome fiends stalk their underpowered investigators.

Unfortunately, that's not too likely. There may certainly be moments like that, but more likely, your group will be sitting around eating nachos and making bad jokes to each other most of the night. The worst thing you can do is try and stop them. Remember that they're there to have a good time and socialize while exercising their own imaginations. Let them enjoy themselves and don't try to be overly oppressive with the spooky stuff.

When the time comes and the weirdness begins, subtly change the tone a bit. Smile and dim the lights, then turn on some creepy music—just loud enough for them to hear it without being too overt. If what you're running is genuinely creepy, your group will be relaxed and willing to go with the flow and let the heebie-jeebies take over. Try and *force* them and it will almost certainly backfire.

Whatever you do, when the group finally encounters some horrid monster, make sure to describe it rather than refer to it by name. A "large, lanky, green-skinned creature with drool dripping from its fangs and beady black eyes" is much more frightening than "a troll."

Running the Game

Savage Worlds has been designed from the ground up to make the job of the Game Master as easy as possible. The designers and playtesters of this game want to concentrate on playing the game and making incredible and exciting memories. We aren't interested in spending hours before the game creating statistics for Karlos the Innkeeper.

That means that when preparing for your game, you can concentrate on creating intricate plots, tricky puzzles, and interesting characters. You don't have to do complex math to make your nonplayer characters and monsters, and you certainly don't need to spend an hour on some computer program just to make up a few bandits.

Your job is kept easy during the game as well since there's very little bookkeeping. You might have to track a few Wild Card villains' wounds, but other than that, the bad guys are up, Shaken, or removed from play. You can focus on describing the action instead of trying to record "2 hit points of damage on the skeleton figure with the chipped paint on his sword."

Take advantage of these things to give yourself a break and run a game like you never have before. If you *want* to spend a lot of time on your campaign, make some cool props or develop your nonplayer characters' personalities and plots—not their game statistics.

Introducing New Players

Getting your friends to try a new game, especially if they're used to one system and don't like to try many others, can be pretty difficult. We recommend downloading the Test Drive rules from our website and giving them to each of your friends. This will show them what *Savage Worlds* is all about and encourage them to try it at least once. If you run one of the free adventures from our site, complete with pregenerated characters, it should be very easy for everyone to jump in, play a short session, and figure out if it's for them. We hope it is of course. If so, you can then try something with a little more meat, such as *Deadlands, Necessary Evil, Slipstream,* or even a world of your own creation. If you like these rules but have a favorite game world, you can convert it over (see page 148).

Balance

Some games have very strict rules for how to balance encounters so that every fight is "fair." The battle might be a tough one, but it's still expected the heroes can win if they play smart and have decent luck.

In *Savage Worlds*, most setpiece encounters should be reasonably balanced for the expected power level of the group. But this isn't always the case. Sometimes it's just as interesting for the players to evaluate a situation and realize they probably can't win—at least not by charging in guns blazing. This is desirable on occasion as it encourages the group to think, talk, plan, and come up with clever solutions to the most challenging situations.

Game Masters should never be afraid to let the opposition flex their muscles. These are *savage* worlds, after all, and triumphing against these foes should be a major accomplishment—not a given.

Combat Ratings

Once you've played *Savage Worlds* for a while you should have a good feel for how many bad guys to throw at your adventurers. New Game Masters might want a little guidance. The system below gives you a baseline to start from, but make sure to also think about additional advantages either side might have (such as traps, support, powerful magic items, or favorable terrain).

- Start your estimate by getting a Combat Rating for each player character equal to half the maximum damage he does with his typical attack. So a fighter with a d8 Strength and a short sword (Str+d6 damage) has a Damage Rating of 7 (14/2). A wizard who typically uses the *bolt* power averages a standard bolt attack of 2d6, or 6 (12/2).
- Add +1 for each Combat Edge or special ability, and another +1 for each point of Toughness over 5.
- Do the same for any allies. If a character isn't a Wild Card, his Combat Rating is halved.
- Now add all the player characters' Combat Ratings together to find the party's Combat Rating.
- Use the same system for the villains (counting combat special abilities as Combat Edges).

Now compare each side's values. If the party's Combat Rating is 50, for example, your opposition should be a little less for an easy encounter, about even for a moderate encounter, and a little more for a tough fight.

If the villains' Combat Rating is two or more times the heroes' total they're likely going to learn how to retreat.

Experience

You should usually award two experience points per game session. That means your players get to upgrade their characters every two or three game.

When you end longer adventures, story arcs that take four to six sessions or so, you might want to award three points, but any more should be reserved for really big events. Keeping your average award to two means your characters progress at a more natural rate, and won't be Legendary warriors after only a few months of play.

Starting With Experienced Characters

In general, player characters at the start of *Savage Worlds* campaigns have a little training and talent, but haven't had many adventures on their own yet.

You may occasionally want to start a campaign with more experienced characters. That's encouraged for really difficult worlds, or for shorter campaigns where the heroes need to get to the heart of the action a little quicker. A commando raid in World War Two, an assault on a lich's lair, or super spies infiltrating a diabolical villain's base are not adventures for the inexperienced.

Start experienced characters as Seasoned, or very rarely, Veterans, when first trying this out. Once you have a good feel for more experienced characters, you can go as high as you want.

It's important to the balancing process to make your players create their characters as Novices and then "bump" them up through their four progressions per Rank. That maintains a more realistic progression of attributes and skills, and ensures they can't take more advanced Edges than they would otherwise be entitled to.

It's also easier to do it this way from a player's perspective. It's a little tricky to add up all the "points" one would have at Seasoned rank. Bump up a character from a Novice however and the advancement system is very simple.

Bennies

Experience is very limited—we encourage you to give out two points just about every game session. Bennies are much more flexible, and allow you to reward creative players on the spot for their actions.

You should hand out a Benny anytime a player does something particularly clever, finds a very important clue, or generally advances the plot. You should also hand out Bennies for great roleplaying, particularly as it concerns their Hindrances. If a Loyal character jeopardizes his life to save his comrade, he definitely deserves a Benny for his efforts. It never hurts to reward a player for a great line, side-splitting in-game joke, or even a rare serious and dramatic moment.

Average players should get one or two extra Bennies per night. Really good roleplayers may wind up with two to three.

Interpret the Die Rolls

Savage Worlds frequently features wild and unpredictable die rolls. When this happens, go with it! If a hero has to jump from a wrecked car as it careens out of control and makes an amazing Agility roll, describe how he leaps into the air, tucks and rolls on the ground, and comes up on his feet with

perfect balance. Similarly, don't be afraid to throw some bad luck at them when they get a really poor roll. Maybe while using the Chase rules a player is skiing down a mountain attempting to escape a rampaging yeti and rolls snake eyes! Describe how he tumbles in the snow, rolling and tumbling as the beast bounds after him and prepares to make its attack!

Your players will love the extra embellishment, and they'll feel powerful and cool when the dice are nice, and feel danger and excitement when the dice betray them.

Pacing

A good Game Master must pay attention to the pace of the game. Sometimes your group will want to take their time roleplaying their characters, interacting with the world, or even just joking out of character and enjoying the social aspect of the game. If this goes on too long, however, your party likely needs a little guidance.

This can be especially true in open adventures such as a murder mystery that requires the players to figure out where their characters go and what they want to do (as opposed to a dungeon crawl or similar adventure where they really only need to decide if they're pressing forward or not).

In general, if most or all of the group is roleplaying, smiling, and having a good time—leave them alone. Let them set

them the pace. If you notice some of your players are left out or looking a little bored, prod them a bit. If they seem a little lost as to what to do next, ask one of the group to recount the clues or situation as they understand it. This will often be enough to spark an idea or lead they want to follow up on. You might also introduce new information via a call or visit from a nonplayer character. Finally, don't be afraid to contrive an encounter that gives the group a new path to follow. Maybe the team is attacked by the bad guys, and in the aftermath are able to gather a new clue from the survivors.

Combat Pacing

Perhaps even more important than pacing at the plot level is making sure combats are fast and furious. As you count down the Action Cards, make each player tell you what his character is doing fairly quickly. If he needs a moment, put his character on Hold and move on to the next player (but probably wait if the next actor is a villain).

If you feel the scene should be particularly dramatic and a player doesn't announce his character's intentions quickly enough, start counting down… "What do you do? 5, 4, 3…!" That will get all the players' blood pumping and reinforce the notion that their characters are in a dangerous situation that requires quick decisions and big heroics.

Design Note - The Countdown

The countdown is a fantastic tool for instilling a sense of urgency into your combats. We've run hundreds of games and when a player takes too long to figure out what they want to do on their turn everyone suffers. That's not to say there aren't times when you want to give them some breathing room—particularly if they have a big plan or need to look up something really important. But most of the time, rush things along. Make them feel the urgency of combat. Make them a little nervous. Make them realize things are desperate and that next die roll better be a good one.

And of course, don't be afraid to back off and give the group time to plan and strategize when that makes sense. Feel the moment and play up the drama befitting your scenario, the environment, and the party's mood.

Extras

The backbone of any good game is the world that surrounds the player characters, and nonplayer characters are a big part of that. This section shows you how to breathe life into the supporting cast of your world.

Creating Extras

Consider this Game Master's Rule #1 when it comes to Extras: Don't "build" them!

Don't create your Extras with the character creation rules. Just give them what you think they ought to have in their various skills and attributes and move on. Remember this game is supposed to be easy for you to set up, run, and play. Don't sit around adding up skill points for Extras when you could be designing fiendish traps and thinking up nasty special abilities for your monsters!

Personality

Far more important than most nonplayer character's statistics are their personalities. Jot down a note or two about any Extras the party is likely to come across so you'll have some idea how to run them. Some Game Masters find it useful to identify prominent Extras with actors or characters from film, television, books, or comics.

Knowing that the Captain of the City Guard is "played by Sam Elliot," for instance, gives you a good handle on how to handle interactions with him. He's likely to be gruff, to the point, and have a deep, throaty voice.

Adding these extra touches to the characters can really make them stand out and be remembered by your players as well. That way the captain becomes a memorable character they may call on in the future rather than just a one-shot resource they forget about by the next scene. Not every Extra needs this kind of depth of course, but those that do add a level of realism and continuity to your game.

Allies

Though it's rarely written, most games assume that the Game Master controls the nonplayer characters, both when they're being talked to and when they fight alongside the player characters in combat. Most of the time, this means the overworked GM simply forgets about the additional characters during a fight, or shoves them off to the side and narratively describes what happens to them. This goes for hirelings as well as animal companions, sidekicks, or love interests. The simple fact is that in most games, allies are a cumbersome complication.

Savage Worlds takes a very different approach—we turn control of allies over to the player characters. The GM acts out these allies when they're spoken to, of course, but he should very rarely, if ever, take them over in combat.

If you allow your heroes to have allies, you can include all the minions your villains should have as well. Picture an ancient lich cornered in his unholy "throne" room. Would he be sitting there alone? No, he'd be surrounded by scores of ghoulish undead. These lesser minions make great complications for your battles, and your players will have fun bashing through them with the Extras while their heroes battle the lich and his more capable lieutenants.

This can take a little getting used to. If you've been Game Mastering other games for a long time and have a hard time letting go of the nonplayer characters, we suggest you try it for a bit and see how it works out. You can always change it if doesn't make sense for your group.

Artificial Inflation

When running *Savage Worlds*, a lot of Game Masters become extremely enamored with the ally aspect of the game. That's great and it's what we intend, but it also sometimes leads to very large parties of player characters and Extras, which then demand very large parties of opponents.

It's okay if you do this—the system can handle it—but be warned that a combat with 50+ combatants will take a bit, even with a fast and furious system. To avoid this kind of "inflation," pay attention to the size of your party and its nonplayer characters, and then remember that you'll need a lot of enemies to challenge a large group.

Creating Worlds

Pinnacle makes many incredible and award-winning settings that we hope you'll check out, but it's also fun to create your own worlds to play in. The game rules and statistics won't give you any trouble after you've played even a single game, and you probably don't *need* to create a single Edge, Hindrance, or power (though you may want to). That means you can concentrate on what your world is about, what the heroes do there, what kinds of fantastic treasures they might find, and who their opponents are.

The Name

It's not necessarily the most important part of the game, but a good name can really help you nail down the theme. *Evernight,* for example, is about a world of perpetual darkness. *Deadlands* has a Western feel, and hints at the underlying horror. You can just guess what *Hell on Earth* is all about.

If you can come up with a good name for your game, it may help everyone instantly realize just what kind of setting it is.

Iconic Adventures

Perhaps the single strongest thing you can think of for your new world is what you expect a typical adventure to be about. If it's a fantasy "dungeon crawler," you expect the heroes to delve into multi-leveled dungeons fighting monsters and gathering treasure. If it's an anti-corporate cyberpunk setting, you expect the team to run missions against secure buildings and battle in cyberspace.

This doesn't mean all your adventures need to follow this pattern, but if you set this as a baseline expectation players will quickly understand the world, what it's about, and most importantly, their role in it. Knowing the game will mostly be about Texas Rangers roaming the frontier fighting crime, for example, gives a player a very strong guideline for what kind of character he could make.

Scripted Adventures

Scripted adventures are more like interactive stories. The players can make choices along the way, but the overall plot advances more or less intact regardless of what they do. Epic tales must sometimes follow this path—it's hard to tell a story if you don't know what chapters are to come.

When running a scripted adventure, try not to make your scenarios *feel* scripted. The group should never feel like they're just observers, going along for the ride no matter what they do. Instead, use the situation, overwhelming opponents, or "down times" to give the group the illusion they control the story more than they really do. In *Evernight*, for example, there's a point where the heroes can do whatever they want for a time. Eventually, however, they are captured by the villains of the tale, and begin the next episode of the story.

Situational Adventures

Situational adventures are much easier to run if you're able to think on your feet as you won't have quite as much preparation. In these epic tales, you present a situation of some sort and then just let the heroes deal with it however they choose. Say an evil lich has risen and is creating an army of undead to destroy the living. What do the heroes do about it? Do they hire on with the local militia? Do they try and sneak into the cursed lands to strike down the necromancer himself?

You will need to prepare a few locations, Extras, and perhaps a few staged encounters ahead of time. You don't want to have to figure out what the lich's lair looks like on the fly, for example. And you might want a few "random" encounters to fill in the gaps between the heroes' actions.

The Genre

Your setting should hint at what genre it's in—you shouldn't pick a genre and then try to shoehorn your setting into it. Maybe you want to make a pulp fantasy game that harkens back to the old Robert E. Howard *Conan*® stories. You could call that pulp, but most people will think you're talking about Indiana Jones® or *The Shadow*®. Call it fantasy and they'll think you're talking about Tolkien or *Dungeons & Dragons*®.

So how about "pulp fantasy?" That tells your friends that there's not likely to be lots of shining knights on white horses saving princesses. It's more likely to feature cunning rogues outwitting incredibly powerful sorcerers, lost races, forgotten ruins, and savage combat.

Having a genre description in your head can go a long way toward helping you figure out what kinds of villains should be present, and what typical adventures your characters might go on.

The World

Now it's time to design the world itself. Start with the area you expect the heroes to adventure in most of the time. If there's a city that serves as their home base, describe it in a paragraph or two. Is it a shining example of law and order? Or is it a wretched hive of scum and villainy? Now sketch out some of the surrounding areas. Are the "Mountains of Dread" just a few miles away? Or are such places relatively far away from the centers of population?

There are several software programs available to help you do this if you like. The nice thing about using a computer program is that it's much easier to make changes should you later decide the Mountains of Dread were just too close. Or perhaps the players themselves can add to the map in exploration campaigns as they discover new areas and lost cities!

Original Settings

When creating your own original setting, start by identifying its core elements. Spend some time writing down just what makes it so special.

What are the themes? Is it fantasy? Is it science fiction? Is it science fantasy? Is there a hook? If so, what is it? (And we highly recommend you have a hook—there are already solid swords and sorcery realms with elves and dwarves. Add something new, like an alien invasion—as we did in *Evernight*.)

Once you have clearly identified the thematic elements that identify your setting, figure out who the heroes are. These "archetypes" are usually the best identifiers of new worlds.

Next figure out what kind of adventures take place. There's no point detailing the undersea world of Caribdus, for example, if 99% of the action in *50 Fathoms* takes place above water and on ships. Focus your efforts where it's important, then fill in the extra details when they come up.

The last step you should take is creating new powers, Edges, and Hindrances. For the most part, we've found you really want to keep the selection to less than a dozen powers, and half that number of new Edges or Hindrances. A lot of new Game Masters go crazy creating scores of each, but at the end of the day find that most of the stuff people actually take is already covered in the main *Savage Worlds* rule book. That's not to say you shouldn't have some cool new powers, Edges, or Hindrances—just that you should think them through very carefully, and add them mostly for flavor or to cover some very unique feature of the setting that the rules don't currently cover.

Converted Settings

There are literally thousands of great roleplaying settings out there made by other companies besides Pinnacle. We're fans of many of these brilliant worlds as well. But we usually like playing them with *Savage Worlds.* Here are some tips we've learned after a few years of watching folks "savage" other games.

Don't reinvent the wheel. *Savage Worlds* was designed for quick play with minimal rule interference. All too often conversions of other games try to account for every element—massive skill lists, minute details, and hundreds of powers. This isn't *Savage Worlds*, and bringing in those elements is likely to burden the rules to the point where the game play is no longer fast, furious, or fun.

Like an original setting, identify the themes of the other game and try to adapt with a very few key world rules. Literal translations of game mechanics from other systems usually just result in cumbersome sub-systems that don't add one

minute of fun to the Savage version.

There is a often a strong desire to create lots of new skills, Edges, and powers to fit your setting. That's understandable, but it isn't always the best path.

Remember that more skills dilutes the pool from which the players can choose. It weakens the overall character, because now their 15 skill points have to be spread further. Creating a list of 20 different firearm skills might be more realistic, but the system wasn't designed that way and it becomes a major burden to the players. Creating one new Edge that allows a person to specialize in a specific gun is a better way to go if that's particularly important to the feel of your game (as it might be in a high-tech military campaign).

Remember too that a lot of what you're looking for might already be in the rules. Do you need a sniper Edge? That's Marksman. Do you need a Mechanic skill? Why not use Repair? Do you need a magic missile power? Why not use *bolt*?

When you do decide to add a new skill, try to let it cover as broad a range of related topics as possible. There's no need to create Dancing, Oratory, Acting, and Singing Skills in most campaigns when a single Perform skill does the trick.

When converting monsters and Extras, compare them to existing creatures in this rule book. That's much easier—and much less confining—than trying to convert every attribute, skill, and hit point.

Design Note - The Elevator Pitch

There's a term used in Hollywood called "the Elevator Pitch." The idea is that you're a young and hungry screenwriter trying to pitch an idea to an executive. You can't get in to see him, but one day he's in the elevator and you have about 30 seconds to make him understand your idea, why it's cool, and why he'd want to make it.

The idea of the elevator pitch is strong for your campaign as well. If it takes many minutes to explain what the game is about to your potential players, it's too much. You can certainly do all the things you've talked about or have them as part of your backstory, but they need to be revealed during play as they're important to the characters.

If your game can be summed up succinctly, the players will get it quickly as well. You'll also know very quickly if they're excited about it and then can ask you for the details they're particularly interested in.

Here are the elevator pitches for some of Pinnacle's games:

- **Deadlands:** Weird Western horror where heroes are sometimes so tough they come back from the dead.
- **50 Fathoms:** A fantastic and colorful world is drowning from a witch's curse. Heroes from that world and our own earth must travel the seas to stop the flooding and defeat the witches.
- **Necessary Evil:** When all the superheroes are gone, the only ones left to save the world from an evil alien invasion are the supervillains!
- **Weird Wars:** The violence of war gives rise to dark things. Soldiers, sailors, and airmen of every nation must battle their enemies as well as the horrible things that grow in the shadows.

Races

A race of super-intelligent titans are simply going to be more powerful in game terms than humans. That's fine if everyone is playing a titan, but if they're not, the GM needs to do a little balancing.

Guidelines for creating new player character races can be found on page 22, but if the entire campaign world is more difficult (or less difficult), don't be afraid to amp up (or tone down) the heroes.

Perhaps the player characters are all giant monsters, as are their foes. Or perhaps the heroes are intelligent rats. Both campaigns could be extremely interesting—and require stronger or weaker starting statistics.

New Edges & Hindrances

Now comes one of the trickiest parts of the game. You may want to create some new Edges & Hindrances for your setting. First, realize that you *probably* don't have to. What's in this book covers an awful lot of character types.

What you really may want to look at are Professional Edges. These help you create the archetypal characters of your world. A *Savage Worlds* character with the Woodsman Edge, for example, is a "ranger" in most swords and sorcery games.

If there's a particular character type common to your world, this is the way to encourage your group to play them. Let's say you're creating a far-future *Matrix*-type world with vampires, for example, and you want to create one or more Professional

Edges for vampire hunters. You could start with something useful but fairly low-powered, let's call it Hunter. These are guys who know the vampires exist and have fought them before. Maybe their special ability is that they never make Fear checks when confronted by vampires. To reflect the fact that they've had to face them before, you set the requirement as Novice, Fighting d8+, and Spirit of d8+.

Maybe later on, you create Vampire Hunter. These guys have learned how to stake the bloodsuckers in the heart, and halve penalties for such called shots. Maybe an improved version negates the penalty altogether.

If there's a cardinal rule to Edges, it's that you don't want to grant flat bonuses to combat or arcane skills. It's okay if they only apply in certain situations, but don't give gunslingers +2 to Shooting all the time, or martial artists +2 to Fighting all the time. You'll really throw off the scale of the game if you do that, particularly as they reach higher Ranks. You can give them flat bonuses to noncombat skills, but be careful not to stack them too high with those already found in this book.

Finally, don't feel you need a ton of new Edges & Hindrances. What you're looking for is those few bits that make the world stand out, or enable a particular character archetype to function more effectively than he could if the new rules weren't there. It's not a good idea to go scouring every other book we've done and import all the Combat Edges into your world—it's overwhelming to the players, unnecessary, and moves the game away from what it's supposed to be: streamlined fun.

Design Note - Less Is More

We've seen hundreds of new settings now, both those which have been published by fans and licensees as well as submissions that have never gone public. One thing we see way too much is the "everything and the kitchen sink" approach. It's overwhelming and it just doesn't make sense. Does your Cthulhu-inspired 1920s campaign really need all the Combat Edges from Weird Wars? Does your expedition to Mars really need all the Professional Edges from 50 Fathoms?

Sometimes less is more. Use the core book and anything you just can't live without. For everything else, let the players decide if they want it. Then you can allow it, or not.

Trim the Fat!

Now that you have your theme and your mechanics are in place, it's time to go back and get rid of the stuff that doesn't fit or isn't needed. Does your fantasy setting really need elves and dwarves? Or did you include them because every fantasy setting since *The Hobbit*® has them? Would anything be lost by their removal? Could something else take their place? Do you really need those extensive computer rules in a sci-fi setting? *Star Trek*® might need extensive computer rules—*Star Wars*® does not. Even then, a Knowledge (Computer Use) skill probably does everything you need.

Final Note

At all times, remember to keep it "FFF"—or Fast, Furious, and Fun! All progress in creating a setting should further the setting's feel, but never at the expense of FFF. These are some of the lessons we think work for most people and most settings, and have been echoed on our forums and listservs since *Savage Worlds* came out in March of 2003. But it's your game, and you need to decide what works best for you.

We've talked about heroes and their antics. Now it's time to deal with the monsters, villains, and bad guys. Below are some abilities common to many monsters and villains.

Nonplayer characters and monsters can have any regular Edges or Hindrances the GM feels are appropriate and are not made like player characters. Just give them the abilities you want them to have and spend your time and mental energy on better things, like the plot of the game or how best to entertain your group.

Monstrous Abilities

Aquatic

The creature is native to the water. It is a natural swimmer and cannot drown. While in the water, its Pace is generally equal to its Swimming skill, but some creatures (usually fish) may have much higher movement rates.

Armor

A creature's Armor adds to the creature's Toughness (already added in to its statistics), usually in all locations. Thick, leathery hide generally offers 2 points of Armor. "Armored" creatures like a stegosaurus generally have 4 or more points of protection. Supernatural creatures may have much higher Armor values. A living statue, for example, might have 8 points of Armor or more.

Burrowing

From massive worms to sand-dwelling humanoids, many creatures are able to burrow beneath the earth and move within it. These creatures can tunnel underground and reappear elsewhere for devastating surprise attacks against their foes. The distance a creature can burrow in a turn is written immediately after its Burrow ability. A burrowing creature may tunnel on its action, and may erupt from the ground at any point within its burrowing Pace the same round if desired. It cannot be attacked while beneath the earth unless the attacker has some special means of detecting it and penetrating the intervening dirt.

Burrowing creatures strike by erupting from beneath their opponents and taking them by surprise. When this occurs, the Burrowing creature makes an opposed Stealth roll versus the target's Notice. If the creature wins, it gains +2 to attack and damage that round, or +4 if it gets a raise. If the victim wins and was on Hold, he may try to interrupt the burrower's attack as usual.

Construct

Robots, golems, and other animated objects are collectively called "constructs." Some are sentient beings while others are mere automatons following the will of a hidden master.

Whatever their origin or material, such beings have several inherent advantages over creatures of flesh and blood:

- Constructs add +2 when attempting to recover from being Shaken.
- Constructs do not suffer additional damage from called shots (unless otherwise specified in their description).
- Construct Wild Cards never suffer from Wound Modifiers.
- Constructs do not suffer from disease or poison.

Elemental

Air, earth, fire, and water form the basis of the elemental realms, wherein dwell strange, unfathomable creatures.

- Elementals suffer no additional damage from called shots.
- Elementals are Fearless.
- Elemental Wild Cards never suffer from Wound Modifiers.
- Elementals do not suffer from disease or poison.

Ethereal

Ghosts, shadows, will-o'-the-wisps, and similar intangible creatures have no form in the physical world (or can turn it on and off at will). They cannot be harmed by physical attacks, and cannot even be seen unless they desire to be. Ethereal creatures are always affected by magical items, weapons, and supernatural powers.

Most ethereal creatures can still affect things in the physical world—throwing objects, wielding ghostly swords, or even pushing heroes down long, dark stairs.

Fear

Particularly frightening monsters cause Fear checks to all who see them. Some truly terrifying monsters may inflict penalties on Fear checks as well. A creature with Fear –2, for instance, causes those who see it to make their Fear checks at –2. See the **Fear** rules on page 97 for effects.

Fearless

Mindless creatures, some undead, robots, and the like don't suffer from the weaknesses of the mortal mind. Fearless creatures never suffer from Fear effects and cannot be affected by Intimidation (though Taunt may still work).

Flight

The creature can fly at the listed Pace and ignores the effects of difficult ground. The flyer also has a Climb score that reflects its in-air maneuverability. The number is entirely relative and is mostly used for Chases to determine if the beast is more maneuverable than its foes (see page 94).

Gargantuan

Gargantuan creatures are those that are at least size 9 or better. Classic movie monsters like *Godzilla* or *King Kong* fit into this category. Gargantuans have Heavy Armor, so they can only be hurt by Heavy Weapons, and all their attacks count as Heavy Weapons as well.

Gargantuans suffer the penalty for being Huge: +4 to attack rolls from man-sized creatures.

When a Gargantuan creature makes a stomp attack (Game Master's call), add its Size to its damage roll, but subtract the Size of the foe as well. Don't add the size of inanimate obstacles such as vehicles, buildings, or ships—that's already figured into their Toughness.

Hardy

Very tough and resilient creatures do not fall from lesser wounds, no matter how many they suffer. A decisive blow is needed to put one of these tenacious creatures down.

If the beast is Shaken, further Shaken results have no further effect—they do not cause a wound.

Infection

A vampire's bite, a horrid spider-like creature that injects eggs into its victim's wounds, or even the disease-born scratching of rats are all examples of Infection.

Whenever a character is Shaken or wounded by a creature with Infection, the victim must make a Vigor roll. Modifiers to the roll are listed in the creature's description, as are the effects of failure.

Infravision

Nocturnal beasts often see in the infrared spectrum—meaning they can "see" by detecting heat. Creatures with Infravision halve penalties (round down) for bad lighting when attacking living targets.

Clever characters may figure out ways to mask their heat from such creatures. Smearing cold mud over one's body or wearing special heat-filtering suits generally obscures the target from those with Infravision. Creatures with Infravision almost always have normal sight as well.

Immunity

Creatures born in fire aren't affected by heat, and a horror made of pure lightning won't suffer from a *bolt* attack with an electrical trapping.

Immunities are always to specific types of attacks, such as fire, cold, electricity, and so on. Such creatures aren't Invulnerable, they just ignore damage from the specific attack types named.

Invulnerability

Savage Settings are filled with violent combat, but many often feature desperate puzzle-solving or dark research into unholy horrors as well. To defeat an Invulnerable creature, you'll need a little of both.

Invulnerable creatures can be Shaken, but they can't be wounded by anything but their Weakness (all such creatures have at least one if not more). An ancient dark god given life by misguided cultists, for example, might be immune to mortal weapons, but is vulnerable to shards of stained glass gathered from a church.

Low Light Vision

Many monsters, and even fantasy races such as elves and dwarves, are typically able to see in all but the blackest darkness. Low light vision ignores penalties for Dim and Dark lighting, allowing the creature to see in all but pitch black conditions.

Paralysis

Certain creatures and poisons can instantly paralyze a foe, rendering the victim easy prey for the thing's dark designs or ravenous appetite. A target who suffers damage or a Shaken result from such a creature must make a Vigor roll or be paralyzed and incapable of any action—even speech—for 2d6 rounds or longer.

Poison

Snakes, venom-coated daggers, and so on afflict their victims with dangerous poison. Poisons are described in more detail in the **Hazards** section.

A creature with the Poison ability typically injects it via a bite or scratch. To do so, the thing must cause at least a Shaken result to the victim, who then makes a Vigor roll modified by the strength of the poison (listed in parentheses after the creature's Poison ability). The effects of failure are described in each creature's description.

Regeneration

Legend has it that trolls, vampires, and certain other types of legendary creatures can Regenerate damage caused to them.

Regeneration comes in two types: Fast and Slow.

- Fast Regeneration lets a wounded creature make a Vigor roll every round to heal any damage it has sustained—even after it has been "killed." A success heals one wound (or removes Incapacitated status), and a raise heals an additional wound. Most creatures with this ability also have a Weakness or Vulnerability, such as fire. Wounds from the creature's Weakness or Vulnerability do not regenerate, but may still heal naturally. Creatures with Fast Regeneration also add +2 to Spirit rolls made to recover from being Shaken.

- Slow Regeneration means the creature won't be suddenly healing itself during a fight, but may recover its wounds quickly between encounters. Slow regenerators make a natural Healing roll once per day.

Size

A creature's size has a lot to do with how much damage it can take, so we add a modifier to its Toughness to reflect its tremendous mass. Note that a beast's size has nothing to do with Vigor—even a mighty kraken can catch a cold or tire out.

The Toughness modifiers on the table below represent average specimens of particular species for comparison, but there are always exceptions. Not every great white has a +4 Toughness bonus. A young specimen might have a +3, while a larger fish might be +5 or even +6. The same is true for humans. Small humans suffer a –1 penalty, while those with the Brawny Edge gain a +1 bonus. Use the table as a baseline when creating your own creatures then adjust for particularly large or smaller versions.

Toughness Modifiers

Mod	Size of a...
−2	Cat, fairy, pixie, large rat, dog
−1	Large dog, bobcat, half-folk, goblin, small human
0	Human
+1	Orc
+2	Bull, gorilla, bear, horse
+3	Ogre, kodiak bear
+4	Rhino, great white shark
+5	Small elephant
+6	Drake, bull elephant
+7	T-Rex, orca
+8	Dragon
+9	Blue whale
+10	Kraken, leviathan

► **Minimum Toughness:** Normal creatures have a minimum Toughness of 2 regardless of modifiers. Only insects and the like have Toughness scores of 1.

Small/Large/Huge

Creatures the size of rats or pixies are very difficult to hit, especially when moving. Assuming such a creature is active, attackers subtract 2 from any attack rolls directed at it.

Large creatures, at least the size of a rhino, are somewhat easier to hit. Attackers may add +2 to any attack rolls directed at Large targets.

Truly Huge creatures, at least as big as a dragon, are +4 to be hit.

This particular special ability is relative and cumulative. Two elephants don't get the bonus when fighting each other, but if a pixie attacks an elephant it adds +4 to its roll. If an elephant strikes back at the tiny pixie, it subtracts 4 from its roll.

Strength

Strength is a Trait, not a special ability, but because very large creatures exceed the normal human range of d4 to d12, you might need a little more information when creating your own creatures.

Creatures of human or lesser Strength should be expressed as a d4 through a d12, as you think appropriate. Stronger creatures, such as gorillas, ogres, and so on, have a d12 plus a bonus. The bonus depends on how strong the creature is and how well it can use that strength in combat. Just as with humans, there is variation within each species, however. A mother gorilla may have a Strength of d12+1, while her much larger mate has a Strength of d12+3.

Here's a quick comparison to help you figure out what Strength creatures of your own creation should have.

Creature Strength

Creature	Strength
Gorilla, bear, ogre	d12+1 to +3
Rhino, great white	d12+3 to +6
Elephant, drake, T-Rex	d12+5 to +8
Dragon	d12+9 to +12

Stun

A creature with this ability often has an electrical attack, mild toxin, mind lash, or similar trapping. When it successfully hits a character (even if it causes no damage), the victim must make a Vigor roll minus any listed penalties or be Shaken. He cannot attempt to recover from being Shaken for 1d6 rounds.

Undead

Zombies, skeletons, and similar Undead horrors are particularly difficult to destroy. Below are the benefits of being such an abomination.

- Undead add +2 to their basic Toughness.
- Undead add +2 when attempting to recover from being Shaken.
- Undead don't suffer additional damage from called shots.
- Undead Wild Cards never suffer from Wound Modifiers.
- Undead do not suffer from disease or poison.

Wall Walker

Some creatures have the ability to walk on walls. These creatures only make Climbing rolls in the most adverse and stressful situations—otherwise they automatically walk on vertical or inverted surfaces just as a human walks on the earth.

A Wall Walker's Pace when walking on walls is its standard movement rate. It may run as usual when walking on walls unless the specific creature's text says otherwise.

Weakness

Some creatures suffer additional damage or other effects when attacked by their Weakness. A creature made of ice, for example, might take double damage from fire. A vampire suffers from a Weakness to sunlight, causing it to catch fire and burn when exposed to its rays.

See the creature's description for the particular effects of its Weakness.

Some creatures can only be killed by their Weakness. They may feel pain or even become

Shaken from other attack types, but only suffer wounds when struck by their Weakness. A vampire, for instance, ignores wounds from swords and bullets, but suffers damage normally if hit in the heart with a wooden stake.

Bestiary

Below is a sampling of some common animals and monsters common to many Savage Settings. Note that for some creatures, Smarts is listed relative to the animal world, and is thus followed by an (A) to remind you that this is animal intelligence, not people intelligence, so don't expect a dolphin to drive off in your tank just because it's *relatively* smart animal. Creatures with animal intelligence do not typically Advance as Allies—this only happens if the animal is gained via an Edge.

Alligator/Crocodile

Alligators and crocs are staples of most pulp-genre adventure games. The statistics here represent an average specimen of either species. Much larger versions are often found in more remote areas.

Attributes: Agility d4, Smarts d4 (A), Spirit d6, Strength d10, Vigor d10
Skills: Fighting d8, Notice d6, Swimming d8
Pace: 3; **Parry:** 6; **Toughness:** 9 (2)
Special Abilities
- **Armor +2:** Thick skin.
- **Aquatic:** Pace 5.
- **Bite:** Str+d6.
- **Rollover:** Both gators and crocs are notorious for grasping their prey in their vice-like jaws and rolling over and over with their flailing victims in their mouth. If one of these large reptiles hits with a raise, it causes an extra 2d4 rollover damage to its prey in addition to its regular Strength damage.

Bear, Large

Large bears covers grizzlies, kodiaks, and massive polar bears.
Attributes: Agility d6, Smarts d6 (A), Spirit d8, Strength d12+4, Vigor d12
Skills: Fighting d8, Notice d8, Swimming d6
Pace: 8; **Parry:** 6; **Toughness:** 10

Special Abilities
- **Bear Hug:** Bears don't actually "hug" their victims, but they do attempt to use their weight to pin their prey and rend it with their claws and teeth. A bear that hits with a raise has pinned his foe. The opponent may only attempt to escape the "hug" on his action, which requires a raise on an opposed Strength roll.
- **Claws:** Str+d6.
- **Size +2:** These creatures can stand up to 8' tall and weigh over 1000 pounds.

Bull

Bulls are usually only aggressive toward humans when enraged. Of course, if you're looking up the statistics here, it's probably already seeing red.
Attributes: Agility d6, Smarts d4 (A), Spirit d8, Strength d12+2, Vigor d12
Skills: Fighting d4, Notice d6
Pace: 7; **Parry:** 4; **Toughness:** 10
Special Abilities
- **Horns:** Str+d6.
- **Gore:** Bulls charge maneuver to gore their opponents with their long horns. If they can move at least 6" before attacking, they add +4 to their damage total.
- **Size +2:** Bulls are large creatures.

Cat, Small

This is an ordinary house cat, the sort that might be a familiar for a spellcaster, a Beast Master's animal friend, or an alternate form for the *shape change* power.
Attributes: Agility d8, Smarts d6 (A), Spirit d10, Strength d4, Vigor d6
Skills: Climbing d6, Notice d6, Stealth d8
Pace: 6; **Parry:** 3; **Toughness:** 3
Special Abilities
- **Acrobat:** +2 to Agility rolls to perform acrobatic maneuvers; +1 to Parry if unencumbered.
- **Bite/Claw:** Str.
- **Low Light Vision:** Cats ignore penalties for Dim and Dark lighting.
- **Size −2:** Cats are typically less than a foot high.
- **Small:** Attackers subtract 2 from their attacks to hit.

Dire Wolf

Dire wolves are very large and feral wolves often used by orcs as attack dogs. They may also be found roaming in packs in the deepest, darkest woods.

Attributes: Agility d8, Smarts d4 (A), Spirit d6, Strength d8, Vigor d8
Skills: Fighting d8, Intimidation d8, Notice d6
Pace: 10; **Parry:** 6; **Toughness:** 6
Special Abilities

- **Bite:** Str+d6.
- **Go for the Throat:** Wolves instinctively go for an opponent's soft spots. With a raise on its attack roll, it hits the target's most weakly armored location.
- **Fleet-Footed:** Dire wolves roll d10s instead of d6s when running.

Dog/Wolf

The stats below are for large attack dogs, such as Rottweilers and Doberman Pinschers, as well as wolves, hyenas, and the like.

Attributes: Agility d8, Smarts d6 (A), Spirit d6, Strength d6, Vigor d6
Skills: Fighting d6, Notice d10
Pace: 8; **Parry:** 5; **Toughness:** 4
Special Abilities

- **Bite:** Str+d4.
- **Fleet-Footed:** Roll a d10 when running instead of a d6.
- **Go for the Throat:** Dogs instinctively go for an opponent's soft spots. With a raise on its attack roll, it hits the target's most weakly armored location.
- **Size −1:** Dogs are relatively small.

✠Drake

Drakes are non-flying dragons with animal intelligence (rather than the more human-like sentience of true dragons). They are much more aggressive in direct combat than their distant cousins, however.

Attributes: Agility d6, Smarts d6 (A), Spirit d10, Strength d12+6, Vigor d12
Skills: Fighting d10, Intimidation d12, Notice d8
Pace: 6; **Parry:** 7; **Toughness:** 17 (4)

Special Abilities

- **Armor +4:** Scaly hide.
- **Claws/Bite:** Str+d8.
- **Fear:** Drakes are frightening creatures to behold.
- **Fiery Breath:** Drakes breathe fire using the Cone Template. Every target within this cone may make an Agility roll at −2 to avoid the attack. Those who fail suffer 2d10 damage and must check to see if they catch fire (see **Fire**). A drake may not attack with its claws or bite in the round it breathes fire.
- **Large:** Attackers add +2 to their attack rolls when attacking a drake due to its large size.
- **Size +5:** Drakes are over 20' long from snout to tail, and weigh in at over 3000 pounds.
- **Tail Lash:** A drake can sweep all opponents in its rear facing in a 3" long by 6" wide rectangle. This is a standard Fighting attack, and damage is equal to the creature's Strength −2.

✠Dragon

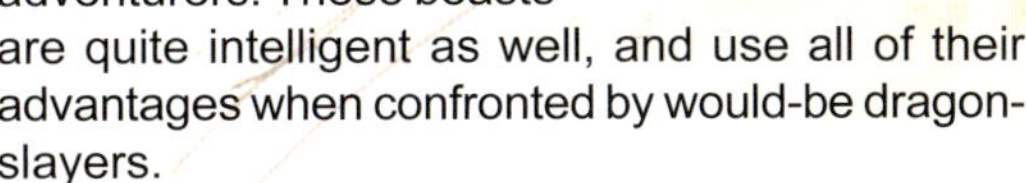

Dragons are fire-breathing monsters that bring doom and despair to the villages they ravage. Such creatures should not be fought lightly as they are more than a match for even a party of experienced adventurers. These beasts are quite intelligent as well, and use all of their advantages when confronted by would-be dragon-slayers.

Attributes: Agility d8, Smarts d8, Spirit d10, Strength d12+9, Vigor d12
Skills: Fighting d10, Intimidation d12, Notice d12
Pace: 8; **Parry:** 7; **Toughness:** 20 (4)
Special Abilities

- **Armor +4:** Scaly hide.
- **Claws/Bite:** Str+d8.
- **Fear −2:** Anyone who sees a mighty dragon must make a Fear check at −2.
- **Fiery Breath:** Dragons breathe fire using the Cone Template. Every target within this cone may make an Agility roll at −2 to avoid the attack. Those who fail suffer 2d10 damage and must check to see if they catch fire. A dragon may not attack with its claws or bite in

the round it breathes fire.

- **Flight:** Dragons have a Flying Pace of 24" and Climb 0.
- **Hardy:** The creature does not suffer a wound from being Shaken twice.
- **Huge:** Attackers add +4 to their Fighting or Shooting rolls when attacking a dragon due to its massive size.
- **Improved Frenzy:** If a dragon does not use its Fiery Breath ability, it may make two Fighting attacks with no penalty.
- **Level Headed:** Act on best of two cards.
- **Size +8:** Dragons are massive creatures. This version is over 40' long from nose to tail, and weighs well over 30,000 pounds.
- **Tail Lash:** The dragon can sweep all opponents in its rear facing in a 3" long by 6" wide square. This is a standard Fighting attack, and damage is equal to the dragon's Strength –2.

Elementals

Elementals are living spirits of earth, fire, water, and air. These are average examples of such creatures. They may be more or less powerful in specific settings.

Earth Elemental

Earth elementals manifest as five-foot tall, vaguely man-shaped collections of earth and stone. Though amazingly strong, they are also quite slow and ponderous.
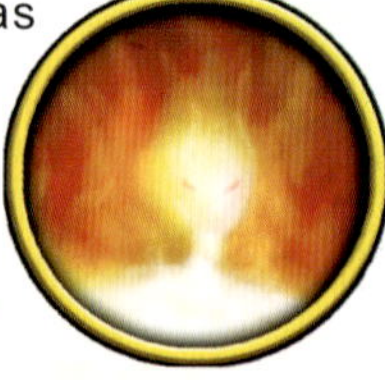
Attributes: Agility d6, Smarts d4, Spirit d6, Strength d12+3, Vigor d10
Skills: Fighting d8, Notice d4
Pace: 4; **Parry:** 6; **Toughness:** 11 (4)
Special Abilities
- **Armor +4:** Rocky hide.
- **Bash:** Str+d6.
- **Burrow (10"):** Earth elementals can meld into and out of the ground.
- **Elemental:** No additional damage from called shots; Fearless; Immune to disease and poison.

Fire Elemental

Fire elementals appear as man-shaped flame.
Attributes: Agility d12+1, Smarts d8, Spirit d8, Strength d4, Vigor d6
Skills: Climbing d8, Fighting d10, Notice d6, Shooting d8

Pace: 6; **Parry:** 7; **Toughness:** 5
Special Abilities
- **Elemental:** No additional damage from called shots; Fearless; Immune to disease and poison.
- **Invulnerability:** Fire Elementals are immune to all non-magical attacks, but suffer 1d6 damage when doused in at least a gallon of water, +2 per additional gallon.
- **Fiery Touch:** Str+d6; chance of catching fire.
- **Flame Strike:** Fire elementals can project a searing blast of flame using the Cone Template. Characters within the cone must beat the spirit's Shooting roll with Agility or suffer 2d10 damage, plus the chance of catching fire.

Water Elemental

Water spirits are frothing, man-shaped creatures of water and sea-foam.

Attributes: Agility d8, Smarts d6, Spirit d6, Strength d10, Vigor d10
Skills: Fighting d8, Notice d6, Shooting d8, Swimming d12+2
Pace: 6; **Parry:** 6; **Toughness:** 7
Special Abilities
- **Aquatic:** Pace 12
- **Elemental:** No additional damage from called shots; Fearless; Immune to disease and poison.
- **Invulnerability:** Water elementals are immune to all non-magical attacks except fire. A torch or lantern causes them 1d6 damage but is instantly put out if it hits.
- **Seep:** Water elementals can squeeze through any porous gap as if it were Difficult Ground.
- **Slam:** Str+d6, nonlethal damage.
- **Waterspout:** Water spirits can project a torrent of water using the Cone Template. Those in the area may make an Agility roll opposed by the spirit's Shooting to avoid it or suffer 2d8 nonlethal damage. This puts out any normal fires.

Air Elemental

Air elementals manifest as sentient whirlwinds.
Attributes: Agility d12, Smarts d6, Spirit d6, Strength d8, Vigor d6
Skills: Fighting d8, Notice d8, Shooting d6
Pace: —; **Parry:** 6; **Toughness:** 5

Special Abilities

- **Elemental:** No additional damage from called shots; Fearless; Immune to disease and poison.
- **Ethereal:** Air Elementals can maneuver through any non-solid surface. They can seep through the cracks in doors, bubble through water, and rush through sails.
- **Flight:** Air Elementals fly at a rate of 6" with a Climb of 3. They may not run.
- **Invulnerability:** Immune to all non-magical attacks except fire.
- **Push:** The air elemental can use an action to push a single adjacent target 1d6" directly away with a concentrated blast of air. The victim makes a Strength roll, with each success and raise reducing the amount moved by 1" (to a minimum of 0).
- **Wind Blast:** Air Elementals can send directed blasts of air at foes using the Cone Template and a Shooting roll. Foes may make an opposed Agility roll to avoid the blast. The damage is 2d6 points of nonlethal damage.
- **Whirlwind:** As long as the air elemental does not move that turn it may attempt to pick up a foe. Make an opposed Strength check and if the air elemental wins then its foe is pulled into the swirling maelstrom of its body. While trapped, the target is at –2 on all rolls including damage, to hit and Strength rolls to free himself. The air elemental cannot move as long as it wants to keep foes trapped inside its form.

Giant Worm

Massive worms tunneling beneath the earth to gobble up unsuspecting adventurers are sometimes found in lonesome flatlands. The things sense vibrations through the earth, hearing a walking person at about 200 yards. The stats below are for a monster some 50' long.

Attributes: Agility d6, Smarts d6 (A), Spirit d10, Strength d12+10, Vigor d12

Skills: Fighting d6, Notice d10, Stealth d10
Pace: 6; **Parry:** 5; **Toughness:** 22 (4)
Special Abilities

- **Armor +4:** Scaly hide.
- **Bite:** Str+d8.
- **Burrow (20"):** Giant worms can disappear and reappear on the following action anywhere within 20".
- **Gargantuan:** The worms are Huge and thus suffer +4 to attacks against them. Their attacks count as Heavy Weapons, and their Armor is Heavy Armor.
- **Hardy:** The creature does not suffer a wound from being Shaken twice.
- **Size +10:** Giant worms are usually well over 50' long and 10' or more in diameter.
- **Slam:** Giant worms attempt to rise up and crush their prey beneath their massive bodies. This is an opposed roll of the creature's Fighting versus the target's Agility. If the worm wins, the victim suffers 4d6 damage.

Ghost

Spectres, shades, and phantoms sometimes return from death to haunt the living or fulfill some lost goal.

Attributes: Agility d6, Smarts d6, Spirit d10, Strength d6, Vigor d6
Skills: Fighting d6, Intimidation d12+2, Notice d12, Taunt d10, Stealth d12+4, Throwing d12
Pace: 6; **Parry:** 5; **Toughness:** 5
Gear: Thrown objects (Str+d4).
Special Abilities

- **Ethereal:** Ghosts are immaterial and can only be harmed by magical attacks.
- **Fear –2:** Ghosts cause Fear checks at –2 when they let themselves be seen.

Goblin

Goblins of myth and legend are far more sinister creatures than some games and fiction portray. In the original tales, they were terrifying creatures that stole into homes in the middle of the night to steal and eat unruly children. The statistics here work for both dark "fairy tale" goblins as well as those found alongside orcs in contemporary roleplaying games.

Attributes: Agility d8, Smarts d6, Spirit d6, Strength d4, Vigor d6

Skills: Climbing d6, Fighting d6, Notice d6, Taunt d6, Shooting d8, Stealth d10, Throwing d6, Swimming d6

Pace: 5; **Parry:** 5; **Toughness:** 4

Gear: Short spears (Str+d4).

Special Abilities

- **Infravision:** Goblins halve penalties for dark lighting against living targets (round down).
- **Size −1:** Goblins stand 3-4' tall.

Horse, Riding

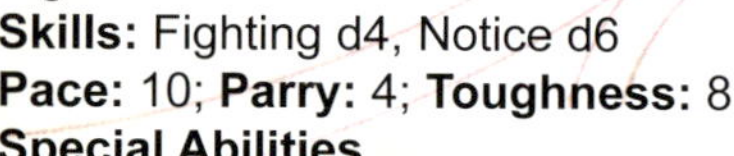

Riding horses are medium-sized animals that manage a good compromise between speed and carrying capacity.

Attributes: Agility d8, Smarts d4 (A), Spirit d6, Strength d12, Vigor d8

Skills: Fighting d4, Notice d6

Pace: 10; **Parry:** 4; **Toughness:** 8

Special Abilities

- **Fleet-Footed:** Horses roll a d8 when running instead of a d6.
- **Kick:** Str.
- **Size +2:** Riding horses weigh between 800 and 1000 pounds.

Horse, War

War horses are large beasts trained for aggression. They are trained to fight with both hooves, either to their front or their rear. In combat, the animal attacks any round its rider doesn't make a trick maneuver of some kind.

Attributes: Agility d6, Smarts d4 (A), Spirit d6, Strength d12+2, Vigor d10

Skills: Fighting d8, Notice d6

Pace: 8; **Parry:** 6; **Toughness:** 10

Special Abilities

- **Fleet-Footed:** War horses roll a d8 when running instead of a d6.
- **Kick:** Str+d4.
- **Size +3:** Warhorses are large creatures bred for their power and stature.

✠ Lich

Perhaps the most diabolical creature in any fantasy land is the lich—a necromancer so consumed with the black arts that he eventually becomes undead himself.

Attributes: Agility d6, Smarts d12+2, Spirit d10, Strength d10, Vigor d10

Skills: Fighting d8, Intimidation d12, Knowledge (Occult) d12+2, Notice d10, Spellcasting d12

Pace: 6; **Parry:** 6; **Toughness:** 15 (6)

Gear: Magical armor (+6), other magical items.

Special Abilities

- **Death Touch:** Liches drain the lives of those around them with a touch. Instead of a normal attack, a lich may make a touch attack. Every raise on its Fighting roll automatically inflicts one wound to its target.
- **Spells:** Liches have 50 Power Points and know most every spell available.
- **Undead:** +2 Toughness; +2 to recover from being Shaken; called shots do no extra damage; ignores wound penalties.
- **Zombie:** Liches are necromancers first and foremost. The undead they raise through the *zombie* spell are permanent, so they are usually surrounded by 4d10 skeletons or zombies as they choose. Some liches have entire armies of the undead at their disposal.

Lion

The kings of the jungle are fierce predators, particularly in open grassland where their prey cannot seek refuge.

Attributes: Agility d8, Smarts d6 (A), Spirit d10, Strength d12, Vigor d8

Skills: Fighting d8, Notice d8

Pace: 8; **Parry:** 6; **Toughness:** 8

Special Abilities

- **Bite or Claw:** Str+d6.
- **Improved Frenzy:** Lions may make two Fighting attacks each action at no penalty.
- **Low Light Vision:** Lions ignore penalties for Dim and Dark lighting.
- **Pounce:** Lions often pounce on their prey to best bring their mass and claws to bear. It can leap 1d6" to gain +4 to its attack and damage. Its Parry is reduced by −2 until its next action when performing the maneuver however.
- **Size +2:** Male lions can weigh over 500 pounds.

Mech (Sentinel)

The stats below are for a 12' high mechanized sentinel such as might be found in a typical hard sci-fi campaign. This is a light patrol-style platform with reasonable intelligence, a sensor package, and high maneuverability.

Larger mechs outfitted for battle have

substantially more armor, are larger, and have more specialized weaponry.

Attributes: Agility d4, Smarts d6, Spirit d4, Strength d6, Vigor d8

Skills: Fighting d6, Notice d10, Shooting d8

Pace: 10; **Parry:** 5; **Toughness:** 10 (4)

Gear: Typically a machine gun or flamethrower.

Special Abilities

- **Armor +4**
- **Construct:** +2 to recover from being Shaken; called shots do no extra damage; does not suffer from disease or poison.
- **Fearless:** Mechs are immune to fear and Intimidation, but may be smart enough to react to fear-causing situations appropriately.
- **Sensors:** Sentinel mechs are equipped with sensor packages that halve penalties for darkness, can detect sounds, or record conversations via directional microphones.

Minotaur

Minotaurs stand over 7' tall and have massive, bull-like heads and horns. In many fantasy worlds, they are used as guardians of labyrinths. In others, they are simply another race of creatures occupying a fantastically savage setting. In all cases, they are fierce beasts eager for battle and the taste of their opponents' flesh.

Attributes: Agility d8, Smarts d6, Spirit d8, Strength d12+2, Vigor d12

Skills: Fighting d10, Intimidation d12, Notice d10, Throwing d6

Pace: 8; **Parry:** 8; **Toughness:** 11 (1)

Gear: Leather armor (+1), spear (Str+d6, Reach 1, Parry+1).

Special Abilities

- **Horns:** Str+d4.
- **Fleet-Footed:** Minotaurs roll d10s instead of d6s when running.
- **Gore:** Minotaurs use this maneuver to gore their opponents with their horns. If they can charge at least 6" before attacking, they add +4 to their damage total.
- **Size +2:** Minotaurs stand over 7' tall.

Mule

Mules are a cross between a donkey and a horse, and are usually used to haul heavy goods or pull wagons.

Like any good pet, the GM should feel free to give the mule a little personality. The expression "stubborn as a mule" certainly comes to mind.

Attributes: Agility d4, Smarts d4 (A), Spirit d6, Strength d8, Vigor d8

Skills: Notice d4

Pace: 6; **Parry:** 2; **Toughness:** 8

Special Abilities

- **Fleet-Footed:** Mules roll d8 instead of d6 when running.
- **Kick:** Str.
- **Ornery:** Mules are contrary creatures. Characters must subtract 1 from their Riding rolls when riding them.
- **Size +2:** Mules are stocky creatures weighing up to 1000 pounds.

Ogre

Ogres are kin to orcs and lesser giants. They are often taken in by orc clans, who respect the dumb brutes for their savagery and strength. Orcs often pit their "pet" ogres in savage combats against their rivals' ogres.

Attributes: Agility d6, Smarts d4, Spirit d6, Strength d12+3, Vigor d12

Skills: Fighting d8, Intimidation d8, Notice d4, Throwing d6

Pace: 7; **Parry:** 6; **Toughness:** 12 (1)

Gear: Thick hides (+1), massive club (Str+d8).

Special Abilities

- **Size +3:** Most ogres are over 8' tall with pot-bellies and massive arms and legs.
- **Sweep:** May attack all adjacent characters at −2.

Orc

Orcs are savage, green-skinned humanoids with pig-like features, including snouts and sometimes even tusks. They have foul temperaments, and rarely take prisoners.

Attributes: Agility d6, Smarts d4, Spirit d6, Strength d8, Vigor d8

Skills: Fighting d6, Intimidation d8, Notice d6, Shooting d6, Stealth d6, Throwing d6

Pace: 6; **Parry:** 5; **Toughness:** 8 (1)

Gear: Leather armor (+1), scimitar (Str+d8).

Special Abilities

- **Size +1:** Orcs are slightly larger than humans.
- **Infravision:** Halves penalties for poor light vs. warm targets.

✠Orc, Chieftain

The leader of small orc clans is always the most deadly brute in the bunch. Orc chieftains generally have a magical item or two in settings where such things are relatively common (most "swords and sorcery" worlds).

Attributes: Agility d8, Smarts d6, Spirit d6, Strength d10, Vigor d10

Skills: Fighting d12, Intimidation d10, Notice d6, Shooting d8, Stealth d6, Throwing d8

Pace: 6; **Parry:** 8; **Toughness:** 11 (3)

Gear: Plate chest plate (+3), chain arms and legs (+2), battle axe (Str+d10).

Special Abilities

- **Infravision:** Halves penalties for poor light vs. heat-producing targets.
- **Size +1:** Orcs are slightly larger than humans.
- **Sweep:** May attack all adjacent characters at −2 penalty.

Shark, Great White

These statistics cover great whites, 18 to 25 feet long. Larger specimens surely exist.

Attributes: Agility d8, Smarts d4 (A), Spirit d8, Strength d12+4, Vigor d12

Skills: Fighting d10, Notice d12, Swimming d10

Pace: —; **Parry:** 7; **Toughness:** 12

Special Abilities

- **Aquatic:** Pace 10.
- **Bite:** Str+d8.
- **Hardy:** The creature does not suffer a wound from being Shaken twice.
- **Large:** Attackers add +2 to their attack rolls when attacking a great white due to its large size.
- **Size +4:** Great whites can grow up to 25' in length.

Shark, Medium Maneater

These statistics cover most medium-sized mankillers, such as tiger sharks and bulls.

Attributes: Agility d8, Smarts d4 (A), Spirit d6, Strength d8, Vigor d6

Skills: Fighting d8, Notice d12, Swimming d10

Pace: —; **Parry:** 6; **Toughness:** 5

Special Abilities

- **Aquatic:** Pace 10.
- **Bite:** Str+d6.

Skeleton

The skin has already rotted from these risen dead, leaving them slightly quicker than their flesh-laden zombie counterparts. They are often found swarming in vile necromancers' legions.

Attributes: Agility d8, Smarts d4, Spirit d4, Strength d6, Vigor d6

Skills: Fighting d6, Intimidation d6, Notice d4, Shooting d6

Pace: 7; **Parry:** 5; **Toughness:** 7

Gear: Varies.

Special Abilities

- **Bony Claws:** Str+d4.
- **Fearless:** Skeletons are immune to Fear and Intimidation.
- **Undead:** +2 Toughness; +2 to recover from being Shaken; called shots do no extra damage.

Snake, Constrictor

Pythons, boa constrictors, and other snakes over 15' long are rarely deadly to man in the real world because they aren't particularly aggressive toward such large prey. In games, however, such snakes might be provoked, drugged, or just plain mean.

Attributes: Agility d4, Smarts d4 (A), Spirit d8, Strength d6, Vigor d6

Skills: Fighting d6, Notice d10

Pace: 4; **Parry:** 5; **Toughness:** 5

Special Abilities

- **Bite:** Str.
- **Constrict:** Large constrictors have very little chance of entangling active man-sized prey in the real world—they must attack while

in the real world—they must attack while their victim is sleeping, stunned, paralyzed, and so on. Constrictors in pulp and other fantastic genres might be far more deadly. These creatures bite when they succeed at a Fighting roll, and entangle when they succeed with a raise. The round they entangle and each round thereafter, they cause damage to their prey equal to Str+d6. The prey may attempt to escape on his action by getting a raise on an opposed Strength roll.

Snake, Venomous

Here are the stats for Taipans (Australian brown snakes), cobras, and similar medium-sized snakes with extremely deadly poison.

Attributes: Agility d8, Smarts d4 (A), Spirit d6, Strength d4, Vigor d4
Skills: Fighting d8, Notice d12
Pace: 4; **Parry:** 6; **Toughness:** 2
Special Abilities

- **Bite:** Str.
- **Poison:** See the Poison rules on page 103.
- **Quick:** Snakes are notoriously fast. They may discard Action Cards of 5 or lower and draw another. They must keep the replacement card, however.
- **Size −2:** Most venomous snakes are 4-6' in length, but only a few inches thick.
- **Small:** Anyone attacking a snake must subtract 2 from his attack rolls.

Spider, Giant

Giant spiders are about the size of large dogs and live in nests of 1d6+2 arachnids. They frequently go hunting in these packs when prey is scarce in their home lair.

Their dens are littered with the bones and treasures of their victims, often providing ripe pickings for those brave enough to venture within.

Attributes: Agility d10, Smarts d4 (A), Spirit d6, Strength d10, Vigor d6
Skills: Climbing d12+2, Fighting d8, Intimidation d10, Notice d8, Shooting d10, Stealth d10
Pace: 8; **Parry:** 6; **Toughness:** 5
Special Abilities

- **Bite:** Str+d4.
- **Poison (−4):** See the poison rules on page 103.
- **Wall Walker:** Can walk on vertical surfaces at Pace 8.

- **Webbing:** The spiders can cast webs from their thorax that are the size of Small Burst Templates. This is a Shooting roll with a range of 3/6/12. Anything in the web must cut or break their way free (Toughness 7). Webbed characters can still fight, but all physical actions are at −4.

Swarm

Sometimes the most deadly foes come in the smallest packages. The swarm described below can be of most anything—from biting ants to stinging wasps to filthy rats.

The swarm is treated just like a creature. When it is wounded, the swarm is effectively dispersed.

Swarms cover an area equal to a Medium Burst Template and attack everyone within every round.

Attributes: Agility d10, Smarts d4 (A), Spirit d12, Strength d8, Vigor d10
Skills: Notice d6
Pace: 10; **Parry:** 4; **Toughness:** 7
Special Abilities

- **Bite or Sting:** Swarms inflict hundreds of tiny bites every round to their victims, hitting automatically and causing 2d4 damage to everyone in the template. Damage is applied to the least armored location (victims in completely sealed suits are immune).
- **Split:** Some swarms are clever enough to split into two smaller swarms (Small Burst Templates) should their foes split up. The Toughness of these smaller swarms is lowered by −2 (to 5 each).
- **Swarm:** Parry +2; Because the swarm is composed of scores, hundreds, or thousands of creatures, cutting and piercing weapons do no real damage. Area-effect weapons work normally, and a character can stomp to inflict his damage in Strength each round. Swarms are usually foiled by jumping in water (unless they are aquatic pests, such as piranha).

Troll

Trolls in myths and legends are horrid, flesh-eating creatures who live in deep woods, beneath bridges, or in hidden mountain caves. In modern games and fiction, trolls are monsters with the ability to

regenerate damage and a weakness to fire. These statistics reflect both backgrounds.

Attributes: Agility d6, Smarts d4, Spirit d6, Strength d12+2, Vigor d10

Skills: Fighting d8, Intimidation d10, Notice d6, Swimming d6, Throwing d6

Pace: 7; **Parry:** 6; **Toughness:** 10 (1)

Gear: Spiked club (Str+d8).

Special Abilities

- **Armor +1:** Rubbery hide.
- **Claws:** Str+d4.
- **Improved Sweep:** May attack all adjacent foes at no penalty.
- **Fast Regeneration:** Trolls may attempt a natural healing roll every round unless their wounds were caused by fire or flame. This occurs whether the troll is a Wild Card leader or an Extra. If the latter, a downed troll actually returns to action if it heals itself (and is not Shaken—even if it was before being Incapacitated).
- **Size +2:** Trolls are tall, lanky creatures over 8' tall.

✠ Vampire, Ancient

Blood-drinkers of lore are common in many fantasy games. The statistics below are for a vampire somewhat below the legendary Dracula, but far above those bloodsuckers fresh from the grave (detailed next). The abilities listed below are standard—the GM may want to add other Edges as befits the vampire's previous lifestyle.

Attributes: Agility d8, Smarts d10, Spirit d10, Strength d12+3, Vigor d12

Skills: Fighting d10, Intimidation d12, Notice d8, Shooting d8, Swimming d8, Throwing d8

Pace: 6; **Parry:** 7; **Toughness:** 10

Special Abilities

- **Change Form:** As an action, a vampire can change into a wolf or bat with a Smarts roll at −2. Changing back into humanoid form requires a Smarts roll.
- **Charm:** Vampires can use the *puppet* power on the opposite sex using their Smarts as their arcane skill. They can cast and maintain the power indefinitely, but may only affect one target at a time.
- **Children of the Night:** Ancient vampires have the ability to summon and control wolves or rats. This requires an action and a Smarts roll at −2. If successful, 1d6 wolves or 1d6 swarms of rats (see Swarm) come from the surrounding wilds in 1d6+2 rounds.
- **Claws:** Str +d4.
- **Improved Frenzy:** Vampires may make two attacks per round without penalty.
- **Invulnerability:** Vampires can only be harmed by their Weaknesses. They may be Shaken by other attacks, but never wounded.
- **Level Headed:** Vampires act on the best of two cards.
- **Mist:** Greater vampires have the ability to turn into mist. This requires an action and a Smarts roll at −2.
- **Sire:** Anyone slain by a vampire has a 50% chance of rising as a vampire themselves in 1d4 days.
- **Undead:** +2 Toughness; +2 to recover from being Shaken; called shots do no extra damage (except to the heart—see below). No wound penalties.
- **Weakness (Sunlight):** Vampires catch fire if any part of their skin is exposed to direct sunlight. After that they suffer 2d10 damage per round until they are dust. Armor does not protect.
- **Weakness (Holy Symbol):** A character may keep a vampire at bay by displaying a holy symbol. A vampire who wants to directly attack the victim must beat her in an opposed test of Spirit.
- **Weakness (Holy Water):** A vampire sprinkled with holy water is Fatigued. If immersed, he combusts as if it were direct sunlight (see above).
- **Weakness (Invitation Only):** Vampires cannot enter a private dwelling without being invited. They may enter public domains as they please.
- **Weakness (Stake Through the Heart):** A vampire hit with a called shot to the heart (−4) must make a Vigor roll versus the damage total. If successful, it takes damage normally. If it fails, it disintegrates to dust.

Vampire, Young

Blood-drinkers of lore are common in many fantasy games. This is a relatively young vampire minion.

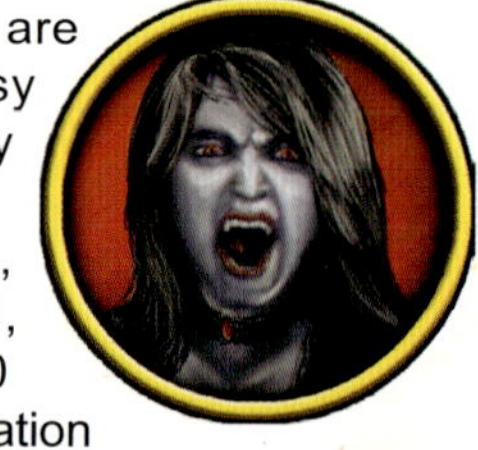

Attributes: Agility d8, Smarts d8, Spirit d8, Strength d12+1, Vigor d10

Skills: Fighting d8, Intimidation

d8, Notice d6, Shooting d6, Swimming d8, Throwing d6
Pace: 6; **Parry:** 6; **Toughness:** 9
Special Abilities

- **Claws:** Str+d4.
- **Frenzy:** Vampires can make two attacks per round with a −2 penalty to each attack.
- **Level Headed:** Vampires act on the best of two cards.
- **Invulnerability:** Vampires can only be harmed by their Weaknesses. They may be Shaken by other attacks, but never wounded.
- **Sire:** Anyone slain by a vampire has a 50% chance of rising as a vampire themselves in 1d4 days.
- **Undead:** +2 Toughness; +2 to recover from being Shaken; called shots do no extra damage (except to the heart—see below).
- **Weakness (Sunlight):** Vampires catch fire if any part of their skin is exposed to direct sunlight. After that they suffer 2d10 damage per round until they are dust. Armor does not protect.
- **Weakness (Holy Symbol):** A character with a holy symbol may keep a vampire at bay by displaying a holy symbol. A vampire who wants to directly attack the victim must beat her in an opposed test of Spirit.
- **Weakness (Holy Water):** A vampire sprinkled with holy water is Fatigued. If immersed, he combusts as if it were direct sunlight (see above).
- **Weakness (Invitation Only):** Vampires cannot enter a private dwelling without being invited. They may enter public domains as they please.
- **Weakness (Stake Through the Heart):** A vampire hit with a called shot to the heart (−4) must make a Vigor roll versus the damage. If successful, it takes damage normally. If it fails, it disintegrates to dust.

Werewolf

When a full moon emerges, humans infected with lycanthropy lose control and become snarling creatures bent on murder. Some embrace their cursed state and revel in the destruction they cause.

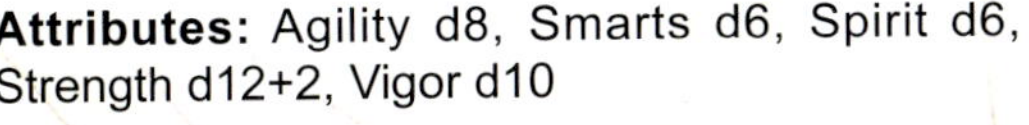

Attributes: Agility d8, Smarts d6, Spirit d6, Strength d12+2, Vigor d10
Skills: Climbing d8, Fighting d12+2, Intimidation d10, Notice d12, Swimming d10, Stealth d10, Tracking d10
Pace: 8; **Parry:** 9; **Toughness:** 7
Special Abilities

- **Claws:** Str+d8.
- **Fear −2:** Werewolves chill the blood of all who see them.
- **Infection:** Anyone slain by a werewolf has a 50% chance of rising as a werewolf themselves. The character involuntarily transforms every full moon. He gains control of his lycanthropy only after 1d6 years as a werewolf.
- **Invulnerability:** Werewolves can only be Shaken by weapons that are not silver—not wounded.
- **Infravision:** Werewolves can see heat and halve penalties for bad lighting when attacking living targets.
- **Weakness:** Werewolves suffer normal damage from silver weapons.

Zombie

These walking dead are typical groaning fiends looking for fresh meat.
Attributes: Agility d6, Smarts d4, Spirit d4, Strength d6, Vigor d6
Skills: Fighting d6, Intimidation d6, Notice d4, Shooting d6
Pace: 4; **Parry:** 5; **Toughness:** 7
Special Abilities

- **Claws:** Str.
- **Fearless:** Zombies are immune to Fear and Intimidation.
- **Undead:** +2 Toughness; +2 to recover from being Shaken; called shots do no extra damage (except to the head).
- **Weakness (Head):** Shots to a zombie's head are +2 damage.

On the following pages are a number of "One Sheet" adventures. You'll find dozens more on our website at www.peginc.com.

Why "One Sheet?" Our goal is to give a Game Master something he can read, understand, and be ready to run in just a few minutes—hence one page (front and back) adventures.

Players can make characters appropriate for the genre (or use the Archetypes on page 18–19) and be ready to play in minutes as well.

One Sheets also demonstrate what we mean by "Fast! Furious! Fun!" We get right to the most important aspects of the adventure—the setup, what is expected to happen, and the statistics for any monsters or villains the heroes are likely to fight.

You won't find details on the surroundings or statistics for nonplayer characters who aren't directly important to the plot. Those are left for you, the Game Master, to make up as you go and as they become important to your session.

If you're not comfortable filling in the blanks, look for full-length adventures on our website. Those are generally designed for multiple sessions and give far more detail on the world and the nonplayer characters.

Share!

Once you've run or played some of these adventures, we invite you to come share your tale on our forums. Our community loves to read about them and see what your group did differently than the last.

Something has awakened at the Orpheum, an old building that has been everything from a theatre to a slaughterhouse. The heroes are employees of Knight Errant, a detective agency that specializes in the macabre—and has a very high turnover rate…

► **Setting Rules:** Critical Failures, Gritty Damage

► **Characters:** The heroes are investigators working with the Knight Errant Detective Agency.

The investigators have been sent to look into the renovation of the Orpheum Theatre in a decaying area of a nearby city's downtown. The work has suffered a number of unexplained setbacks and the company insuring the project has come to suspect that the owner of the theater, Silas Linden, is deliberately sabotaging the effort in an attempt at insurance fraud. The insurance company has hired Knight Errant to look into these grave matters.

In reality, the construction crew has disturbed a vampire that has lain in a comatose state for over half a century. It was unwittingly brought to the theater as a display in a freak show and abandoned in the basement when the theater closed.

The monster was once a poor Chinese railroad worker who fell victim to another such fiend long ago. It speaks no English, and in fact is far too mentally disturbed at this point to speak at all. It stirred briefly when the building was used as a slaughterhouse, feeding on the blood of the animals that drained down to it only to once again lapse into torpor when that business closed as well. The thing was awakened recently by a tragic accident involving one of the workers.

Visiting the Orpheum

The Orpheum is an old building in a rundown section of the city. Most of the buildings nearby are abandoned and in poor repair. The theater, thanks to its renovations, stands out like a diamond in a coal pile. Inside, ornate filigree, marble tiling, and generous use of opulent red curtains ooze a sense of nostalgia for an earlier, more stylish time.

Meeting Linden

The investigators find Linden, a short, somewhat heavy-set man, very receptive to their arrival. Linden seems genuinely concerned about the delays his project has suffered. A number of workmen have been injured since the job started and rumors are beginning to circulate amongst the men that the building is either haunted or cursed. A few have apparently been so spooked they simply walked off the job and never returned.

He answers any of their questions to the best of his ability. Linden also provides them with unfettered access to the theater while the work progresses, warning them that it is a construction site and the project has been plagued by no shortage of accidents.

A Little History

If asked, Linden tells the heroes the Orpheum began as a theater back at the turn of the 20th century, but closed its doors in the early 1920s. The building was converted to a slaughterhouse during the Depression, however that business folded around the time of the second World War. Much of the renovation has involved removing and repairing modifications made during the building's time as a slaughterhouse.

It has sat unused and unoccupied since then—except, he adds, for the usual transients and drug addicts. Linden admits he never actually saw any in the theater, but the neighborhood was overrun with shady characters. Now, most seem to have moved to less active areas in the city.

Legwork

Depending on how they approach the investigation, the characters can discover a number of clues. Reveal the information as the team investigates the theater and the neighborhood. Let them ask questions and think about how to get these clues—don't just give them info based on skill rolls.

- **Accidents:** The first accident occurred while the crew was removing the old slaughterhouse equipment. One of the men nearly severed an arm on a rusty saw and bled out before the ambulance arrived.
- **Basement:** The lower level is a cluttered mess of boxes, crates, and furniture forming a virtual maze. A prop elevator sits at the stage end and a large area has been cleared around a floor drain under the old orchestra pit. There are deep red stains around the drain—left over from the slaughterhouse blood sluices. A Notice roll spots recent scrapes around the drain cover, indicating it may have been moved.
- **Financial Ledger:** Any investigator scouring Linden's financial records can make an Investigation or Knowledge (Accounting) roll.

Success finds that the man is so far in debt on the project that even if he defaults and collects the insurance, he will have to declare bankruptcy.

- **Missing Workers:** None of the crew has heard from any of the other workers who left the site. In fact, in many cases, no one ever saw them leave. A Streetwise roll finds that most of the missing crewmen had been assigned to work clearing the basement level.
- **Neighborhood:** A Streetwise roll discovers that most of the former homeless inhabitants of the area left not because of the work at the Orpheum. The few who remain tell the investigators that "something woke up" in the Orpheum and it preys on anyone foolish enough to be caught alone at night.
- **Newspaper Reports:** An Investigation roll on recent newspaper articles finds that shortly after the first accident at the Orpheum, a homeless man was found dead not far from the theater. The cause of death was massive blood loss.
- **Orpheum Records:** The records from the first Orpheum are intact, buried in the basement. The original theater turned to displays of the unusual or macabre toward the end of its run in an attempt to keep its doors open. An Investigation roll uncovers the last display was purchased from "Nightlinger's Traveling Expedition of the Extraordinary" and included, among other things, "one coffin and contents."

The Final Act

The vampire has created a few offspring from workers and homeless victims during its recent feedings. The creatures hide in the sewers under the theater, crawling up through the drain mainly at night. Rarely, they may snatch a lone worker from the basement during the day.

If the investigators enter the sewers, the undead immediately attack. Should they set up watch on the theater during the night hours to catch vandals or saboteurs, whether inside or out, allow them Notice rolls to spot the monsters creeping out to seek prey.

The young vampires, driven by bloodlust, are feral and fight to the death. The ancient vampire tries to flee if it suffers two Wounds, attempting to escape into the sewers under the theater.

- **Vampire (WC):** Use the stats for the Ancient Vampire found on page 164.
- **Vampire Spawn (1, plus 1 per 2 heroes):** Use the stats for Young Vampire found on page 164.

furnace
prop elevator
drain
loading elevator
stairs up

The Orpheum

dressing rooms
prop storage
office
stairs down
stage
prop elevator
(former orchestra pit)
auditorium
concessions
lobby
box office

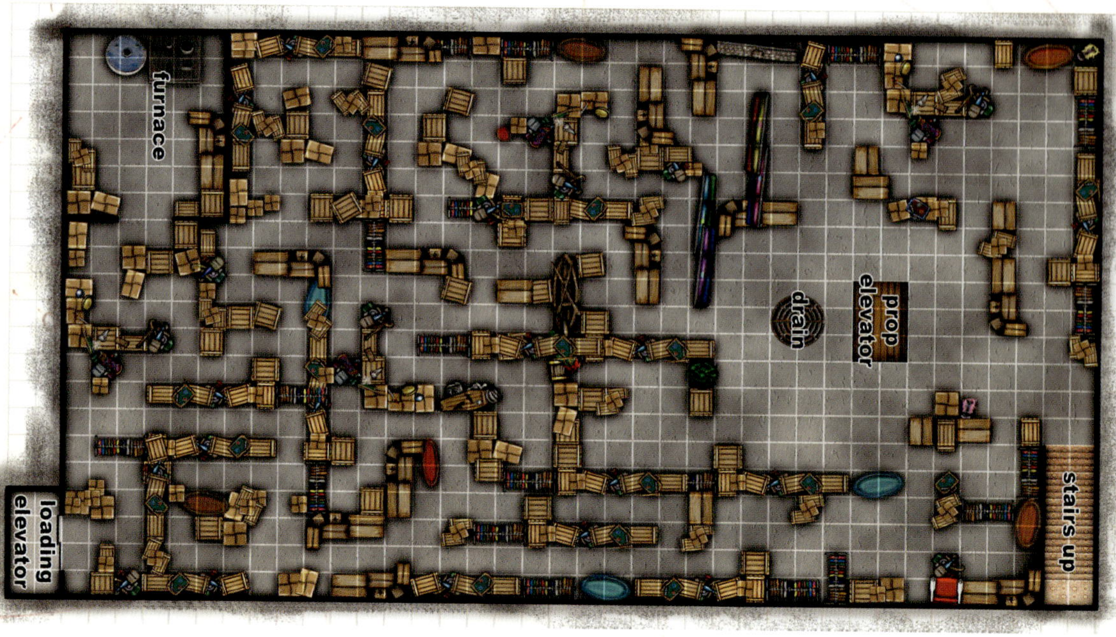

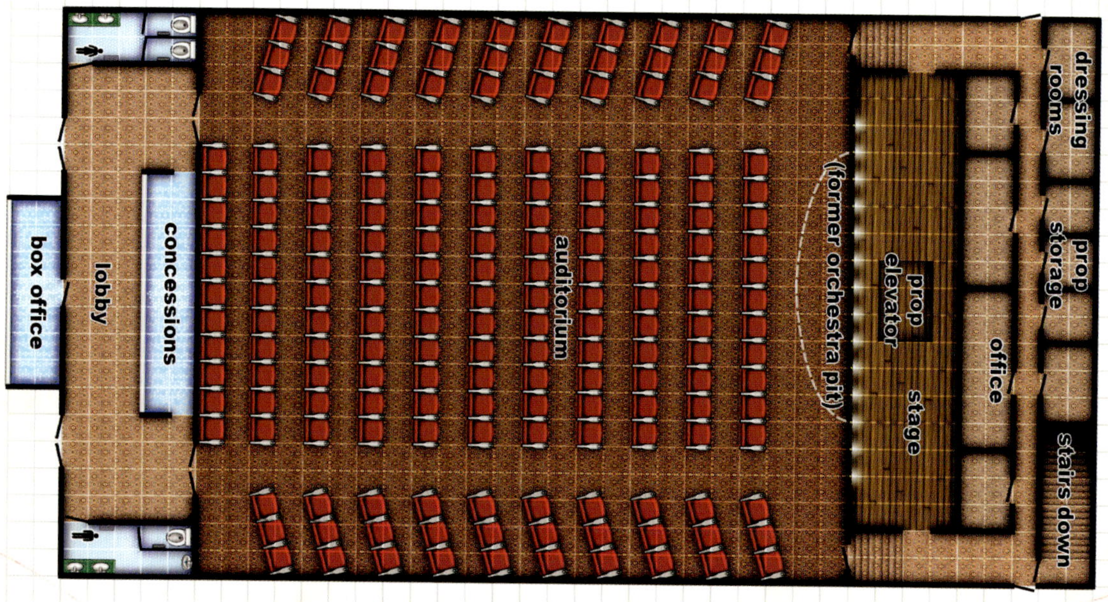

The following is a tale of vikings, ice, and death. It can take place in a fantasy or historical setting as the Game Master chooses. Players should be Viking warriors, scouts, or shamans with mystical powers.

▶ **Setting Rules:** Born a Hero, Blood & Guts
▶ **Characters:** Viking warriors, scouts, shamans, or villagers. At least one of the characters should have Tracking.

The heroes are members of a village called Trundheim somewhere in the frigid north. They are raiders and warriors, but this is the winter season when they spend the harsh days and nights enjoying their ill-gotten gains with their families and friends.

To the south are ice-laden seas. To the east and west are rival clans. To the north are tall mountains said to be home to fierce trolls and massive packs of hungry wolves. It is the trolls that pose the most recent threat to Trundheim.

Two nights ago trolls descended into the village and took one of the village's most beautiful girls—the Jarl's daughter, Brynhilde. The warriors are tasked with venturing out during one of the worst blizzards the elders can remember to bring her back—or avenge her death with the heads of the mysterious trolls.

The Ice Trolls

The adventure starts in the small hours of dawn. Sven Sjurson, who was on guard duty the last part of the night, wakes the village with a cry. He is covered in blood and suffers from a nasty blow to the head. Nearby is the home of Jarl Steinar, headman of the village. The log wall of the longhall has been pulled down and the jarl lies dead in a pool of frozen gore. Sven tells the following tale:

> *Something terrible came through the darkness. I turned to fight but the thing was so tall it blocked out the moon! I was about to strike when it swung a massive club at my head. The next thing I know I was lying in the snow here and…Jarl Steinar was dead.*

The Jarl is a bloody mess. Long claw marks cover his body, and it appears the death blow was delivered to his throat. A quick search of the rest of the longhall reveals the Jarl's daughter, Brynhilde, is missing—her bed violently overturned and furs strewn about the floor. If anyone thinks to look, the Jarl's few valuables are still present.

In the nearby snow are massive barefoot tracks—the feet at least a foot and a half long. Farther out the tracks vanish—a fierce snow is setting in and covering them quickly.

The clan is without leadership, but if the heroes don't think of it on their own, the town elders strongly encourage them to form a rescue party and set out immediately. The rest of the warriors will need to stay in town to prevent further raids and to protect against opportunistic rival clans to the east and west.

The tracks are fading fast, but they lead to the mountainous north. A Tracking roll points the rescue party in the right direction. A raise on the Tracking roll reveals there are three distinct sets of tracks.

What Really Happened

Bjorn Thorkellson is the Jarl of the nearby village of Aldavig. He desperately wants the favor of the king, but to do so he must expand his control to more than a single settlement. Trundheim is small but rich thanks to particularly successful raids the last few years. Fighting such successful warriors would be difficult and likely destroy much of the village, so Thorkellson came up with a more subtle plan. He gathered a group of his most veteran warriors and tasked them with feigning an attack by a monster on the village, killing Jarl Steinar in his sleep, and kidnapping his daughter. His own hunting band would then "chance" across the beasts, kill them, and return as heroes to Trundheim with the princess. Thorkellson would be the new Jarl, and with luck, a legend sung about by the skalds for ages to come for killing the terrible trolls.

Thorkellson has an ally in the treacherous Sven the Sjurson, who has been promised land in the new fiefdom. Sven and the raiders killed the Jarl in his sleep and knocked his daughter unconscious (the Jarl's wife died long ago). Then they quietly tore down the walls and bashed Sven over the head before stealing off into the howling storm.

Following the Raiders

The kidnappers have headed due north. A Tracking roll at −4 for the gathering snow leads the rescuers quickly to their trail. If the roll is failed, the group must make a Vigor roll to resist the cold and try again. If the party decides to stop and recover (mandatory if one of the heroes becomes Incapacitated), they must build a temporary shelter and bundle up. Every 30 minutes in the shelter removes one level of Fatigue.

Pack Tactics

After about half-a-day's journey north the group comes to the foothills. The blizzard picks up and the scattered trees are leafless and bare. As the rescuers pick their way through the blasted landscape they hear sudden barking from behind. Two black wolves stand out against the snow field. Unless the characters specifically state they are not turning to look at the predators they are ambushed by the rest of the pack hiding behind scrub-covered hills to their front.

- **Wolf Pack (6):** See Wolves on page 157.

After the fight, the vikings can skin the wolves for fur and meat. If they do so, this extra layer of warmth and fresh food grants them +1 to their Vigor rolls versus Fatigue for the rest of the adventure.

As they go about the bloody task, have the group make Notice rolls. Whoever rolls highest finds a scrap of red cloth on one of the scraggly trees. It is the rich cloth of a chief's daughter—Brynhilde.

Icy Cliffs

By now all traces of the trolls' footprints are lost, but legend says the trolls live in the caves higher in the mountains. To get to those caves the party must climb a series of sheer cliffs.

Have the group make three Climbing rolls. The rolls are made at –2 if the party had to find shelter after leaving the village as the blizzard has grown in intensity.

- **Total of 1 or less:** The character falls for 2d6 damage if failed on the first roll, 3d6 on the second, and 4d6 on the third.
- **Failure:** The character suffers a Fatigue level.
- **Success:** The climber ascends this section of the mountain.

After each of the three ascents the heroes must rest. Pick a character at random and draw a card for an Interlude. Give the player a few minutes to tell his tale, then move on to the next roll, or the next scene if it was the third Interlude.

The Trolls

After the grueling ascent, have everyone make Notice rolls. The highest roll spots smoke coming from somewhere in the mountains. With a Survival roll the rescuers find the cave quickly. If failed, the group must make a Vigor roll at –2 before stumbling upon the troll's lair.

The "trolls" wait with the captive Brynhilde beyond a bend in the cave. They have a warm fire and stocks of meat and mead. Assuming the rescuers approach quietly, they overhear the raiders talking to their victim.

A heavy voice says: "You were taken by trolls, girl. Say otherwise and we'll kill you. You'll marry Jarl Thorkellson and keep your mouth shut."

A girl's voice answers in angry reply, "My father raised no weaklings. I'll not be bullied into betraying my clan."

"More's the pity for you then. Thorkellson will have his way with you and slit your throat. Then he'll take your broken body back to Trundheim with the sad tale of how we tried to rescue you, but with your last words you pledged your love and legacy to Thorkellson."

The trolls laugh heartily and then grow quiet, feasting on hot broth and mead. It's the perfect time for the heroes to strike. Five raiders are in the cave with their war gear nearby. A Notice roll also spots false "troll feet" made from various hides lying in a pile near the fire.

The group should be able to strike with surprise against the raiders. Unfortunately, the round after the fight begins, Jarl Thorkellson and his personal guard show up to the rendezvous and attack from behind.

Troll-Raiders (3)

Attributes: Agility d6, Smarts d4, Spirit d6, Strength d8, Vigor d8
Skills: Climbing d6, Fighting d8, Intimidation d6, Notice d6, Stealth d8, Survival d6, Throwing d6, Tracking d6
Charisma: –; **Pace:** 6; **Parry:** 7; **Toughness:** 8 (1)
Hindrances: —
Edges: Brawny
Gear: Leather armor (+1), axe (Str+d6), wooden shield (+1 Parry), 2 x throwing axes (Range 3/6/12, Damage Str+d6).

Thorkellson's House Guard (2 + 1 per Hero)

Attributes: Agility d6, Smarts d4, Spirit d6, Strength d10, Vigor d8
Skills: Climbing d6, Fighting d8, Intimidation d6, Notice d6, Stealth d8, Survival d6, Throwing d6, Tracking d6

Charisma: –; **Pace:** 6;
Parry: 7; **Toughness:** 8 (1)
Hindrances: Loyal
Edges: Brawny
Gear: Leather armor (+1),
axe (Str+d6), wooden shield
(+1 Parry), 2 x throwing axes
(Range 3/6/12, Damage Str+d6).

✠ Jarl Thorkellson

Attributes: Agility d6, Smarts
d8, Spirit d10, Strength d12,
Vigor d10
Skills: Climbing d6, Fighting
d10, Intimidation d6, Notice
d6, Survival d6, Throwing d6,
Tracking d6
Charisma: –2; **Pace:** 4;
Parry: 6; **Toughness:** 9 (2)
Hindrances: Arrogant,
Lame, Mean
Edges: Improved Sweep
Gear: Chain armor (+2),
great axe (Str+d10, –1
Parry), 2 x throwing axes
(Range 3/6/12, Damage
Str+d6).

The *USS Kaine* drifts in the cold reaches of space. The crew of the salvage vessel *USS Clark* discovers the *Kaine* and ventures out to discover its dark secret.

▶ **Setting Rules:** Critical Failure, Gritty Damage

▶ **Characters:** The heroes are members of a rescue vessel, the *USS Clark*. One of them must be the captain and have Piloting and Knowledge (Astronavigation) at d8 or higher. All of the crew members must have Repair at d4 or higher.

The USS Kaine

The *USS Kaine* is a deep-space probe designed by the United States Navy to investigate anomalies—including signs of alien life. It was reported missing after a dangerous mission to investigate Black Hole C1263. The ship was to approach within scanning distance of the black hole and take detailed readings on some unusual energy signals detected there.

Unfortunately, the *Kaine* got too close. It wasn't sucked in—that would have destroyed it—but gravitational distortions warped the crew's mind, reducing them to blood-crazed lunatics.

The USS Clark

The *Clark's* computer picked up the *Kaine's* faint distress signal eight hours ago and the captain set course immediately. The vessel is still located near Black Hole C1263, but not dangerously so. The *Clark* will arrive within 10 minutes—just enough time to allow the group to make any preparations they want.

Their vessel is equipped with tools of all sorts, deep space suits with 10 minutes of continuous propulsion and four hours of oxygen, and any other necessities they might think of. The crew does not have weapons, but the captain has a pistol and a box of 20 ceramic bullets in his cabin if he wants it (Range 24/48/96, Damage 2d6-2, Shots 7, will not puncture most inorganic materials—such as the ship's hull!)

The thick suits add +1 Toughness due to their thick material. A hero who suffers a wound or more from a cutting or piercing attack must repair the suit before heading out of life support or he decompresses and dies in 2d6 rounds.

The Approach

The *USS Kaine* is largely intact, though some of the extending structures have all warped strangely toward the bow (an effect of the black hole). There

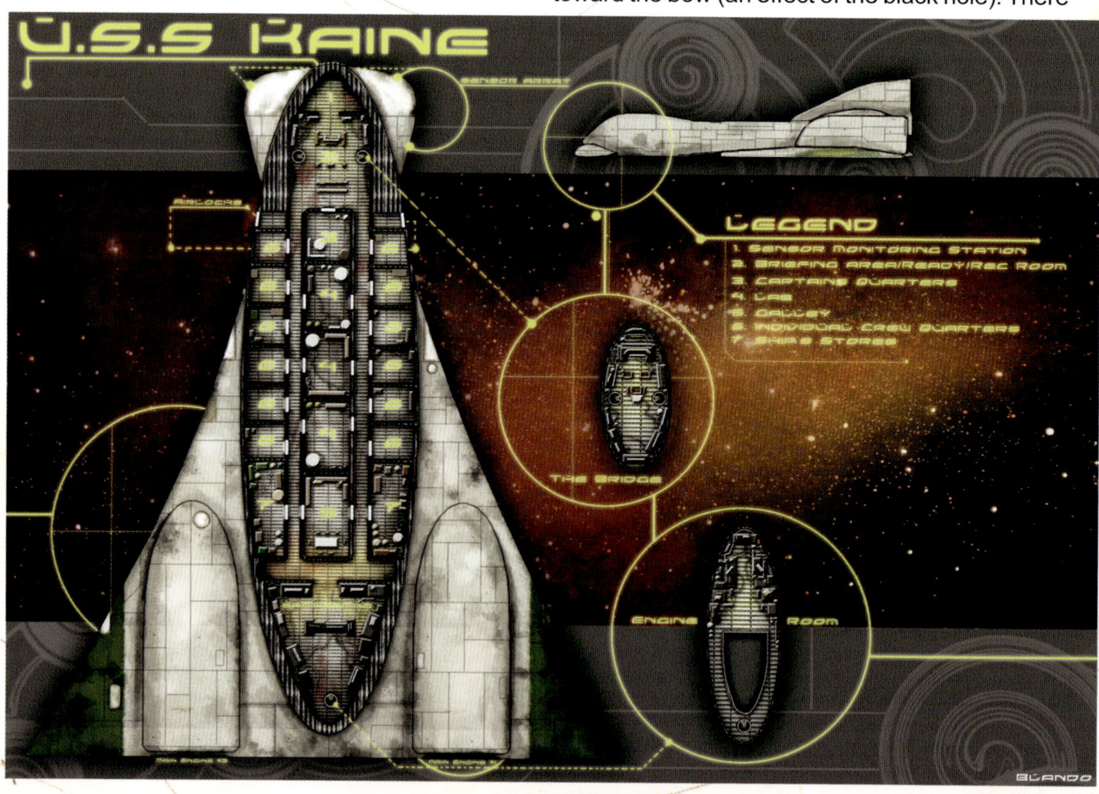

is no obvious damage other than the warped superstructure. Scans of the ship show there is still residual power and life support functioning.

Docking with the *Kaine* requires a standard Piloting roll. A critical failure means the airlock is jammed and the salvagers have to go EV (extra-vehicular—meaning they move around outside the vessels) to enter from the airlock on the opposite side. This uses two minutes of propulsion for each spacesuit.

Life Support & Gravity

Life support is functioning, but the artificial gravity generator was overloaded in the surge. The scavengers wear electromagnetic boots that allow them to walk normally (including on the walls and ceilings!), but cuts their Pace by half and inflicts a –2 penalty to all physical actions.

Should a character turn off the electromagnets in his boots, he drifts in whatever direction he moved last. Initial Pace while drifting is equal to whatever it was last round, but a scavenger may increase or decrease his Pace by 1 or 2 per round by using their suit's microthrusters.

Maneuvering at a Pace of 6 or less requires no roll. At Pace 7 or higher, the hero must make an Agility roll to turn sharp corners, get through hatchways, make a melee attack, etc. If failed at a Pace of less than 10, the character suffers a Fatigue level from Bumps and Bruises. At a Pace of 11 or higher, he suffers 1d6 damage for every 5" of Pace (round normally).

The crew of the *Kaine* does not suffer any penalties due to the absence of gravity. They're quite mad and have adjusted by now, so they move effortlessly through the ship, scampering along the walls and ceilings like some sort of insectoids.

Should the scavengers succeed in repairing the *Kaine's* artificial gravity, however, the situation is reversed. and the deranged crew suffers a –2 to all their physical actions!

Map of the Kaine

▶ **Bridge:** The *Kaine's* navigational equipment needs extensive repairs before she can be piloted. Each Repair attempt takes an entire day and is made at –2 (in addition to any penalties for zero-g).

▶ **Captain's Cabin:** A once neatly maintained cabin, it is now a cluttered mess as a variety of old maritime antiques and curios float through the room.

▶ **Crew Quarters:** Each cabin is a reflection of the former occupant. Some are orderly and clean while others are in varying degrees of disarray. Nothing of note is to be found in any of the rooms.

▶ **Engineering:** The engineering section takes up two levels, with a balcony overlooking much of the main deck portion. The ship's drive is functional, but the artificial gravity generator is temporarily overloaded. Ten minutes labor and a Repair roll (–2) can bring it back online.

▶ **Galley:** Lightweight tables and chairs float throughout the room, along with the body of another of the *Kaine's* crew. A Healing or Knowledge (Medicine) roll easily identifies the cause of death as multiple stab wounds. If the team searches the galley, a Notice roll uncovers a butcher knife (Str+d4).

▶ **Laboratories:** The *Kaine* contained three state-of-the-art laboratories. With a successful Notice roll, the team members can find one small improvised weapon in each lab if they are specifically looking for them.

▶ **Ship's Stores:** A variety of standard equipment is kept in these rooms, including spare space suits and repair gear, but little is of immediate use. A Notice roll spots a pneumatic bolt gun (Range 6/12/24, Damage 2d6, Shots 6) which can be fired using Shooting or Repair.

Something's Amiss

Regardless of how the salvagers proceed in investigating the *Kaine,* they encounter a corpse in the third compartment they enter after boarding the ship. The body floats, limbs askew, twirling slowly in the absence of gravity. A mist of blood globules seems to almost orbit around it. A successful Healing or Knowledge (Medicine) roll determines the cause of death to be blood loss from numerous cuts, tears, and even bites.

Ambush

Immediately after leaving the room where they discover the body, the team is attacked by a band of three of the former crew of the *Kaine.* If possible, the lunatics attack in a passageway, coming at the party from both sides as they scuttle along the walls and ceilings. They have no weapons other than their teeth, hands, and feet.

Marooned!

Moments after the ambush begins, four other members of the *Kaine's* crew rush the airlock to the *Clark.* Any characters at the airlock are attacked. If there is no one there, the madmen rush into the airlock and manually release the docking tube. The airlock protects the integrity of both vessels' atmosphere, but the decompression of the tube blows the vessels apart.

Unless one of the team has remained on the *Clark,* the only way the salvagers can get back to their vessel is through an extended EVA. This requires a successful Agility or Smarts roll to navigate the gap. On a failure, the spacefarer expends two minutes of propulsion and requires another attempt. On a critical failure, it uses five minutes. Once a hero is out of fuel, he drifts into the void unless rescued.

Last Stand

The *Kaine's* captain, Bill Weir, and the remaining five of his crew have laired in the engineering section. One floats limply through the main deck pretending to be dead while the others hide in the shadows of the balcony. If a team member approaches the "dead" man, he suddenly comes to life and attacks. The hapless victim must make a Fear check unless she specifically states she is expecting a trick. Regardless, the salvagers must check for surprise.

The captain and crew attack the next round, diving from above. Treat this as a Wild Attack (see page 87). The lunatics fight to the death.

Two of the crewmen on the balcony are armed with butcher knives from the galley (Str+d4). Use the *Kaine* crewman stats for Captain Weir, but treat him as a Wild Card. He is also armed with a bolt gun, as above.

Kaine Crewman

Attributes: Agility d8, Smarts d4, Spirit d6, Strength d8, Vigor d6
Skills: Fighting d8, Stealth d8, Throwing d6
Charisma: +0
Pace: 6; **Parry:** 6; **Toughness:** 5
Edges & Hindrances: Frenzy
Special Abilities:

- Bite/Fist/Kick: Str. (Treat as armed.)

The Fires of Ascalon

The ravaging hordes are coming and a party of elven scouts must deny them sustenance. The town of Ascalon lies in the way and must be burned to the ground—if the villagers can be convinced.

▶ **Setting Rules:** None.
▶ **Characters:** The heroes are all elves or friends of the elves fighting in a terrible war against a savage foe.

The premise of this Savage Tale is that there is a massive war in a typical fantasy world of elves, dwarves, men, and orcs. The party is assumed to be made exclusively of elves, who in this world are viewed as aloof at best or outsiders at worst by human society.

The adventure can be altered to fit other settings—including those without elves and humans. The important circumstance is that the player character's party is made up primarily of a race or nationality the villagers of Ascalon won't trust easily.

The orcs may be any force of chaos and destruction—the only thing that matters is that allowing the village's precious resources to fall into the horde's hands would cause devastation for the locals and hardship for the rest of the kingdom.

The Mission

The heroes are scouts of the elves tasked with an important mission. While the main force harries the orcish horde, the adventurers are sent to burn the village of Ascalon. This was a decision reached by the allied war council, which includes humans, but the elves were closest and so were appointed with the destruction of the village.

Read or paraphrase the following from their commander when you're ready to begin:

The horde approaches more rapidly than anyone had believed. But all armies march on their stomachs. I will lead our main force in a bitter defense against the orcs at Gallows Woods. Your mission will be to race to the human village of Ascalon and...I'm afraid... burn it to the ground.

Ascalon has rich farmlands and abundant crops that will feed the orcs and prolong their rampage for months. Even the wood from the houses and inns must be destroyed lest it be turned into weapons or siege equipment.

The horde has approached too quickly. The villagers have not been told of this decision by our allied war council and will likely have to be forcibly removed. Convince them to leave and do not harm them—but Ascalon must burn. You leave immediately.

The heroes are given torches covered in pitch and two flasks of quick-burning oil to get the largest buildings burning as fast as possible. Ascalon is an hour's run away and no horses can be spared, so they must get moving immediately.

The run is long and tiring. Have each scout make a Vigor roll or suffer Fatigue before they reach Ascalon. Those with the Fleet-Footed Edge add +2. This Fatigue can be recovered after 30 minutes of rest—precious time the adventures won't likely have.

Foraging Party

The road to Ascalon from the elven camp winds through green, scrub-covered foothills. Halfway along the trek, have the group make Notice rolls. Those who make it hear sounds of fighting on the path ahead and can gain surprise on the first round if they so choose.

The scene they see before them is an overturned cart laden with fruits, vegetables, and flour. Two horses struggle to free themselves from the twisted yokes, and three farmers are doing their best to fend off three circling orcs riding mangy boars. The orcs are foraging for the main horde and chased the cart for several hundred yards before the driver took a sharp turn and unfortunately overturned the wagon.

- **Orcs (3):** The orcs ride boars. Use the statistics at the end of this adventure. The raiders have Riding at d6.

Assuming the orcs are slain or driven off, the humans thank their rescuers and say that the supplies were a gift to the war council from the town. The leader of this small group is Nathan Crenshaw, a strong, soft-spoken man of about 50. If the elves tell Crenshaw their plan, he and his boys begin to right the wagon (it takes 10 minutes). Then he heads back to Ascalon to warn the elders and take part in any debate. If the elves don't mention their task, he heads on to the allied war camp none the wiser.

The Elders

In Ascalon, adults seem alarmed as they spy the mysterious elves brazenly enter their town, while the children gather in delight at their strange and wondrous visitors. If the elves look for someone of authority, they are pointed to Elder Elias Stosham, the leader of this village.

Convincing Stosham of the elves' mission is an extremely difficult task. To do so, use the Social Conflict system on page 110. The outsiders roll at −4 unless Crenshaw accompanied them back from the ambush. If so, his testimony that the

elves saved him and his companions reduces the penalty to –2.

If the heroes tie or lose the conflict, the villagers turn hostile and attack unless the elves seem willing to leave.

If the elves win the debate by 1 or 2 successes, Stosham orders the villagers to comply with the elves' "demands." The villagers slowly gather their loved ones and belongings and fade off into the countryside.

If the heroes succeed by three successes or more, the villagers gather their belongings and send the women, children, and elderly to destinations further behind the lines. The men, however, join the allied army, hoping to defeat the orcs before any more villages must be sacrificed.

Village Fighting Men (15)
Attributes: Agility d6, Smarts d4, Spirit d6, Strength d6, Vigor d6
Skills: Fighting d4, Notice d6
Charisma: —; **Pace:** 6; **Parry:** 4; **Toughness:** 5
Gear: Pitchforks (Str+d4, add Parry +1) or scythes (Str+d6).

Fire, Fire, Burning Bright

Whether they are defeated or reluctantly agree to the plan, the villagers disperse, and no matter how convincing the elves were, they will not help burn their town. The moment the heroes begin to set the fires themselves, a raiding party of orcs arrives.

There are four points that must be lit to effectively raze the town: the Rampant Lion Inn, the granary silo, the bridge, and the livery. The livery still has 2d6 horses and mules in it, so the heroes will need to decide if they want to take the time to evacuate them first. A loud yell and successful Intimidation roll gets 1d4 animals per round, a raise doubles that. Anyone with Animal Companion or Beast Bond adds +2 to the roll. The *beast friend* power can also be used on the "lead" horse in the livery. All of the other animals follow the round thereafter.

Setting fire to these four areas ensures the town and its supplies are denied to the rampaging greenskins. A hero can set one of the objectives on fire as long as he starts his turn in contact with it, has a lit torch and oil flask, isn't Shaken, and makes a successful Smarts roll. A failed Smarts roll means a small flame is started but isn't enough to set the building truly ablaze.

If any of these conditions aren't met, the arsonist must try again next round.

- **Orc Chieftain:** See the statistics on page 162, and add Riding d8.
- **Orc Raiders:** There are 20 orcs riding giant boars (see below), though they roam in groups of five so the Game Master should space them out accordingly so as not to overwhelm the heroes. Orc raiders have Riding d6 in addition to their usual skills.

War Boar
These massive boars serve as the orcish horde's mounts. They're 700 pounds of muscle, tusk, stench, and attitude. Only orcs are typically tough enough to breed and ride them.
Attributes: Agility d4, Smarts d4 (A), Spirit d6, Strength d10, Vigor d10
Skills: Fighting d8, Intimidation d8, Notice d8
Pace: 10; **Parry:** 6; **Toughness:** 9
Special Abilities
- **Tusk Slash:** Str+d6
- **Gore:** If a boar can charge at least 6" before attacking, it adds +4 to its damage total that round. It cannot slash and gore in the same action.
- **Fleet-Footed:** War boars roll d10s instead of d6s when running.
- **Size:** +2. War boars weigh 700 pounds.

Crime City was first introduced in the free One Sheet *The Moscow Connection,* available on our website at www.peginc.com. This adventure takes place immediately afterward, so we recommend you download and run that adventure first, but it's certainly not necessary.

Our action begins moments after a small group of Russian mafia members stop a terrorist cell from bringing in a mysterious cargo. Now they must escape with it!

▶ **Setting Rules:** Blood & Guts, Critical Failures, Gritty Damage, Joker's Wild, Skill Specialization

▶ **Characters:** The player characters are all criminals belonging to—or in the employ of—the Russian Mafia. The default characters can be found on the opposite page.

In Media Res

At the end of *The Moscow Connection,* the group stopped Mahmoud Abbas and a cell of the Red Hand, and took possession of a mysterious cargo loaded in the back of a large panel truck. What's the cargo? That's up to you, the Game Master, but it must be big enough to require moving with the panel truck. The cargo might be a nuclear bomb, or a dirty bomb, or something far more bizarre—such as debris from the 1908 Tunguska Blast, or an artifact from Chernobyl (since it came in on a ship called the *Chernobyl Revenge).* Or maybe it's a strange device the gangsters don't even understand.

Regardless of the nature of the cargo, the Russians need to get it out of the area to one of their own warehouses fast. Reinforcements of the Red Hand are already on their way and a chase through the streets of New York City are on.

Choose Your Poison

Start the action as one of the Russians (Ivan if you're using the pregenerated characters as he speaks Farsi) hear reinforcements state they're "almost there" on one of the dead terrorists' radios.

Then give the players exactly one minute to discuss which vehicles they want to take, and who's driving or riding in each. They have to take the truck since it holds the cargo, and Mahmoud Abbas' motorcycle still idles around the corner. Alexy also has a black 2005 Ford Tahoe nearby with armored plates in the doors as well.

- **Motorcycle (2009 Kawasaki Ninja):** Acc/TS 20/40, Toughness 8(2), Crew 1.
- **SUV (2005 Ford Tahoe):** Acc/TS 15/35, Toughness 17(7) on sides, or 14(3) to front and back, Crew 1+7, Airbags. Note that the Tahoe is slightly slower and tougher than normal due to the armor-plated side panels.
- **Panel Truck:** Acc/TS 5/25, Toughness 14(1), Crew 1.

The Chase Begins

This entire adventure is a Chase. Tell the group that their goal is to get the cargo away from the Red Hand, and there's no telling how many reinforcements are swarming in. Even if they defeat the first wave, more may come. If the Russians are defeated, the mysterious cargo will fall right back into their enemies' hands.

This is an Extended Chase of 10 rounds. See page 94 for details on running Chases. The heroes' goal is to escape with the panel truck and its cargo intact. If the truck and the heroes are still moving after 10 rounds, they lose their pursuers and escape. If the truck is stopped, see "Last Stand," below.

The enemy is composed of fanatical members of the Red Hand, riding in two cars and six motorcycles.

- **6 x Motorcycle (variety of older models):** Acc/TS 15/35, Toughness 8(2), Crew 1 each.
- **2 x Mid-Size Cars:** Acc/TS 20/40, Toughness 11(3), Crew 1+3 each.

The motorcycles have one driver each. The cars have a driver, who does not attack, and three passengers, two of which can attack on any given action.

Remember that when the terrorists have Advantage, no more than a third of them can attack a particular target at once as the various vehicles weave in and out of traffic.

Complications

The inevitable Complications represent traffic, construction work, or blind alleys. In addition, if a red Ace is drawn and used by either of the groups, it means the police have been drawn to the pursuit. There's a single police cruiser after the first round the Ace is used. After that, roll a d6 at the beginning of each new round. On a 4+, another police cruiser shows up.

- **Police Cruiser:** Acc/TS 20/45, Toughness 12(3), Crew 2. Use Soldiers for the policemen (page 93). They're equipped with pump-action shotguns and 9mm pistols. Only one policeman per cruiser can attack each round, but he only shoots at Medium Range or better for fear of wild shots hitting civilians.

Last Stand

If the Russians stop for any reason, the remaining members of the Red Hand dismount and fight on through the next two rounds. At the start of the third, another wave (two more cars and six more bikes) show up and attack as well. Deal this new wave in as a separate group. The cars might try to ram the Tahoe, while those on motorcycles might circle and strafe in hopes that their fast movement will keep them from getting shot. After three more rounds have passed, a truck with a dozen more terrorists arrive.

If the Russians can't drive away at this point (which renews the Extended Chase), they'd best abandon their cargo and duck down an alley. The Red Hand won't pursue—they came in force to escort their package. The group might want to figure out how they want to get it back before the terrorists put the device—whatever it is—to use.

Red Hand Terrorist

Attributes: Agility d6, Smarts d8, Spirit d8, Strength d6, Vigor d10
Skills: Driving d6, Fighting d8, Knowledge (English) d6, Notice d8, Shooting d8, Stealth d6
Charisma: –2, **Pace:** 6, **Parry:** 6, **Toughness:** 7
Hindrances: Mean, Loyal (to Red Hand)
Gear: AK47, large knife.

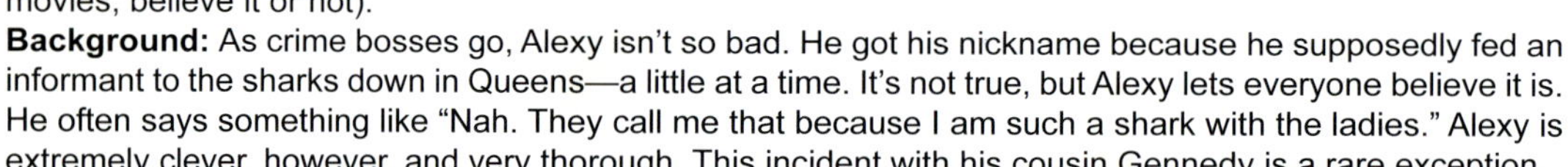

Pregenerated Characters

Below are the five characters assumed to be used for "The Chase," as well as *The Moscow Connection* you can find online at www.peginc.com. If you decide to have the players create their own characters, these can serve as guides for the types of anti-heroes they might make.

Alexy "The Shark" Petrovich

Rank: Seasoned
Attributes: Agility d8, Smarts d8, Spirit d6, Strength d6, Vigor d8
Skills: Driving d8, Fighting d8, Healing d4, Intimidation d6, Knowledge (English) d6, Notice d8, Persuasion d6, Shooting d8, Stealth d6
Charisma: 0, **Pace:** 6, **Parry:** 6, **Toughness:** 6
Hindrances: Loyal (to family and friends), Outsider (Russian), Wanted (Major, Alexy is being watched by the FBI—and maybe certain Russian factions as well, but that's a tale for another day).
Edges: Noble (the Petrovich Crime Family)
Gear: 9mm Glock Pistol. In Alexy's Tahoe is also a pump-action shotgun, a very good first aid kit (+2 to Healing, 4 uses), a gallon of water, five gallons of gas, and a couple of DVDs he hasn't returned to the video store yet (Disney movies, believe it or not).

Background: As crime bosses go, Alexy isn't so bad. He got his nickname because he supposedly fed an informant to the sharks down in Queens—a little at a time. It's not true, but Alexy lets everyone believe it is. He often says something like "Nah. They call me that because I am such a shark with the ladies." Alexy is extremely clever, however, and very thorough. This incident with his cousin Gennedy is a rare exception.

Ivan "Soldier Boy" Petrovich

Rank: Seasoned
Attributes: Agility d8, Smarts d6, Spirit d8, Strength d6, Vigor d6
Skills: Driving d6, Fighting d8, Intimidation d8, Knowledge (English) d6, Notice d6, Shooting d8, Stealth d6, Taunt d6, Tracking d6
Charisma: -2, **Pace:** 4, **Parry:** 6, **Toughness:** 5
Hindrances: Lame, Loyal (to family and friends), Outsider (Russian)
Edges: Rock and Roll, Strong Willed
Gear: MP5 Submachine gun, 2 extra clips.

Background: Ivan Petrovich idolizes his older brother, and strives to show him how strong and independent he is. He joined the US Army after 9/11 and later spent two tours in Iraq before getting hit with an IED that left him with a permanent limp. He's scrappy, tough, and very skilled, but his stint with real soldiers occasionally makes him doubt his family's activities.

Irina "The Skirt" Gregorovna

Rank: Seasoned
Attributes: Agility d8, Smarts d6, Spirit d8, Strength d6, Vigor d6
Skills: Driving d4, Fighting d6, Knowledge (English) d6, Notice d6, Persuasion d8, Shooting d8, Stealth d8, Streetwise d6
Charisma: +2, **Pace:** 6, **Parry:** 5, **Toughness:** 5
Hindrances: Loyal (to family and friends), Outsider (Russian), Vengeful
Edges: Combat Reflexes, Very Attractive
Gear: 9mm Pistol, 2 extra clips, switchblade.
Background: Alexy's main girl is Irina. Irina reflects the new era in the family—one which is very slowly starting to embrace women as well. She's gorgeous and knows it, and frequently uses her charms to distract or spy on Alexy's rivals.

Piotr "The Bull" Fydorovich

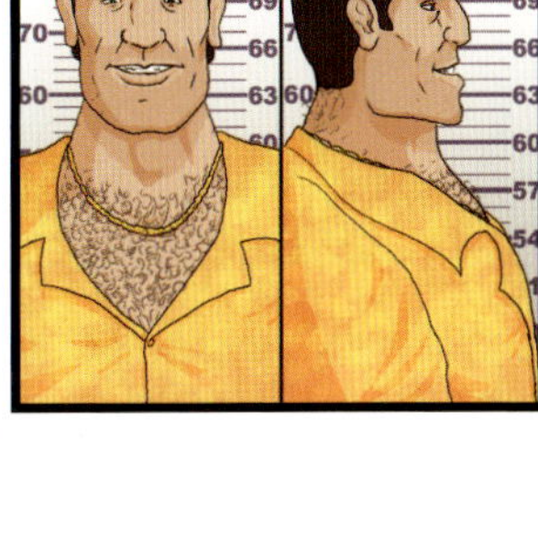

Rank: Seasoned
Attributes: Agility d6, Smarts d4, Spirit d6, Strength d10, Vigor d10
Skills: Driving d6, Fighting d10, Intimidation d6, Knowledge (English) d4, Notice d4, Shooting d4, Stealth d4, Throwing d4
Charisma: -2, Pace: 6, **Parry:** 7, **Toughness:** 8
Hindrances: Loyal (to family and friends), Outsider (Russian), Clueless
Edges: Brawny, Frenzy, Sweep, Trademark Weapon (Louisville Slugger)
Gear: Louisville Slugger (Str+d6), chewing gum, hair spray and comb.
Background: "The Bull" grew up with Alexy, but spent most of his time in the gym or playing sports. He's a massive, mountain of a man, and he likes to prove it by foregoing firearms and blades—though he's not unskilled in their use. His trademark weapon is a Louisville slugger he loves to kiss just before going to work.

Johnny "Remora" Mancebo

Rank: Seasoned
Attributes: Agility d10, Smarts d4, Spirit d6, Strength d6, Vigor d8
Skills: Climbing d6, Fighting d10, Knowledge (Russian) d4, Lockpicking d8, Notice d6, Shooting d4, Stealth d8
Charisma: -2, Pace: 6, **Parry:** 7, **Toughness:** 5
Hindrances: Loyal (to family and friends), Outsider (non-Russian in Russian gang), Small
Edges: First Strike, Quick, Quick Draw, Thief
Gear: Lockpicks, switchblade.
Background: Johnny isn't Russian, but he grew up around them and speaks the language reasonably well. He's a sly little man, and frequently people don't even realize he's around until he knifes some poor schmuck in the back. His nickname comes from the way he follows Alexy around ("the shark").

Look for the prequel to this adventure, The Moscow Connection, online at www.peginc.com!

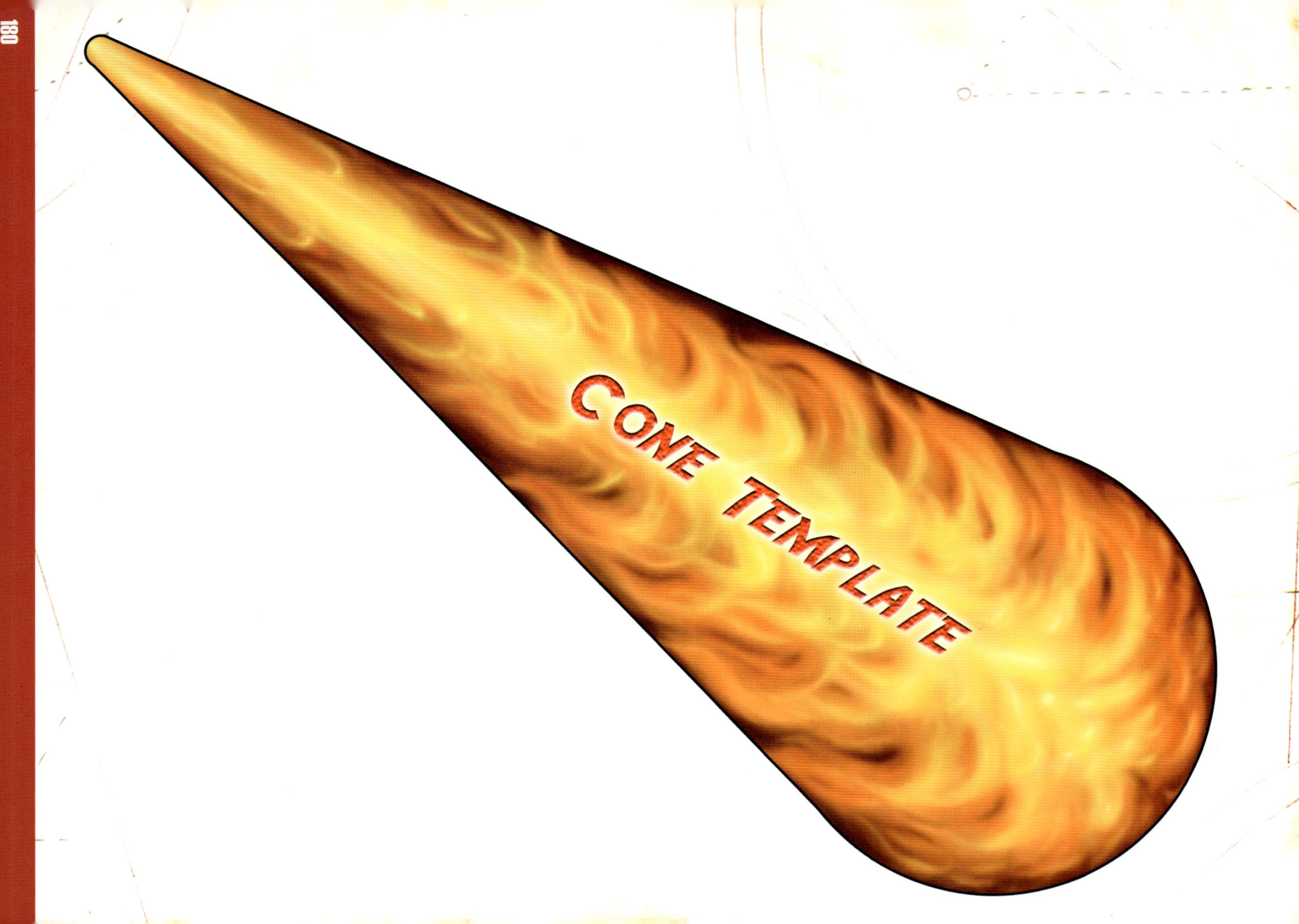
CONE TEMPLATE

LARGE BURST
TEMPLATE

TURNING TEMPLATE

SMALL BURST
TEMPLATE

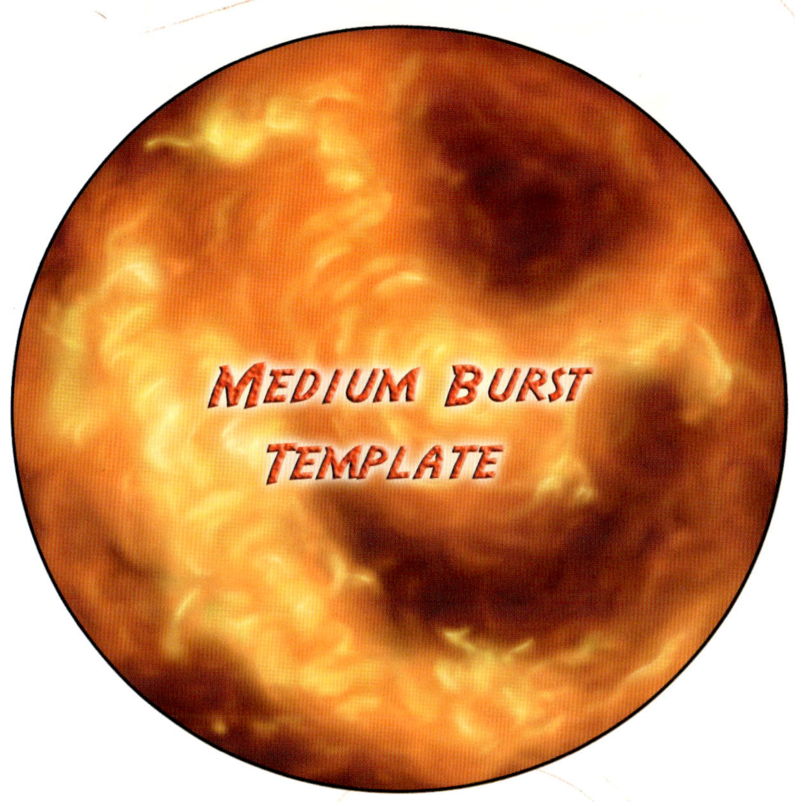

- Cone Templates are 9" long and 3" wide at their widest point.
- Large Burst Templates are 6" in diameter.
- Medium Burst Templates are 4" in diameter.
- Small Burst Templates are 2" in diameter.
- The Turning Template is a 45 degree angle.

Permission is granted to photocopy these templates for personal use.

Climbing Modifiers

Modifier	Situation
+2	Antique or medieval climbing equipment
+4	Modern climbing equipment
–2	Scarce or thin handholds
–2	Wet or slippery surface

Stealth Modifiers

Situation	Modifier
Crawling	+2
Running	–2
Dim light	+1
Darkness	+2
Pitch darkness	+4
Light cover	+1
Medium cover	+2
Heavy cover	+4

Tracking Modifiers

Modifier	Situation
+2	Tracking more than 5 individuals
+4	Recent snow
+2	Mud
+1	Dusty area
–4	Raining
–2	Tracking in poor light
–2	Tracks are more than one day old
–2	Target attempted to hide tracks

Knowledge (Language) Table

Skill	Ability
d4	The character can read, write, and speak common words and phrases
d6	The speaker can carry on a prolonged but occasionally halting conversation
d8	The character can speak fluently
d10	The hero can mimic other dialects within the language
d12	The speaker can masterfully recite important literary or oral works

Reaction Table

2d6	Initial Reaction
2	**Hostile:** The target is openly hostile and does his best to stand in the hero's way. He won't help without an overwhelming reward or payment of some kind.
3-4	**Uncooperative:** The target isn't willing to help unless there's a significant advantage to himself.
5-9	**Neutral:** The target has no particular attitude and will help for little reward if the task at hand is very easy. If the task is difficult, he'll require substantial payment of some kind.
10-11	**Friendly:** The target will go out of his way for the hero. He'll likely do easy tasks for free (or very little), and is willing to do more dangerous tasks for fair pay or other favors.
12	**Helpful:** The target is anxious to help the hero, and will probably do so for little or no pay depending on the nature of the task.

Range Modifiers

Range	Modifier
Short	—
Medium	–2
Long	–4

Cover Modifiers

Cover	Modifier
Light	–1
Medium	–2
Heavy	–4
Near Total	–6

Test of Wills Table

"Attack" Skill		Resisted By…
Taunt	vs.	Smarts
Intimidation	vs.	Spirit

Vehicular Attack Modifiers

Penalty	Situation
–2	Unstable Platform
–1 per 10" of Speed	Fast Targets

Natural Healing Modifiers

Modifier	Condition
–2	Rough traveling
–2	No medical attention
–2	Poor environmental conditions, such as intense cold, heat, or rain
—	Medical attention (1940 or earlier)
+1	Medical attention (1941 or better)
+2	Medical attention (2010 and beyond)

Toughness Modifiers

Mod	Size of a...
–2	Cat, fairy, pixie, large rat, dog
–1	Large dog, bobcat, half-folk, goblin, small human
0	Human
+1	Orc
+2	Bull, gorilla, bear, horse
+3	Ogre, kodiak bear
+4	Rhino, great white shark
+5	Small elephant
+6	Drake, bull elephant
+7	T-Rex, orca
+8	Dragon
+9	Blue whale
+10	Kraken, leviathan

Creature Strength

Creature	Strength
Gorilla, bear, ogre	d12+1 to +3
Rhino, great white	d12+3 to +6
Elephant, drake, T-Rex	d12+5 to +8
Dragon	d12+9 to +12

Experience Awards

Award	Situation
1	The group accomplished little or had a very short session.
2	The group had more successes than failures.
3	The group succeeded greatly, and their adventure had a significant impact on the overall story.

Social Conflict Results

Margin of Victory	Result
Tie	The issue is unsettled and no action is taken until new and more compelling evidence can be presented to reopen the negotiation. In a court case, the defense would win as the burden of proof is on the prosecution.
1-2	The target isn't truly convinced but decides it's better to be safe than sorry. He provides the minimum amount of support possible. In a court case, the jury barely finds reasonable doubt if the defense wins, or assigns minimal sentencing if the prosecution wins.
3-4	The target is reasonably convinced. He grants the help requested, more or less, but may have conditions or ask favors in return. In a court case, the judge invokes severe sentencing if the prosecution wins. If the defense wins the defendant is cleared of all charges.
5+	The target is sure of his decision. He provides more support than requested. If the prosecution wins in a court case, the defendant receives the maximum penalty.

Obstacle Toughness

Armor	Obstacle
+1	Glass, leather
+2	Plate glass window, shield
+3	Modern interior wall, sheet metal, car door
+4	Oak door, thick sheet metal
+6	Cinder block wall
+8	Brick wall
+10	Stone wall, bulletproof glass

Object Toughness

Object	Toughness	Damage Type
Light Door	8	Blunt, Cutting
Heavy Door	10	Blunt, Cutting
Lock	8	Blunt, Piercing
Handcuffs	12	Blunt, Piercing, Cutting
Knife, Sword	10	Blunt, Cutting
Rope	4	Cutting, Piercing
Small Shield	8	Blunt, Cutting
Medium Shield	10	Blunt, Cutting
Large Shield	12	Blunt, Cutting

Fright Table

1d20*	Effect
1-4	**Adrenaline Surge:** The hero's "fight" response takes over. He adds +2 to all Trait and damage rolls on his next action.
5-8	**Shaken:** The character is Shaken.
9-12	**Panicked:** The character immediately moves his full Pace plus running die away from the danger and is Shaken.
13-16	**Minor Phobia:** The character gains a Minor Phobia Hindrance somehow associated with the trauma.
17-18	**Major Phobia:** The character gains a Major Phobia Hindrance.
19-20	**The Mark of Fear:** The hero is Shaken and also suffers some cosmetic physical alteration—a white streak forms in the hero's hair, his eyes twitch constantly, or some other minor physical alteration. This reduces his Charisma by 1.
21+	**Heart Attack:** The hero is so overwhelmed with fear that his heart stutters. He becomes Incapacitated and must make a Vigor roll at –2. If successful, he's Shaken and can't attempt to recover for 1d4 rounds. If he fails, he dies in 2d6 rounds. A Healing roll at –4 saves the victim's life, but he remains Incapacitated.

Injury Table

2d6	Wound
2	**Unmentionables:** If the injury is permanent, reproduction is out of the question without miracle surgery or magic. There is no other effect from this result.
3-4	**Arm:** Roll left or right arm randomly; it's unusable like the One Arm Hindrance (though if the primary arm is affected, off-hand penalties still apply to the other).
5-9	**Guts:** Your hero catches one somewhere between the crotch and the chin. Roll 1d6: *1-2 Broken:* Agility reduced a die type (minimum d4). *3-4 Battered:* Vigor reduced a die type (minimum d4). *5-6 Busted:* Strength reduced a die type (minimum d4).
10	**Leg:** Gain the Lame Hindrance (or the One Leg Hindrance if already Lame).
11-12	**Head:** A grievous injury to the head. Roll 1d6: *1-2 Hideous Scar:* Your hero now has the Ugly Hindrance. *3-4 Blinded:* An eye is damaged. Gain the One Eye Hindrance (or the Blind Hindrance if he only had one good eye). *5-6 Brain Damage:* Massive trauma to the head. Smarts reduced one die type (min d4).

Out of Control

2d6	Effect
2	**Roll Over:** The vehicle performs a Slip and rolls over 1d6 times in that direction. Roll collision damage for the vehicle and everyone inside. Any exterior-mounted weapons or accessories are ruined.
3–4	**Spin:** Move the vehicle 1d6" in the direction of the maneuver, or 1d6" away from a damaging blow. Roll a d12, read it like a clock facing, and point the vehicle in that direction.
5-9	**Skid:** Move the vehicle 1d4" left or right (in the direction of a failed maneuver, or away from a damaging attack).
10–11	**Slip:** Move the vehicle 1d6" left or right (in the direction of a failed maneuver, or away from a damaging attack).
12	**Flip:** The vehicle flips end over end 1d4 times. Move it forward that many increments of its own length. Roll collision damage for the vehicle, its passengers, and anything it hits. Slow and heavy vehicles such as tanks (GM's discretion) don't flip but suffer a Slip or Skid instead.

Critical Hits

2d6	Effect
2	**Scratch and Dent:** The attack merely scratches the paint. There's no permanent damage.
3	**Engine:** The engine is hit. Oil leaks, pistons misfire, etc. Acceleration is halved (round down). This does not affect deceleration, however.
4	**Locomotion:** The wheels, tracks, or whatever have been hit. Halve the vehicle's Top Speed immediately. If the vehicle is pulled by animals, the shot hits one of them instead.
5	**Controls:** The control system is hit. Until a Repair roll is made, the vehicle can only perform turns to one side (1–3 left, 4–6 right). This may prohibit certain maneuvers as well.
6–8	**Chassis:** The vehicle suffers a hit in the body with no special effects.
9–10	**Crew:** A random crew member is hit. The damage from the attack is rerolled. If the character is inside the vehicle, subtract the vehicle's Armor from the damage. Damage caused by an explosion affects all passengers in the vehicle.
11	**Weapon:** A random weapon on the side of the vehicle that was hit is destroyed and may no longer be used. If there is no weapon, this is a Chassis hit instead.
12	**Wrecked:** The vehicle is wrecked and automatically goes Out of Control.

Index

A

B

C

D

SAVAGE WORLDS

Charisma Pace Parry Toughness

Attributes

4 6 8 10 12 Agility
4 6 8 10 12 Smarts
4 6 8 10 12 Strength
4 6 8 10 12 Spirit
4 6 8 10 12 Vigor

Name

Profession

Setting Rules

Quote

Skills

4 6 8 10 12 ______
4 6 8 10 12 ______
4 6 8 10 12 ______
4 6 8 10 12 ______
4 6 8 10 12 ______
4 6 8 10 12 ______
4 6 8 10 12 ______
4 6 8 10 12 ______

4 6 8 10 12 ______
4 6 8 10 12 ______
4 6 8 10 12 ______
4 6 8 10 12 ______
4 6 8 10 12 ______
4 6 8 10 12 ______
4 6 8 10 12 ______
4 6 8 10 12 ______

Armor

Head:
Torso:
Arms:
Legs:

Total WT Carried:
Weight Limit:
Encumbrance Penalty:

Equipment

Hindrances:

Edges:

N
5
10
15

S
25
30
35

V
45
50
55

H
65
70
75

L
90
100
110

Wounds

-2

-3

Permanent Injuries

In

-2

Fatigue

Power/Trapping	Cost	Range	Damage/Effect	Duration

Weapon	Range	ROF	Damage	AP	WT	Notes

5   10   15   20   25   30